L. A. Marzulli bridges the ga
spiratorial musings, ancient
astonishing evidence our gov
years. With this evidence now confirmed by military
experts and some of the intelligence community's most
credible individuals, *Rungs of Disclosure* takes the reader
on a riveting journey and exposes the nefarious plan
revealed thousands of years ago in the pages of Scripture.

—MARK CONN, PHD
ADJUNCT PROFESSOR, LIBERTY UNIVERSITY

A tireless researcher, anointed speaker, and gifted author,
L. A. Marzulli has steered at the helm of UFO research
for decades, and the veracity and logic of his books
were instrumental in my initial conversion to Jesus. He
answered questions the church was not willing to answer.

Despite opposition—and sometimes outright anger—
from secular and religious folks alike, as well as imitation
from others in his field of research, LA has continued to
educate people on the satanic UFO agenda, shining a light
and drawing attention to the imminent return of our King.
Rungs of Disclosure is the magnum opus of a lifetime's
worth of dedication, research, and passion.

—MATTHEW FISHER
SENIOR PASTOR, CALVARY CHAPEL STROUDSBURG
SCIOTA, PENNSYLVANIA

The world is fascinated with the supernatural, the occult,
and events that cannot be naturally explained. We are
living in perilous times of great deception. Can we trust
what we see? Are the words of the secular experts true?
Does anyone have the ability to challenge the conven-
tional wisdom of the media? Yes! There is a man, and
his name is Dr. L. A. Marzulli. With many years of experience and research, he has unmasked the enemy and
revealed the truth. Dr. Marzulli is the real deal, and this
book is a game changer.

—LARRY OLLISON, PHD
LARRY OLLISON MINISTRIES

L. A. Marzulli has knocked it out of the park in this all-too-important release. In an increasingly darkening world searching for answers, Marzulli has provided a guiding light. Every Christian needs this book!

—Josh Peck
Award-winning Filmmaker and Author

LA never fails to deliver. *Rungs of Disclosure* is insightful, eye-opening, and riveting—a deep dive into the fascinating and prophetic events happening all around us in these last days. I could not put it down.

—Dan Plourde
Pastor, Calvary Church
Jupiter, Florida

Dr. L. A. Marzulli has been on the cutting edge of UFO research for decades. His research in this field is extremely thorough, and the way he connects this burgeoning phenomena with biblical prophecy sets him apart from the rest. This book is a must-read for anyone interested in what may take place in the not-too-distant future.

—Bill Salus, DLitt
Founder, Prophecy Depot Ministries

Nearly four decades of research and countless hours of interviews have culminated in this seminal work, proving once again why L. A. Marzulli remains the leading Christian voice in the UAP/UFO research community.

—Gil Zimmerman
Producer/Director, Member of the Academy of
Motion Picture Arts and Sciences

I've often wondered if L. A. Marzulli was a fan of *Star Trek*. I can picture him glued to the 19-inch family television as Captain Kirk uttered those now famous words, to "go where no man has gone before." Marzulli is that man. The majority of the Christian community has been curiously silent about the prince of the power of the air (Satan) and his demonic hordes. The church seems to go the extra mile to sweep him under the rug. As hard as it is to believe, about 60 percent of people who call themselves Christians do not believe in a literal Satan. Marzulli's mission in life is to expose the works of darkness and bring the uninformed masses into God's marvelous light. His boots-on-the-ground, hard-hitting research and interviews are opening eyes. From the whistleblowers to the military pilots to the sworn-to-secrecy government insiders, they're all carefully watching their steps as they navigate the final rungs on the UFO disclosure ladder. Buckle up and read about things you'll never hear in church. A shocking day awaits this world—the great deception. Will you or your family be deceived by the evil one? Or will *Rungs of Disclosure* prepare you for the future?

—Bob Ulrich
COO, Prophecy Watchers

In a moment of transparency in July 1947, the Roswell incident was reported as a disc-shaped craft that crashed in the desert. The following day, the decades-long obfuscation by the U.S. government began and remained unabated—until 2017. There is no better filmmaker and writer than L. A. Marzulli to document the recent path of disclosure. This new book on the rungs of disclosure is exactly what every prophecy watcher needs as they seek to share this truth with others who might not yet understand its full significance. I highly recommend LA's work on this very important topic.

—Mondo Gonzales
Co-host, Prophecy Watchers

RUNGS OF DISCLOSURE

RUNGS OF DISCLOSURE

L. A. MARZULLI

FRONT
LINE

For more resources like this, visit MyCharismaShop.com and the author's website at LAMarzulli.com.

Cataloging-in-Publication Data is on file with the Library of Congress.

International Standard Book Number: 978-1-63641-448-5
E-book ISBN: 978-1-63641-449-2

3 2024
Printed in the United States of America

Most Charisma Media products are available at special quantity discounts for bulk purchase for sales promotions, premiums, fund-raising, and educational needs. For details, call us at (407) 333-0600 or visit our website at www.charismamedia.com.

CONTENTS

EDITOR'S NOTE

I REMEMBER WHEN *ANCIENT Aliens* was first broadcast on the History Channel in 2009. I was riveted to the television, seeing for the first time video of archaeological sites I'd always wanted to explore. At that time, it was much more difficult to get your hands on information about these ancient sites than it is today. Some books, most of them very expensive, with small photographs summed up the bulk of available literature. I scrutinized the photos with a magnifying glass as I was scanning Scripture in my mind to view these enigmatic structures and carvings through a biblical lens.

I was watching one of the *Ancient Aliens* episodes during its first season, and someone named L. A. Marzulli was interviewed. He was offering a theory different from the ancient astronaut view, and I sat up, paying even closer attention. Wait...that can't be right. Is he a Christian? I had never heard a Christian talk about any of this.

Now fifteen seasons of *Ancient Aliens* are in the rearview mirror, and in spite of its massive popularity, the church at large remains completely silent on the subject. Congress has had hearings on UFO/UAP phenomenon, and former intelligence staff have testified under oath that there have been UFO craft and nonhuman biologics retrieved. Pastors smile and play the music as the Titanic is taking on water, and as occult themes and practices are steadily invading their congregations.

The research LA has done on this subject is considerable. There are few Christian researchers in the world who can offer a similar track record and bona fides. LA has earned respect with the countless hours of research; real expeditions to real archaeological sites; top-notch, professionally conducted, history-changing DNA studies; the spiritual warfare that goes along with the calling; and most importantly his unyielding commitment and adherence to the Word of God.

I've worked with LA since 2016. There is such a pastor's heart operating in the center of the Spiral of Life ministry, and I use the word *ministry* intentionally. God always uses the experience from the battles we've endured, limped through, and cried over to minister to others. In this case, part of that calling is ministering to people who have been deceived by Eastern religious concepts and the New Age. LA is usually the only Christian researcher presenting at UFO conferences.

I think it was in 2022 or early 2023 that several of us felt the Holy Spirit was saying that LA was entering the most important time for his ministry. I kept praying for God to cause everything LA needs to accomplish God's to-do list to be brought to him. It is for a time such as this. Now is the time.

Just today I was again reading in 1 Kings 18. Elijah challenged the prophets of Baal to a showdown. I love the portion where he told them to call with a louder voice since maybe their god couldn't hear them: "'He is on a journey, or perhaps he is asleep and must be awakened'" (v. 27). After all of their drama, Elijah said, "Lord God of Abraham, Isaac, and of Israel, let it be known this day that thou art God in Israel, and that I am thy servant, and that I have done all these things at thy word. Hear me, O Lord, hear me, that this people may know that thou art the Lord God, and that thou hast turned their heart back again" (vv. 36–37, kjv).

LA has these encounters with false prophets, mediums,

self-proclaimed hybrids, and space-brother preachers nearly daily. And God uses him powerfully. He talks with them, while asking thought-provoking questions and sharing the gospel in a gentle and respectful way, showing them that "the LORD, He is God!" (1 Kings 18:39).

This message is needed today more than ever. The United States has been beaten back from the biblical principles that gave it strength and stability. Churches have no understanding of prophecy because they have intentionally shunned it, rejecting nearly a third of Scripture Jehovah Sabaoth included to warn His beloved children. Churches have no understanding of spiritual warfare or of the heretical doctrines and prophets of Baal that now occupy their pews and work to cause division and destruction and to poison the minds of the ill-equipped flock.

We certainly seem to be in a window of time that is talked about in Scripture, described as deception, *pharmakeia*, war, instability, DNA manipulation, and more, all at once. If this isn't the space shuttle engines revving up just before takeoff, it must be a test run. One of the great deceptions almost certainly involves the UFO/ UAP phenomenon, with cruel Grays who kidnap children and adults for their own evil purposes, the same Grays sought by the space brother devotees, the same Grays who more and more secular researchers are recognizing as fitting the biblical description of the demonic. This ticks all the boxes of a religion. The picture that forms once you get all the pieces on the table is more than just sobering. Pretending it isn't there is not a solution. As Spirit-filled believers, we are to be unafraid of these dark beings and schemes; we are to ride out and meet them, fully clad in the gleaming armor of God, and in the name of Yeshua (Jesus) deliver the biggest supernatural smackdown in the history of man.

This book is gleaned from decades of research, prayer, and Holy Spirit dot-connecting. LA can see the picture that forms from the pixels, and he endeavors to equip you to see the picture that forms for yourself. And he doesn't leave you there; he frequently refers to the Scripture that keeps him and his work—and by extension, you, the reader—thoroughly grounded.

The timing of this book is important. We are in the middle of chaos on every side, and UFO/UAP and abduction videos and reports fill our video feeds, email inboxes, and text message threads. The world needs the message, the answers that LA has put in this book. Rip the cloaking device off the evil ones by learning what their grand scheme is. If you know what they're up to, it will be a lot harder for them to succeed at deceiving you. Pray as you read, and answer the call on all spiritual warriors for the King, the Lion of the tribe of Judah; then we will frustrate the enemy forces, and they will have a massive headache. Any day we can give the dark forces a migraine is a good day, and LA does that with this important work.

—SANDA ALLYSON
EDITOR, *SPIRAL OF LIFE*

FOREWORD

THIS BRIEF FOREWORD is written to give you, the reader, an understanding of the driving passion that brought this book to completion. L. A. Marzulli, a good friend of mine for many years, strongly believes that the marvels we've all known as "flying saucers" or "lights in the sky" are only the leading edge of a much larger truth: Those UFOs, now labeled as UAPs, are hiding a dark reality.

"Flying objects" have become known as "aerial phenomena." Their variety seems unlimited. Now accepted as reality, these worldwide occurrences are in truth part of a war that has long been waged against humanity, the majority of which is hidden in a fog of false perception, mythology, pseudo-scientific speculation, and deliberate obfuscation by researchers around the globe. Denial of this obvious truth takes many forms.

World governments see this phenomenon as an opportunity to take the next step on the ladder of technological superiority. For many years they've been reverse engineering UFO wreckage—and succeeding in their efforts. In 1947 the "Roswell incident" changed the world! From then until now, top-secret operations around the world have rushed to unlock the secrets of wreckage they regard as technology from the stars—or perhaps the future.

But from my perspective, Marzulli's devotion to the Lord Jesus Christ and our mutual interest in Bible prophecy is what caused our paths to cross years ago. We were convinced that one of the chief driving factors of the latter-day plunge toward judgment day could be seen in the increasing occurrence of UAP events.

At our first meeting I was struck by his appetite for learning, absorbing, theorizing, and following the trails that would lead him to understanding the pathways the Holy Spirit had opened to him. In fact, "on the trail" is his guiding slogan. He is devoted to deep scriptural research, and his commitment has given him an increasingly detailed understanding of the amazing truth behind the high-tech research and top-secret activities around the world. Furthermore, grotesque human abductions and cattle mutilations both point to a sinister demonic plan.

What Marzulli has known for some time is that the real understanding of the global UAP phenomenon is to be found only from a scriptural point of view. In fact, we came to know each other through a mutual study of biblical prophecy.

From cover to cover, the Bible describes the activities of the evil followers of the fallen one, Satan. In the Book of Ephesians, he is called "the prince of the power of the air" (2:2). His minions are on constant patrol. Throughout the Bible we find references to their sinister activities, as well as God's angelic opposition to Satan's diabolical efforts to corrupt humanity.

Now there is a call for full disclosure! On that note, L. A. Marzulli has made great strides, going beyond mere disclosure to a deeper understanding: exposing the motives of the dark side.

Thinking back, among all the Christians I've ever known, none has surpassed his passion and gusto for biblical research. He regards the Bible as the centerpiece of understanding all things spiritual, historical, and scientific. And he gives us good reason to believe that our time is short.

All those years ago we immediately realized that we both viewed the Bible as pertinent to everything we are seeing in the dramatic events happening around the world. And we share the strong belief that we now live in the midst of a rapidly unfolding series of events that will bring latter-day Bible prophecy into its next great era.

—GARY STEARMAN
CEO AND HOST, *PROPHECY WATCHERS*

FOREWORD

Even him, whose coming is after the working of Satan with
all power and signs and lying wonders, and with all deceiv-
ableness of unrighteousness in them that perish; because they
received not the love of the truth, that they might be saved.
And for this cause God shall send them strong delusion, that
they should believe a lie: that they all might be damned who
believed not the truth, but had pleasure in unrighteousness.

—2 THESSALONIANS 2:9–12, KJV

D O NOT READ this foreword and do not read this book if
you are not interested in the truth—the raw and honest
truth about what the world calls aliens and UFOs and
UAPs. When Dr. L. A. Marzulli asked me to write this foreword, I
was both greatly honored and somewhat taken aback. I thought to
myself, "Who am I that he would want me to write the foreword for
his book? He could choose from so many well-known theologians
and talented authors. Why did he choose me?"

LA later said to me, "This is the most important book I've ever
written. I do believe when we go up, they show up."

I absolutely agree with LA, and that is why this book is so very
important, both for those who believe in the Christian Bible and
for those who do not. In the pages that follow you will find the
wisdom and knowledge of decades of boots-on-the-ground research
unmatched by any ufologist, filmmaker, or author in the world to
date. The information is critically important and relevant to the
times that we live in. How do I know? Because I am a former alien
abductee, and that is why LA asked me to write this foreword.

I was abducted by sinister, nonhuman alien entities as early in my childhood as I can remember. As a former UFO abductee, my experience with UFOs and alien entities has not been positive—it has been downright evil. UFO abductees are not treated with kindness. The alien entities can control thoughts and emotions. They cause physical and emotional pain and trauma and have the technology to leave you without a memory of their actions. Brutal torture and visceral trauma are the order of the day for abductees. No one knows, notices, cares, or believes. Nights are plagued with nightmares, fear, and sleep paralysis. Children are groomed and trafficked; fetuses are stolen. There is no place to hide. There is no freedom. If all this sounds too bizarre to believe, too dark and hopeless, I guarantee you it feels worse for those of us who have experienced these cruel, uninvited seizures. Does that sound friendly? Benevolent? I think not!

We are inundated with media of all sorts reporting on the UFO phenomenon. Today, dozens of channels dedicate hours of daily programming to unexplained and unknown phenomena. UFOs are becoming a topic of mainstream media and, for some, a part of everyday conversation. What would have been a taboo conversation just ten years ago is now widely accepted in our modern society. Unfortunately the vast majority of the information being pushed on popular mainstream media outlets is propagating a lie that these alien entities are, as George Adamski put it, our benevolent space brothers and ancestral seeders.[1] I do not believe this for a minute, and I believe this incredible book by the talented Dr. L. A. Marzulli will help you come to the same conclusion.

Be careful whom you listen to regarding UFOs and nonhuman alien entities. There are many self-proclaimed experts out there sharing a false narrative based on nothing more than their opinions. Pray for discernment, and look for verification always. I can guarantee to the reader that this book is based on thousands of hours of valid, boots-on-the-ground research, accurate and precise data collection, and incredibly impactful information from first-hand experiencers and experts. This is the real deal!

It is my great honor to introduce this latest and most incredible book in the vast library of works form Dr. L. A. Marzulli.

Pay attention!

Take notes!

Share the invaluable information within these pages far and wide!

Be ready!

Be encouraged!

I pray this book will be a blessing for you all.

And remember, don't go looking up for UFOs and aliens—they are not coming to help us, and they are not our benevolent ancestral seeders. They are evil.

Instead, look up for Jesus. Look for the return of our Lord, our Savior, Jesus Christ!

—KARIN WILKINSON
AUTHOR, *STOLEN SEED, EVIL HARVEST*

PREFACE

U FOs ARE REAL, burgeoning, and *not* going away." I coined that phrase years ago, and I repeat it every week in my UFO update on my YouTube channel. For those of us who have studied the UFO/UAP phenomenon, it is indeed what the late J. Allen Hynek called "high strangeness."[1]

What are we to make of craft that move faster than a bullet or make impossible right-angle turns, or of silver discs that morph into other shapes right before our eyes and then suddenly disappear? What about crop circles? Yes, there are fake ones created by the hoaxers, but there are real ones too that are, in some cases, three-dimensional!

Then there is the dark side of the phenomenon—including cattle mutilations, where all the blood is drained from the animal and parts of its flesh, such as the udder, eye, tongue, or sex organs, are cored out with surgical precision. Men and women are taken against their will, and after they are abducted, sperm is taken from the men and ova from the women. This is not science fiction. It is a fact. Hybrids are being created, and witnesses have encountered these entities, which are a mixing of the seed.

Genesis 3:15 is the gateway to all this seemingly "high strangeness," as it lays out the battle plan the human race has unwittingly been engaged in since the chaos that ensued in the Garden of Eden, when the serpent deceived Eve. However, in this passage of Scripture is the promise of the Messiah—Jesus—the One who will crush the Dragon's head.

The revealing of the so-called extraterrestrial presence is the *coming great deception*, and in the pages of this book you will discover how this ongoing phenomenon dovetails perfectly with Scripture. We need only to connect the dots.

Put on your armor and be prepared to go to the deep end of the pool. This book is not for the faint of heart. However, I believe that what is contained herein will arm you, dear reader, with the information that is critical to the time in which we find ourselves.

The time is near.

—L. A. Marzulli
Summer 2024

RUNGS ON THE LADDER
OF UFO DISCLOSURE

UFOs ARE REAL, burgeoning, and *not* going away!
There! I said it. This is a phrase that I coined years ago, and I have repeated this mantra over and over again at conferences, while giving interviews and lectures, on TV programs, and across all types of media.

We are living in a time where it is no longer only "your intrepid host, L. A. Marzulli" that is making this statement, but as former U.S. Department of Defense intelligence officer Luis Elizondo said, "The government has acknowledged the reality" of UFOs.[1]

However, they have changed the name of UFOs to something more agreeable to the folks out there who are NOT "conspiracy-minded individuals." The proper term is now UAP, or unidentified aerial phenomenon.

And just like that, the common man is now allowed to discuss flying saucers, also known as UFOs, without fear of being called a conspiracy kook—or worse.

I have written many books on the subject of UFOs, and I have tried to warn that, in my opinion, the revealing of the so-called *extraterrestrial presence* is the *strong delusion* that is mentioned in 2 Thessalonians. Here are the verses:

> The coming of the lawless one is according to the working
> of Satan, with all power, signs, and lying wonders, and with
> all unrighteous deception among those who perish, because
> they did not receive the love of the truth, that they might be
> saved. And for this reason God will send them *strong delu-
> sion*, that they should believe the lie, that they all may be con-
> demned who did not believe the truth but had pleasure in
> unrighteousness.
> —2 Thessalonians 2:9–12, emphasis added

What is the truth?

> In the beginning was the Word, and the Word was with God,
> and the Word was God. He was in the beginning with God.
> All things were made through Him, and without Him nothing
> was made that was made. In Him was life, and the life was the
> light of men. And the light shines in the darkness, and the
> darkness did not comprehend it.
> —John 1:1–5

We either believe this statement, which is profound in its implications and scope, or we can believe the fallacy of the *Darwinian
paradigm*:

> *The process by which populations change over time and new
> species arise* is known as the "Darwinian Paradigm," or evo-
> lution by natural selection. Though Charles Darwin first
> formulated this scientific theory by observing life on Earth,
> scientists expect that this process will shape life anywhere in
> the universe.[2]

I do not believe in what is called *theistic evolution*, the concept that God started life but then stepped back and let things
go their own way over time through the process of evolution.
I believe emphatically in John's statement that "all things were

made through Him." And there is another scripture that states this:

> For in him all things were created: things in heaven and on earth, visible and invisible, whether thrones or powers or rulers or authorities; all things have been created through him and for him. He is before all things, and in him all things hold together.
>
> —COLOSSIANS 1:16–17, NIV

One of my favorite lines is, "in him all things hold together." And I'll address this further in one of our closing chapters.

I think we have two very clear choices. The first is the biblical model that states God created everything *and* He holds all things together. The second is the Darwinian theory—which, by the way, is still nothing more than a theory, yet it is taught as fact in our "higher" schools of learning.

The prophecy we read in 2 Thessalonians—which informs us that because "they" did not believe the truth, God will send them *strong delusion*—is where we are on the prophetic timeline. God is allowing the strong delusion to manifest, and it is manifesting in ways that I have never seen.

This book will discuss the ongoing revealing of the so-called *extraterrestrial presence,* which is being reported across all media and is now being discussed on established networks such as Fox News and CNN. The revealing and discussion of UFOs is no longer assigned exclusively to *Coast to Coast AM* and George Noory, where I'm honored to have been a guest for almost two decades now.

We are, as I have coined, climbing up the *ladder of disclosure.*

We will discuss this *ladder* in great detail, and how this revealing of the validity of the UFO phenomenon is changing peoples' perspectives on the possibility of life on other planets. But, as we are warned, is this the *strong delusion*?

The short answer to this is yes, as I do not believe in the plurality of worlds (i.e., life elsewhere in the universe).

I often hear this: "But there are millions of galaxies out there; surely we shouldn't be so narrow minded to think that we are alone."

Here is my response: The New Jerusalem descends to earth; the New Jerusalem is the real mothership! It is 1,500 miles wide!

Here are two pertinent scriptures:

> And all the host of heaven shall be dissolved, and the heavens shall be rolled together as a scroll: and all their host shall fall down, as the leaf falleth off from the vine, and as a falling fig from the fig tree.
>
> —Isaiah 34:4, kjv

> Then I saw "a new heaven and a new earth," for the first heaven and the first earth had passed away, and there was no longer any sea.
>
> —Revelation 21:1, niv

There are those who believe that we might be living in a holographic universe.[3] If so, this would make a lot of sense to me; it would lend itself to the concept of rolling the heavens up like a scroll.

We are living in what I describe as a *cosmic chess match, a battle between the forces of darkness and deception led by the Dragon, and those of light and truth led by Jesus, the King of kings,* who will, at some point in the near future, vanquish His enemies.[4]

As you will read in the following pages, we are climbing the *ladder of disclosure,* and the top rung will be full disclosure of the so-called *extraterrestrial presence.* But are these *extraterrestrials* from Epsilon Eridani, as Gary Stearman, host of *Prophecy Watchers,* likes to quip, or are these the fallen ones,

Rungs on the Ladder of UFO Disclosure

masquerading as extraterrestrials in what amounts to a cosmic charade?

Follow me as we explore the rungs on the *ladder of disclosure*, and its implications for everyone who is alive on the earth at this time. Also check out the website **rungsofdisclosure.com** for videos, interviews, and other content.

Chapter 1

ROSWELL: THE BACKSTORY

B EFORE I GET into what I call the rungs on the ladder of disclosure, I must go back in time to 1947 to a little town in the
middle of nowhere that, at the time, housed the only nuclear
bombing group in the world. This was the 509th Bombardment
Group, and it was in Roswell, New Mexico. What transpired there
so long ago set the stage for the way the UFO phenomenon was to
be put before the public eye for decades to come.

America had just come out of World War II, the bloodiest conflict in human history, and millions of lives were lost. Added to this
was the revealing of the atrocities that the Germans had committed
with their network of over twenty thousand detention areas, death
camps, and forced labor factories.[1]

However, what transpired at the end of WWII after the Germans
had surrendered unconditionally was even more chilling and
caused the entire world to collectively peer into the abyss of anni-
hilation. The United States of America dropped not one but two
atomic bombs—the first at Hiroshima, the second at Nagasaki.
What is incredibly sobering is that some of the scientists weren't
sure what would happen when the chain reaction of atoms began.[2]

Shortly after the detonation of these death bombs, UFOs
appeared in our skies.[3] Why?

The last chapter of this book will delve into what I think the *why* is.

In 1947 Kenneth Arnold was airborne in his small private plane when he saw a group of disc-shaped objects, which he described as looking like nine saucers in an echelon formation skipping through the sky in front of him. Thus the modern moniker of *flying saucer* was born.[4]

Flying saucer then became *UFO* (*unidentified flying object*). During this time, Hollywood became involved, and there was a series of sci-fi films about aliens from outer space; one of the most notable was the movie *War of the Worlds*. In my book *UFO Disclosure* I list many of the TV shows as well as films that have dealt with UFOs and life on other planets.[5] The list is long!

So what we have here was a very charged moment in time. Something was going on, and it had gripped the public. Added to this was the infamous 1952 Invasion of Washington, when UFOs flew directly over the Capitol building in Washington, DC.[6] Nothing to see here!

Many books have been written about what I have just outlined, so I won't do a deep dive on any of these points.

On or around July 8, 1947, rancher Mac Brazel notified the sheriff's office in the little town of Roswell, New Mexico, that something had crashed on his ranch. The sheriff contacted the 509th Composite Group, which, at the time, was the only unit like it in the world. The base intelligence officer, Lieutenant Colonel Jesse Marcel Sr., was dispatched to the area to see what may have crashed on the isolated ranch.

When Marcel arrived at the crash site, he realized the wreckage was unlike anything that he had seen before. According to Marcel's own testimony, he realized that he was looking at something *from another world*. Marcel packed up some of the wreckage and headed back to his home. It was late that night when he awakened his wife and his son, Jesse Marcel Jr., and then displayed the wreckage on the kitchen table and floor.

The local newspaper, *Roswell Daily Record*, published a headline that went around the world: "RAAF Captures Flying Saucer on Ranch in Roswell Region."

According to those who were involved, the tiny town of Roswell was inundated with phone calls from all over the globe. Twenty-four hours later, the story was officially redacted. General Roger Ramey, the Eighth Air Force commander, told the paper that the so-called UFO was a case of mistaken identity, that what had been found was nothing more than a weather balloon.

General Ramey held a press conference where he marched Jesse Marcel Sr. out and had him hold pieces of the supposed weather balloon while the press took a series of photos. One look at Marcel's face says it all. It was a set up. Marcel became a patsy and thus began the deliberate obfuscation of the events that happened in Roswell, New Mexico, in July of 1947.

Jesse Marcel Sr. went to his grave insisting that his version of the story was the correct one, and that he had been set up with the bogus weather balloon story, which was nothing more than a bold-faced lie. Marcel handled weather balloons frequently—he was the intelligence officer of the 509th Bomb Group. He had been

9

trained in looking for and identifying all sorts of radar targets. To think that he would mistake a weather balloon for something more exotic—like a craft from another world—is an insult to Marcel.

In our *UFO Disclosure* film series we have created two films on the Roswell incident. We went to Montana and interviewed Dr. Richard O'Connor, who worked with Jesse Marcel Jr. for decades. We also interviewed Jesse Marcel Jr.'s widow, Linda Marcel, as well as his daughter Denice. All three stated that the official story was bogus and that the government and military had besmirched Jesse Marcel Sr.'s reputation by creating the bogus cover story.

Nevertheless, this became the official, accepted story, and this is what the public was told to believe. In that window of time right after WWII, the public trusted our government and military—to their own peril.

Years later Stanton Friedman contacted Jesse Sr. and interviewed him; then the real story finally came out.[7]

I would highly recommend picking up a copy of Jesse Marcel Jr.'s book about Roswell; it's as close to the truth of the event as you will ever get.[8]

I had the privilege of interviewing Marcel before he passed away, and that interview can be found in my book *UFO Disclosure: The 70 Year Cover-Up Exposed!*

Jesse Jr. stated, on the record, that what he had handled as an eleven-year-old boy on that night so long ago was something not from this world. Here is that interview, an excerpt from chapter 2, "New Information from Roswell New Mexico."

LA: Can you give us a thumbnail sketch of the Roswell Event?

JM: Late June or early July 1947, an unknown object crashed outside of Roswell on a ranch northwest of Roswell. The Army Air Force authorities recovered the debris and sent a portion of it to Fort Worth Army Air Field for their information. General Ramey determined that the debris was of unknown origin and floated the cover story that this was just a misidentified weather balloon and sent the debris for further study to Wright Patterson Air Force Base in Dayton, Ohio. Most people who actually saw the debris felt that it was of extraterrestrial origin, in that there were apparent non-human remains associated with a portion of the debris.

LA: How old were you at the time?

JM: I was born 30 August 1936, which would have made me eleven years old.

LA: What did your father do in the Army Air Force?

JM: He was the Intelligence Officer for the 509th Composite Group, which dropped the two atomic bombs on Japan to end the war. As an intelligence officer, a part of his responsibilities was to interpret photographs and brief bomb crews on appropriate targets. He was with the 509th at Wendover, Utah, where the crews practiced dropping what they called the pumpkin, which was a dummy atomic bomb, in order to practice their skills on targets. After the war he received raw intelligence, and it was his job to decipher this intelligence and give briefings to the appropriate personnel.

LA: Tell us the account of the night your dad brought the debris home.

JM: I had been asleep for several hours when my dad came into my bedroom and awakened me. He was very excited and led me into the kitchen where my mother was standing in the corner. On the floor there were pre-positioned pieces of metallic foil, beam-like structures, and black plastic fragments like pieces of a broken phonograph record. My dad said, "Take a close look at this as you will probably never see anything like this again." I think he used words like *parts of a flying saucer* to describe the debris. He first wanted us to look for anything that could have come from a radio, such as vacuum tubes, resistors, or condensers, which there wasn't anything like that. I think he already knew but wanted my mother and myself to satisfy our curiosity. We looked at the debris for a total of about fifteen or twenty minutes, then my dad boxed it back up and brought it out to the car.

LA: What was the wreckage like?

JM: There were primarily foil-like metal beams that resembled "I" beams to my recollection, and the black plastic debris. The foil was very light but tough, and the beams were metallic with a peculiar type of writing along their length. The writing resembled hieroglyphics—but not exactly. There were more geometric shapes and figures that were of a purple violet hue. The black plastic pieces resembled a broken phonograph record (or Bakelite).

LA: What was the "memory" metal like?

JM: I did not try to bend or tear the metal, but just felt it so I did not witness the metal unfolding, etc.

LA: What did your father say to you that night?

JM: I remember him saying words like, "these are parts of a flying saucer," or something along that line.

LA: When did the story change?

JM: After my father returned from Ft. Worth, he was firm in his instructions never to talk about this again, treat it like it never happened. I think it was at Ft. Worth where the cover-up was started, that he was pressured into saying that this "never happened."

LA: How did your mother react to this?

JM: She was pretty closed mouth about this, never really talking about it.

LA: When did he go public with the story?

JM: In 1978 or 1979 Stan Friedman, who was given a heads-up about the Roswell story from a fellow radio amateur friend my dad had (who apparently was told about the Roswell debris during a ham radio conversation with my dad), interviewed him.

LA: Was there pressure from the military to confuse your dad's memory of the event?

JM: I am not aware of any pressure from the military, except for perhaps a verbal order not to discuss this.

LA: Have you ever been pressured to back off the story?

JM: No.

LA: What do you think the Roswell event was?

JM: I think that it was as advertised—the downing of a probe that came from another civilization. Whether it was crewed or not, I do not know.

LA: Has the validation by Edgar Mitchell of your dad's story about Roswell changed anything for you?

JM: It just reinforces what I had thought all along.

LA: What do you think the alien agenda is? Good or bad?

JM: I think that they are scientists with a curiosity about other civilizations just like we would be. I do not think they are malevolent. If they were, we would not be here—certainly we don't have anything they want.

LA: Why the government secrecy? What are they afraid of?

JM: I have thought long and hard about this and don't have any good answer for it. I don't think they would be afraid of causing public panic like the *War of the Worlds* broadcast in the 1930s. They may think they are protecting us from ourselves, which, of course, is not true.

LA: Do you think there may be an event that will trigger full disclosure?

JM: I think the aliens themselves will disclose their presence in a dramatic fashion when they are good and ready. I don't think there has been any official contact with any of the world's governments, although I may be wrong. It may be that the aliens have more to fear from us than we from them.

LA: Final thoughts.

JM: I would hope that full disclosure will be made in my lifetime, but even if it isn't, I know what the truth is.[9]

THE LIE BECAME THE OFFICIAL POSITION

The weather balloon canard was the official story that was circulated in all forms of media to the American people. The story became accepted as fact, living on unchallenged, and soon the public forgot all about Roswell. But for the Marcels, the story became a lingering wound that never went away; it impacted the family and caused division and embarrassment. One of the reasons we made our two films on Roswell was to help set the record straight and clear Lieutenant Colonel Jesse Marcel's good name.

However, there was now a paradigm that was set firmly in place, a *response protocol* that would be adhered to for decades, an "official" response to anyone who claimed to see a UFO.

In other words, in my opinion, the initial report that went out from the Roswell paper had the story correct—a flying disc had crashed on Mac Brazel's ranch. We now know from years of research that bodies were also recovered. We know from Colonel Hill's deathbed confession (more about Hill later) that the wreckage was not a weather balloon and that it was shipped to Wright Field.[10]

During the decades that followed, people who claimed to have an encounter with a UFO were labeled as nutjobs and thought to be unstable. Commercial airline pilots would not report seeing them for fear of losing their jobs. The label *tinfoil hat* was foisted upon anyone who claimed to have seen a UFO. Another term that the powers that be used was *conspiracy theorist*. Things changed a bit with the Barney and Betty Hill abduction case,[11] but for the most part the topic of UFOs was not something polite society discussed.

Whitley Strieber's *Communion*, a book about people being abducted by UFOs, became a bestseller, as did another tome, *Abduction* by Pulitzer Prize winner Dr. John E. Mack. These were landmark publications and piqued the public's interest in the UFO phenomenon. However, the official narrative remained, and many people just didn't talk about UFOs for fear of being thought of as a kook.

There were actually professional debunkers who were employed to debunk any sightings that people reported. One such debunker was Philip Klass. I actually created a character in my series *The Nephilim Trilogy* that was based on him.[12] If you've never seen this guy in action, it's worth a trip to YouTube to check him out. He has answers for everything. He's a real pro, the classic disinformation spook.

One of the late Richard Shaw's favorite quotes, and mine too, is from the film *Men in Black* when they tell the witness the government explanation for what they saw: *"Swamp gas from a weather balloon was trapped in a thermal pocket and reflected the light from Venus.*"[13]

Untimely Deaths

There is also a very unsettling dynamic that went along with the official government narrative. I will admit that in some ways it is conjecture on my part, but a number of investigators and researchers who got a little too close to the UFO phenomenon were either mysteriously killed, suddenly got cancer and died, or were threatened and silenced.

Here's a brief list of some of the people.

Phil Schneider

Phil Schneider was a whistleblower who claimed to have been in a firefight with some alien species deep below the earth.

> Schneider died on January 17, 1996, allegedly strangled by a catheter found wrapped around his neck. Schneider claimed to have worked in 13 of the 129 deep underground facilities the U.S. government constructed after World War II. One of these bases was the bioengineering facility at Dulce, New Mexico, where according to Schneider, humanoid extraterrestrials worked side by side with American technicians.[14]

David Flynn

I spoke with David Flynn several times by phone shortly after my first novel *Nephilim: The Truth is Here* was published.[15] David contacted me, and we spent some time talking shop. We never met face-to-face, but we would talk occasionally about all things ufology. When David was diagnosed with a brain tumor at forty-nine years of age, I was suspicious. He was young, and he also has a twin brother who is fine and doing well.

David had a website called Watcher Website, and while I was researching for my first novel, I went to the site almost daily. David Flynn, like others, was exposing the UFO agenda, and I would go so far as to state that the powers that be, in other words, the deep state, took him out. This was the protocol of the 1990s.

The Roswell Witnesses

There were many witnesses of the Roswell event in and around Roswell, New Mexico. Researchers like me have heard time and again that these civilians were threatened, sometimes by what we would call the *men in black*. Some witnesses were told that they would be taken out into the desert and never found again, or "Somebody might be picking your bones out of the sand."

Most of the witnesses have died, so there's not much to go on at this point, but I have heard this numerous times. These testimonies are written down and can be accessed in books, and some remaining interviews can still be found on YouTube.[16]

L. A. Marzulli

While I was not threatened for my work on UFOs, I was threatened in three different ways by a guy from one of the alphabet agencies. This happened at the Hear the Watchman Conference in Dallas circa 2016. When I met this man, I had a bodyguard with me, so I have a witness to everything that was said. According to a recent conversation with one of the security guards for the conference, there were also death threats against me.

I was informed that our film *Watchers 10: DNA*,[17] which dealt with the Kandahar giant, was what put me on the radar. I was told by this man—whom I had never met—that I was on a list of names and that I should back off on the story. The conversation in the lobby of the hotel went something like this:

Agent: Do you have a cell phone?

LA: Yes, of course.

Agent: Is it encrypted?

LA: No, why?

Agent: When they come to arrest you, they can find kiddy porn on it.

(I took a step back.)

Agent: What kind of car do you drive?

LA: I drive my go-cart, which is 1991 Mercedes SL 500 that I restored.

Agent: Does it have a computer?

LA: Yes, why?

Agent: We can make you have an accident by messing with the computer.

(Needless to say, this guy had my attention. The last threat was the most disturbing.)

Agent: Do you have any children?

LA: Yes, I have two daughters.

Agent: Well, one of them can go missing and never be found.

I paused for a moment. It wasn't my hubris but my faith in the Lord that made me bold, and I stated this: "I agree, you can do that and more as I'm a worm and you can crush me. *But you can't do anything unless the Lord allows you to.*"

Now he took a step back—he had never heard this kind of a response.

The conference ended, and I went home. A few months passed, and I was driving the go-cart up one of the canyons in the Santa Monica Mountains. Suddenly, as I was going around a turn, I heard something snap or pop. The power steering stopped working, and I immediately lost control of the car. I was headed toward a cliff with no guardrail. I slammed on the brakes and skidded to a stop. I took a deep breath, exited the car, and popped the hood. The timing belt was snapped in two.

I called for roadside service from my motor club, and they sent a tow truck. When the tow truck driver arrived, I showed him the timing belt. He held it close to his face, examining it, then looked me right in the eye and asked, "Do you have any enemies?"

The moment was not lost on me, and I remembered what the spook in Dallas had threatened. I write this here to put everything on the record so if you hear in the future that I have committed suicide, you'll know the story is false—I would never commit suicide.

SUMMATION

In my opinion there has been a concentrated effort to quash the research into the UFO phenomenon, starting with Jesse Marcel Sr. and going up to 2017, when we got our first rung on the ladder of disclosure. Until 2017 officially *there was nothing to see—it's all swamp gas!*

However, the members of the old guard who controlled the narrative have all died, and in my opinion, what we are seeing is the beginning of disclosure that will lead up to the final rung.

The Roswell event framed the way in which the entire phenomenon was handled for decades. At first the Army and the powers that be told the public the truth, but then twenty-four hours later they rolled out the bogus weather balloon story. In short, they had it right the first time. The American people were lied to then, and even now we see the ongoing Texas two-step, as I like to call it.

In the following chapters, I will present what I believe are the successive rungs on the ladder of disclosure.

Chapter 2

THE FIRST RUNG: THE 2017 COMMANDER DAVID FRAVOR INTERVIEW

A s some of you know, I have written about the UFO phenomenon for decades. The UFO phenomenon has become,
in some ways, my life's work. Starting with the Nephilim
Trilogy, which was published in 1999 by Zondervan, to my last book,
Countermove: How the Nephilim Returned After the Flood, which
came out in 2020, everything ties together—there is convergence.

There are now, as of this writing, thirty films in our catalogue.
Many of these films, such as *Fátima: Harbinger of Deception* and
the follow-up film *Fátima: Strange Phenomenon*, deal explicitly with
the UFO phenomenon. Then, of course, there is our ten-episode
film series *UFO Disclosure*, where we discuss the different aspects
of the phenomenon, from CE1 events (which are close encounters of
the first kind) to so-called alien abductions, cattle mutilations, and
our two films on the Roswell event. Finally, our latest addition to
the *UFO Disclosure* series, *What Is the Truth?*, is a two-part documentary that examines some of the different paradigms that are
associated with the phenomenon, from people who believe these
so-called aliens are our creators and space brothers, to people, like

me, who posit that these are not our space brothers but are in fact interdimensional entities—fallen angels.

In the Nephilim Trilogy I coined the term *the coming great deception*. Recently an associate of mine, Brad Myers, asked where I got the term. I told him that I had come up with it, but here's the rub—Brad came up with the same term around the same time I did. So I'm giving him a shout out and thanking him for his work on the UFO subject. There is always a possibility I first heard the term from some of his work; I'll never really know.

That being established, what is important is that both Brad and I have been warning about the UFO phenomena, and both of us have stated our belief that these are interdimensional entities, or fallen angels. I will delve more into this in a later chapter.

So let's discuss the first rung on the ladder of disclosure. I'm using this analogy of a ladder because, like the rungs on a ladder, we seem to be going toward some kind of full disclosure event, which is the top rung on the ladder.

In December of 2017 I was watching *Tucker Carlson Tonight* on Fox News. I enjoyed him and thought his show was one of the last bastions of conservative speech on cable news and mainstream media in general. On a Friday night Tucker announced his last segment, and his introduction went like this: "UFOs have been the stuff of conspiracy theorists for decades, often mocked for talking about it, but maybe they shouldn't be mocked."[1]

This immediately captured my attention, so I was listening and watching this introduction with great interest. This was, after all, my wheelhouse. This was what I had been investigating since I saw my first UFO at Camp Horseshoe, a scouting camp in Rising Sun, Maryland, circa 1962.

Commander David Fravor, a naval aviator, appeared on the screen shortly after an introduction. Then shortly afterward the screen became a triptych with Tucker on the left, Fravor in the middle, and a gunsight film of what is now the famous Tic Tac–shaped UFO on the right.

At this point, I was riveted to the television. I remember calling out to my wife, Peggy, "You're not going to believe what's going on! Get in here!" We were glued to the set as the following interview unfolded.

TC: Commander David Fravor spent eighteen years as a naval aviator, or pilot. In 2004 he had an unforgettable encounter with an aircraft he said was defying the laws of physics. Former Commander Fravor joins us tonight. Thanks a lot for coming on tonight. Tell us what you saw.

CF: ...We had launched on a routine training mission. When we joined up, we were told that the event was going to be canceled, and that we have real-world tasking, and we were sent out to the west. Now, take in mind that this has taken place about a hundred miles southwest of San Diego, between San Diego and Ensenada, Mexico, on a clear, perfect day, blue waters. We get out to the spot where they tell us it's at. We start looking around, and both of us, both airplanes, see disturbance in the water, and a white, forty-foot long, Tic-Tac-shaped object just hovering above the water, going forward, back, left, right. There's no rotor wash, there's no wings; nothing. So as we drive around in a clockwise flow, we get to about the nine o'clock position, and I said, "Well, I'm gonna go down and check it out." And the other jet is gonna stay high. So as we go down, and when we get to the twelve o'clock position, it starts to mirror us. So it's in a clockwise flow and it's on the opposite side of the circle from us. And we continue this. It's in a climb; we're in a descent. We're getting a great look at it. This whole thing takes about probably up to five minutes from the time we show up. I get over to the eight o'clock position, it's at about the two o'clock position, and I decide I'm gonna go and see what it is. And it's about 2,000 feet below me, and I cut across the circle. And as I get within about a half mile of it, it rapidly accelerates to the south in about two seconds and disappears.

TC: What would you estimate the speed?

CF: Oh, well above supersonic....Like a bullet out of a gun, it took off.

TC: So from what you know about aerodynamics, mechanics, physics, should this be possible, what you saw?

CF: Not with the technology that we have today; not at all.

TC: Even now, even thirteen years later, is there anything that you know of capable of this kind of behavior?

CF: No, there's nothing I know of....When we saw the video with the IR, it has no exhaust...no discernible things of [any] form of propulsion. And this thing came from a dead hover over the water, just kind of moving around, to a climb up to about 12,000 feet, to rapidly accelerating away in a climb. And in less than two seconds, it was gone. And you figure, you're talking fifty miles of visibility, and you can easily see an object that size easily out to ten miles. And it just disappeared in seconds.

TC: ...What would be the effects on a human pilot of the g-forces involved in that altitude change?

CF: Well, the altitude wouldn't be bad, it would be the acceleration of the object...Well, honestly, I wanted to fly it.

TC: Yeah, I bet.

CF: ...Talking to some physicists, they don't think the human body could handle that kind of force.

TC: Yeah, it doesn't sound like the human body could. So, bottom line. what do you think this was?

CF: I believe, as do the other folks that were on the flight that, when we visually saw it, that it was something not from this world.

TC: When presumably you expressed that belief to your superiors, what did they say?

CF: Actually, we caught a lot of grief getting back to the boat. And it got passed off as an event that no one could explain. Now, keep in mind they had been tracking these for two weeks prior to us seeing it, and this was the first time that manned airplanes had been airborne when the objects appeared.

TC: This feels like a really big story to me....It's not exactly clear why Vladimir Putin's more interesting than this. I think this seems like a big deal. And Commander, I appreciate your taking the time to talk to us about it. You seem sober and believable, and I appreciate it.[2]

Toward the end of the interview Tucker asked Commander Fravor what he thought he had seen. Without hesitation Fravor stated, on the record, "I believe, as do the other folks that were on the flight that, when we visually saw it, that it was something not from this world."

I about fell out of my chair and told the wifey, "Brace yourself because the phone and our email inbox are going to blow up!"

We prepared and waited. Shockingly, nothing happened! I think I only received one call from a friend who wondered if I had seen the Tucker interview and what my thoughts were on it.

This became the first rung on the ladder of disclosure. So let's walk through it.

The first interesting dynamic here is this: How does someone like Commander Fravor get on prime-time television? He is essentially an unknown; he doesn't have a book he's promoting, and he's not involved in a documentary film. I have two questions: Who calls up Tucker's producers and gets Commander Fravor on the show? And more importantly, why?

Think about it. Commander Fravor, as far as we know, up until that point in time had little to no media experience. Yet here he was on one of the most watched shows on cable news.

So, circling back to my first question, who has the power to call up Tucker's producers and set this up? Why now? Why in 2017 was this rolled out, and why choose Tucker to break the story?

I think this was deliberate. Tucker's audience is primarily conservative and Christian, so the powers that be, or what I would call the shadow government, rolls this out on Tucker to see what, if anything, these pesky conservative Christians will do when they hear about flying saucers.

To our shame, the church at large, of which I am a part, essentially didn't do anything; it was business as usual. In other words, to coin something from the medical profession, *it was flatlined*—essentially there was zero response.

Commander Fravor's statement that what he saw *was not from this world* is life changing in that it creates a new paradigm. It is what I would call a *mega-lever*, something that changes the existing worldview. This was being stated by a credible, trained witness whose record, from what I understand, is impeccable. He's down to earth, as it were. He's not part of the UFO world. He's levelheaded. He's reliable, supposedly someone we can trust. He just revealed information that should have impacted everyone on the planet—caused people to stop and think about what was being said—and it should have made every pastor in America and the world give an answer to their congregations the following Sunday. Sadly none of this occurred. Like I said earlier, the response to Fravor's segment on Tucker was underwhelming.

The church for the most part didn't address it. There was no reaction from most of America. It was just another news day. Even though the footage showed the Tic Tac–shaped UFO, and even though Fravor stated on the record that it shot away from him like a bullet out of a gun, not many people cared. They went about their business, not realizing that, in my opinion, everything changed that night with that broadcast. It was, in fact, the first rung on the ladder of disclosure.

That weekend I was speaking at a conference in Southern California, and my wife and I had a three-hour drive home. We stopped at a wonderful restaurant, and on a napkin—which burned in the 2018 Malibu fire that turned our home into dust—I scrawled the chapter titles for the book that came out shortly after: *UFO Disclosure: The 70-Year Cover-up Exposed.*

I was on a mission, and in record time, it was published.

On July 24, 2020, Commander Fravor showed up again on Tucker Carlson's show as the government began releasing some of the UFO files, including footage that includes the Tic Tac–shaped craft Commander Fravor witnessed.

Here is the transcript of that interview:

> TC: Well, much of the media have mocked the existence of unidentified flying objects. The U.S. Pentagon has been studying this subject for quite a long time and apparently will soon release some of its findings, which remain classified. According to a new report in the *New York Times*, the U.S. government may have physical evidence of—and we're quoting—"off-world vehicles, not made on this earth." Huh.
>
> The government has also released footage of UFO sightings, including a 2004 encounter recorded from an advanced navy fighter jet.
>
> Commander David Fravor is a retired naval aviator who once saw something he could not explain, that science can't explain. We're honored to have him on tonight. Mr. Favor, thanks so much for coming on.
>
> So...tell us if you think this is being misinterpreted. According to the *New York Times*, the U.S. government has physical evidence of some sort of vehicle made not on this earth. Is it what it sounds like?

CF: Well, that sounds that way to me, Tucker....I never want to speculate what the government truly has. But I would say there's stuff out there. I mean, the four of us that chased the Tic Tac in 2004 have attested to it multiple times, that what we saw exceeded anything that we had in our inventory, far superior to the airplanes that we were flying in at the time—they were brand new. So, I would say, yes, there's something out there. And hopefully the government does have stuff.

TC: So, when we spoke before about this and you suggested that the object you saw, that you chased, the Tic Tac, behaved in ways that challenged your understanding of aeronautics, of physics, and that you didn't think it was likely that that object...belonged to a foreign military. Do you think the U.S. government has concluded that this is not Russia, China, or some other country?

CF: I'm pretty sure of that...you know, just by some of the phone calls that we've gotten, some of the people that we have talked to in the government, that they are unaware of what this is. And I think that ties directly with the East Coast sighting, with the Gimbal video.[3] And I'd be willing to say, just because I'm in contact with a lot of these people, that there are more incidents that are starting to come out, that people are starting to report inside the government channels, of things that they've seen. And I think you're seeing it from people in the past, because it always had that taboo to come out and talk about these things. You're not finding people from the past that are saying, "Hey, I saw this; I just was never told to report it," or "When I did, I was told not to say anything." So I think since 2017, the world is starting to change because of the publicity, because of the attention of the Senate and the Congress, because of people like Marco Rubio on the intel committee, of telling the DOD, "Hey, I want a report." I think you're starting to see more and more of that. And I would say if the government does have stuff, and I don't know what they have, but if they do, I would think that, you know, there's probably stuff. [unintelligible] Roswell was seventy-three years ago. If something did happen, because there's a lot of speculation that there was something other than a weather balloon, where's all that at? I mean, if just by odds something would be here.

TC: So that raises the question, why all the secrecy? I mean, clearly the U.S. government has lied to the public for maybe seventy-three years. Why do you think?

CF: Well, you know, if we go back to like Project Blue Book and go, you know, it was done. It really did two things. One, it investigated occurrences and sightings that people saw. The other one was it primarily was sent...out to debunk, to prove that it wasn't, or to make excuses of why it wasn't. I don't know why. I think some of it was trying to capture that technology. But if something lands in your front yard, there's no reason to deny that it existed or, you know, for the government to cover it up because, you know, if it's not collected by some means that's gonna question our national security or our defender or our offensive or defensive capabilities, then why would you hide it? That just baffles me. Just like our incident. Why wasn't it thoroughly investigated at the time? For something that literally could penetrate a battlegroup spaces, and they did nothing. I mean, there was nothing done until, really, about 2009.

TC: I mean, there's a story here that a lot of us can't wait to see. Finally, do you feel vindicated?

CF: I never...You could say that. But I never...You know, most of the fellow aviators that know the group of us, we were never like chastised or...I mean, you get ribbed, but it was never like you're crazy or anything like that. But I know there are people that do have that fear of coming out saying, you know, that it's going to ruin their career, and for me, it just wasn't…it was never the case with us.

TC: Right. Well, that's the beauty of being a naval aviator; people take you seriously, by definition. Commander, thanks so much.[4]

SUMMATION

In my opinion what transpired on *Tucker Carlson Tonight* was life-changing. It was in some ways a paradigm shift. It was the first rung on the ladder of disclosure. It was information that every American should have gone over and over and over, and then asked questions. It was a moment in time that changed everything. Fravor's testimony was an admission that UFOs are *real, burgeoning, and not going away.*

Chapter 3

THE SECOND RUNG: THE LUIS ELIZONDO INTERVIEW

THE SECOND RUNG of the disclosure ladder was on Tucker Carlson's show once again on a Friday. This is where I was introduced to Luis Elizondo. Elizondo headed up what is now a defunct government task force, AATIP, which stands for *Advanced Aerospace Threat Identification Program.*[1] This program was initiated by then Senator Harry Reid. There was, as far as I know, no congressional oversight, which immediately poses questions. How was its funding tucked into a defense appropriations bill? Why don't the taxpayers know more about this? Oh wait! Is this once again proof that there is a shadow government that has been in place since WWII? Am I going down the conspiracy rabbit hole? Somebody, stop me please!

I remember standing behind the grassy knoll in Dallas. There was some graffiti in black marker scrawled on one of the fence pickets: "Magic bullet, magic buildings, magic birth certificate."

Let me explain; I apologize for going down this rabbit hole, but I am going to digress for a moment.

JFK was gunned down in Dallas, and in my opinion, we have never had a real president since except two: Ronald Reagan and Donald Trump. They tried to kill Reagan, and Trump recently was injured in an assassination attempt. Before that, he had been hit with incessant lies about supposed Russian collusion, which in 2022 was conclusively proven to be a 100 percent hoax, and it turns out the plan to release the uncorroborated information about Trump was approved by none other than...wait for it...Hillary Clinton![2] Say it isn't so.

Kennedy was trying to bring our boys home from Vietnam, abolish the Federal Reserve, and splinter the CIA into a thousand pieces. Strike three.

In 2022 Tucker Carlson spoke to a former CIA spook, and he reported on his show that he asked if the agency had been involved in the assassination. The man, who was not on camera, answered yes.[3] Then there's a meeting I had with a former agent who got out of the CIA when he witnessed the corruption firsthand. He, too, told me that the agency had been involved. The Warren Commission insisted that the lone gunman theory was the correct narrative, laying all three shots at the feet of Lee Harvey Oswald, but I'm not buying any of it for a minute, and most Americans don't either. Still nothing happens. No one dares challenge the official record, and our elected officials don't do squat. I could go on, but I'll restrain myself.

Then we have the events of 9/11. We saw the Twin Towers collapse at free-fall speed and turn to dust before our eyes. However, the smoking gun is Building 7, which was not hit by a plane yet collapsed into its own footprint about eight hours later. Nothing to see here. Now we are patted down, our baggage searched, and our eyeballs scanned. Police state anyone?

Then there's the unknown man whose college records are sealed; therefore, we know very little about him. He supposedly rose from being a community organizer to a junior senator, and then he became president of the United States. Of course, I'm speaking about Barry Soetoro. Oh, wait, Mr. Barry changed his name to Barak Hussein Obama. Most of us know about the dustup with Obama's birth certificate. Is it real? Fake? Where was Mr. Obama born? When the Obama administration presented the birth certificate, Sheriff Joe Arpaio pointed out multiple and at times glaring discrepancies.[4]

The bottom line for me is this. We, the American people, have a right to know the truth, but we will likely never see or hear the truth concerning what I've presented here. It is a managed agenda, a controlled narrative. And because the church is anemic and many Americans are asleep, there is little to no pushback in search for the truth.

I feel so much better now having cleared the air with all the conspiracy stuff. Thanks for listening! So let's get on with what Elizondo stated.

———•———

Tucker Carlson: Do you think the U.S. government has debris from a UFO in its possession right now?

Luis Elizondo: ...Simply put, yes.[5]

This admission by Luis Elizondo was essentially the *second rung* on the ladder of disclosure. Elizondo admitted on camera that our government has in its possession debris from crashed UFOs. For those of us who have been in the field of ufology for decades, this is nothing new. In fact we shall see as we climb further up the ladder that this debris that was covered by the mainstream media over the ensuing months morphed into a full-blown, working UFO craft *from another world*! Not so fast, citizen! We'll address this claim when we get to that rung of the ladder. Let's continue with this short, terse statement from our good friend, ex-military, head of AATIP—the secret government program—Mr. Elizondo. I trust everything he says; don't you?

When I saw this segment on Tucker Carlson's show, I immediately thought about the so-called Roswell crash of 1947. I have always believed that the official story from our military-industrial complex was 100 percent bogus, double talk, spin. The original story that was released is the true one—the Army did recover a crashed disc.

In our two films on Roswell we delve into this, in addition to the interviews I conducted with Dr. Jesse Marcel Jr., his widow, and his daughter, Denice. Our film crew went out to the Roswell debris site. Until you drive to the debris field location, you do not get the perspective of just how far out in the middle of nowhere the site is. Gil Zimmerman (my business partner in our film works), Jim Petersen (who runs all the sound equipment when we are filming), Chuck Zukowski, Frank Kimbler, and I drove out to the debris field. It really is in a very isolated area. There's nothing for miles.

When we arrived, I had to pinch myself. There I was, in the legendary debris field of the 1947 Roswell crash. So when Elizondo stated in front of millions of Americans that we, the United States of America, have in our possession the debris of a craft from another world, what are we to make of that? It is a bold statement, but in my opinion, it is part of a managed agenda to roll out the reality of UFOs/UAPs.

> Luis Elizondo's very brief answer to Tucker Carlson's question about whether the U.S. government is in possession of recovered crashed and landed UFO technology hardware is 1,000% accurate. My national security NDAs prevent me from adding any further comment on this.[6]
>
> —Dr. Eric Davis, Astrophysicist and Consultant to AATIP

I just love the statement here. It's hilarious and is an example of the typical type of doublespeak we get from nonelected officials: "My national security NDAs prevent me from adding any further comment on this."

In essence Dr. Davis already violated his NDA by admitting that

Luis Elizondo's statement is "1,000% accurate." Once again we see someone who is tied to the military-industrial complex, Dr. Eric Davis, an astrophysicist and consultant to AATIP, the Pentagon UAP study program.

Another managed agenda brought to you by the military-industrial complex. Remember, President Eisenhower warned us about this in his farewell address. A clip of his statement was featured in Oliver Stone's Oscar-winning *JFK*. There's a link to clips of the statement with commentary in the endnotes.[7]

———

> I won't talk to you about what I know about [Roswell], but it's very interesting...[His son asks him if he will declassify it.] Well, I'll have to think about that one.[8]
>
> —PRESIDENT DONALD TRUMP

President Trump, like some but not all of his predecessors, seems to have been briefed, at least in part, about the events of Roswell.

A few years ago there was a film created by a group of Christian filmmakers. Richard Shaw and I went to see it. And while we gave it two thumbs up, we stated that we had a different opinion, and that difference still stands today. These well-meaning folks declared that UFOs were *not* nuts-and-bolts craft and that the idea of the physicality of these craft was all demonic delusion. I'm not quoting them exactly, but that was the essence of their message. At the end of their film they went to great lengths to state that the Roswell incident was nothing more than a weather balloon. I think our two films on Roswell greatly clarify the matter. They prove that the Army lied, and that what crashed in Roswell was something *not of this earth*. Where have we heard that statement before?

I will tell you—I have never said this before—but I have been told by multiple people who have credentials and access that there is some truth to these stories [about Roswell]. So I don't discount this when people say this. I have had people tell me... people that have substantial scientific or military credentials that they believe it's true. So I encourage people on the Hill to pursue it.[9]

—CHRISTOPHER MELLON, FORMER DEPUTY ASSISTANT
SECRETARY OF DEFENSE FOR INTELLIGENCE

Take notice that once again we see the connection of Christopher Mellon to the military-industrial complex. It's a club, and the players who appear—out of nowhere, mind you—have been, in my opinion, handpicked for a time such as this. All this rhetoric is nothing more than a dog and pony show or Kabuki theater. Mellon told us this: "I have been told by multiple people who have credentials and access that there is some truth to these stories [about Roswell]."

As I stated earlier, we spent half a day on the Roswell debris field, and we found two pieces of metal that may be remnants of the wreckage missed by the remediation crew. And we had the metal tested—I'll get into this in depth in a later chapter.

However, Mellon was circling back to where all the disinformation started in the first place—the 1947 Roswell crash. It was not a weather balloon. Period. End of story. This canard, this lie, this bogus construct has been disproven by many credible investigators, including yours truly. My two in-depth films on the Roswell incident put an end to the lie that was foisted upon the American people and the world. So I find it really interesting that Mellon is now peddling the Roswell incident and signaling to us that there is some truth to it! What doublespeak.

I can only wonder if at some point on the ladder of disclosure we will see the actual footage of the debris field, along with the dead "alien" bodies. I use the term *alien*, but I do not believe that these recovered bodies are from another world. They are, in my opinion, avatars to house the disembodied spirits of the Nephilim that were destroyed in the Flood but wander the earth as demons. Please read the Book of Enoch for further details, or you can purchase *Countermove: How the Nephilim Returned After the Flood*.

———•*•———

> After looking into this, I came to the conclusion that there were reports—some were substantive, some not so substantive—that there were actual [UAP] materials that the government and the private sector had in their possession....It is extremely important that information about the discovery of physical materials or retrieved craft come out.[10]
> —Senator Harry Reid

What's interesting about Senator Reid's statement is that Harry Reid was the Senate majority leader, someone very high up in our government, and he stated—on the record—that UFOs are real! That's right. In the statement above Reid plainly admitted that there is actual material from UFOs. Then he added, "It is extremely important that information about the discovery of physical materials or retrieved craft come out."

As I was writing this, I was keeping an eye on the whistleblower hearings that were taking place in Congress (July–August 2023), where David Grusch—also ex-military—stated that we have "biologics" from downed UFOs.[11] In other words, without the typical doublespeak that these guys wield, they have the bodies.

Harry Reid's statement in 2021 was a deliberate rollout of the UFO phenomenon, yet what did the public do? Yawn. What did the church do? Pass the collection plate.

This is, once again, a managed agenda we are seeing. In my opinion it's deliberate.

———•———

> There was so much [debris at Roswell]. It was scattered over such a vast area [12 football fields]. We found a piece of metal, about a foot and a half or two feet wide, about two to three feet long, felt like [you] had nothing in your hands. It wasn't any thicker than the foil out of a pack of cigarettes. The thing that got me is that you couldn't even bend it; you couldn't dent it; even a sledge hammer would bounce off of it....All I could do was keep my mouth shut. Being an intelligence officer, I was familiar with every, just about all the materials used in aircraft, and in air travel, this was nothing like that. It was not anything from this earth, that I am quite sure of.[12]
>
> —JESSE MARCEL SR.

Here are the questions we must ask ourselves from the get-go: Is Jesse Marcel Sr. lying to us? Is he delusional? Mistaken? Remember his credentials: he was an intelligence officer. As an intelligence officer, Marcel was very familiar with the weather balloons that were launched from the Roswell base on a daily basis. To paint Marcel as somehow incompetent or untrained is absurd. This is why in our two films on Roswell we drilled down into who Marcel was, his credentials, what he knew, and the fact that he went to his grave stating that he had been set up and was essentially made to be a patsy. He was just another "lone gunman."

As I mentioned earlier, in our search of the crash location we found two pieces of metal that could be debris from the craft. We had it analyzed, and the results were shocking. Test results show it is *not an exact match to any known metal*. The pieces of this metal we found were buried about six inches beneath the surface, each piece folded in on itself. They didn't get all of it!

———•———

Podcast host Joe Rogan asked Christopher Mellon about the possibility that we have obtained an extraterrestrial craft and are in the process of trying to back engineer it. Mellon answered:

> That's a really ticklish question for me and awkward. And if I were to say "Yep, it's true," nobody would believe me. If I really knew, I couldn't say yes. And…so it's hard to give good answers to that question. I think it's plausible. I don't say that I think people should rule that out. It's a legitimate question to ask. There's enough information to suggest something like that may have happened. We may have recovered some debris….It would be so deeply squirreled away that you wouldn't be able to bring in the best scientists, you wouldn't be able to bring in world-class scientists. You would have available maybe a few people inside some aerospace company, and they would probably be very hamstrung in their ability to test and examine the material and so forth. And it would just be locked away somewhere.[13]

Just remember who Christopher Mellon is. He is in intelligence. He's trained. How come he gets interviewed? Who sets that up? Why Mellon? In my opinion it's a controlled narrative, a managed agenda.

———•———

> [Astrophysicist Eric] Davis, who now works for Aerospace Corporation, a defense contractor, said he gave a classified briefing to a Defense Department agency as recently as March about retrievals from "off-world vehicles not made on this earth." Mr. Davis said he also gave classified briefings on retrievals of unexplained objects to staff members of the Senate Armed Services Committee on Oct. 21, 2019, and to

staff members of the Senate Intelligence Committee two days later.[14]

"'Off-world vehicles not made on this earth'"! You would think that with statements like this the church would be clamoring for answers. You would think pastors would be reaching out to those of us in the body of Christ—admittedly there are few—who have the answers from a biblical paradigm. Sadly this is not the case. My phone doesn't ring. And I may get one or two emails a month from a pastor who wants to know more.

This is the sad state of affairs that we find ourselves in. I can sum it up in one word concerning the church—ambivalence. Just so there's no mistaking this, here's the definition: "the state of having mixed feelings or contradictory ideas about something or someone."[15]

Here are some examples:

- "Well, there's something out there, but we will most likely never really know what it is."
- "What do UFOs have to do with the gospel?"
- "We'll be raptured, so we won't have to deal with any of this."
- "We should concentrate on the salvation message rather than waste our time with so-called aliens."

I could go on, but I think you get the point.

We have crash retrievals, and they have been analyzed and unfortunately our laboratory diagnostic technologies and our material sciences and the understanding of physics that we had were not advanced enough to be able to make heads or tails of what it is, of what they had their hands on.[16]

—Dr. Eric Davis

In the Book of Enoch (chapters 7 and 8), we read about a quid pro quo between the fallen angels and the men who are in the world at the time. We see that technology is given to mankind in exchange for access to the women. In other words, just like the vampire lore that is part of our culture, there has to be *permission* granted. These fallen beings just can't take what they want when they want it. There are certain protocols in place.

Investigative journalist and author Ross Coulthart asked Nat Kobitz, former director of U.S. Navy science and technology development, "Are you able to confirm to me that the U.S. has been trying to develop recovered alien technology?"

Kobitz's response was, "Yes, I can say that's so."[17]

How many times do we have to hear the same thing before we realize that something is happening right under our noses? We better take notice. I was speaking to someone on the phone a few days ago about the ongoing revealing of the so-called alien presence. We agreed that the ambivalence amongst the populace regarding the so-called disclosure is unbelievable. It's like no one cares. The churches, for the most part, are neither discussing it nor addressing it in any way. This gross lack of discernment and not alerting their congregations to what is going on will come back to haunt them in the days ahead. In my opinion much of the church has lost its salt; it is more concerned with having people feel good and view themselves positively than warning them of what is right now manifesting all around them. It's all in the prophetic passages in our Bibles.

Men will faint from fear and anxiety over what is coming upon the earth, for the powers of the heavens will be shaken.
—LUKE 21:26, BSB

...to deceive, if possible, even the elect.
—MATTHEW 24:24, NIV

The coming of the lawless one is by the activity of Satan with all power and false signs and wonders, and with all wicked deception for those who are perishing, because they refused to love the truth and so be saved. Therefore God sends them a strong delusion, so that they may believe what is false.
—2 THESSALONIANS 2:9–11, ESV

I remember speaking at a church in Alabama. The pastor's son was sitting in the front row during my presentation, and I could tell that he wasn't buying what I was saying. As I usually do when giving presentations, I asked the audience, "Please raise your hand if you have seen lights in the sky, UFOs, orbs, entities, or had sleep paralysis." About a third of the people raised their hands. Shocked, the pastor's son came up to me after my lecture and said that he expected only two or three people would respond. He was blown away by the percentage of people who raised their hands in confirmation. Even more shocking, this number is consistent when I give lectures: *about one-third raise their hands as having experienced these phenomena.* With that said, why isn't the church addressing this?

———

Even before this 'whistleblower' legislation was signed into law, credible individuals were providing Congress information alleging that the U.S. government has recovered extraterrestrial technology. This process began in 2019 when I brought astrophysicist Dr. Eric Davis to Capitol Hill to meet with staff from the Senate Intelligence and Armed Services committees.

Dr. Davis, author of the famous Wilson-Davis memo, provided specific information lending credence to sensational reports that an official U.S. government program is actively seeking to exploit recovered technology that was fashioned by some other species or perhaps advanced AI machines.[18]

—CHRISTOPHER MELLON

Lieutenant Colonel Philip J. Corso's book, *The Day After Roswell*, which was first published in 1997, was sort of a deathbed confession revealing the fact that our government was involved in the reverse engineering of so-called extraterrestrial craft. Bob Lazar stated as much about eight years before Corso's publication; the early whistleblower's story has been vindicated. Lazar stated, on the record, that he was involved in back engineering the propulsion system from a UFO. He also stated that he saw what he termed the "sport model" hovering at a secret military base known as S4,[19] which is part of the enigmatic and mysterious—and by the way, even presidents have never been there—Area 51. How is it that presidents are *not* allowed to see what's there? A shadow government is the only plausible answer. "They" have been in control since the 1947 Roswell crash.

When I was threatened in 2016 by a guy from the deep state, the man stated that it didn't matter who was elected or in the White House. "They," the agency he worked for, were autonomous. They did what they wanted to do and essentially were accountable to no one.

I've never forgotten that conversation.

Lazar worked on the propulsion system. He claimed he was working with element 115. Corso stated that he disseminated material from the Roswell crash site to the private sector, where some of it was back engineered successfully.[20]

In one of our Roswell films we show the testimony of Jim and Carolyn Rankin, who stated on the record that Colonel Hill (whom they were taking care of in the last days of Hill's life) said that the wreckage from Roswell was shipped to Wright-Patterson Field (Wright Field in 1947).[21]

Once again, the powers that be lie, obfuscate, threaten, and are never straight with the public. These people are essentially above the law. They answer to no one. However, I would posit that they have made a Faustian pact and they don't know who it is they are dealing with. In the end these demonic forces will totally control the narrative.

———•———

> I talk over the following weeks with other anonymous insiders. To protect their identities, I cannot reveal much of the astonishing detail of what they told me but I am left in no doubt that they all assert that the U.S. military, almost certainly the U.S. Air Force, is in possession of retrieved non-terrestrial—alien—technology. Intriguingly, what I am told matches the claims made in the Admiral Wilson memo, that a private aerospace company now exercises control over this alien technology.[22]
>
> —Ross Coulthart

Need I say more? You would think that bombshell statements like this would be talked about from every pulpit in America and beyond. Sadly this is not the case. "My people are destroyed for lack of knowledge" (Hos. 4:6).

———•———

> I was told for decades that Lockheed had some of these retrieved materials. And I tried to get, as I recall, a classified approval by the Pentagon to have me go look at the stuff. They would not approve that. I don't know what all the numbers were, what kind of classification it was, but they would not give that to me....That's why I wanted [AATIP to get special

access program status] to take a look at it. But they wouldn't give me the clearance.[23]

—SENATOR HARRY REID

Why can't Reid get permission? Who is controlling whom? Who stops him from doing what, frankly, every elected official should be doing? Why is this information so secretive? What branch of government is in control of this? Are these elected officials or a rogue element?

SUMMATION

The second rung is Elizondo's admission that we have debris from crashed UFOs. However, this opens the floodgates from other "players," who seem to make it very clear that not only do we have the debris but we're in the process of back engineering it. Meanwhile the American people are left in the dark, and anyone who wants to find out more is labeled a conspiracy theorist. *Nothing to see here... please keep moving.*

Chapter 4

THE THIRD RUNG: WE
TESTED THE METAL

W HAT I FIND interesting about this rung on the ladder of disclosure is twofold. The first is that the information was released once again on Tucker Carlson's show when it was on Fox News. The second is that the man who delivered the information was Christopher Mellon, who is linked with the CIA.

You will notice that the information highway seems to be Tucker Carlson's show. Why, you ask? Well, I have an idea. While this is conjecture on my part, I think it makes a lot of sense.

Who has the power to call up Tucker's producers and "insist" perhaps that Commander David Fravor be scheduled as a guest on the show? I covered some of this in chapter 2, but please remember, Fravor, at the time of his appearing on *Tucker Carlson Tonight,* was an unknown. He didn't have a book to sell, hadn't starred in a new feature film, and hadn't produced an award-winning documentary. Essentially he was an unknown, and to me this raises several red flags. The first question is the timing. Why did they start revealing the so-called extraterrestrial presence in 2017? Why then? Why, after all the years of deliberate obfuscation, did they start to roll out to the public that UAPs were real? Second, why Fravor? Third, who are the people that make these decisions from the shadows?

I think Tucker was chosen to release this information in a test run to see how his audience would react. Essentially there was little or no response. I would also add that Tucker's audience is made up primarily of Christian conservatives, and they, for the most part, did not react. As I stated already, my phone didn't ring, and I received only one or two emails the day after the broadcast that addressed what had been revealed on Tucker's show. Several of the rungs on the ladder of disclosure were first revealed on Tucker Carlson's show, and I think Tucker was deliberately chosen because of the makeup of his audience.

To put it another way, the powers that be are testing to see how Christians will couch the revealing of the so-called extraterrestrial presence. I think they are doing this because the church did not believe in the plurality of worlds before the so-called Age of Enlightenment. In their view there was no other life in the universe, and earth was the only place where life as we know it existed.

I was at a New Age conference right before COVID-19 hit, and not surprisingly, I was the only Christian speaker. I've spoken to these audiences many times over the years; it is a part of my calling in ministry. George Noory was the host, and some of the speakers included Nick Pope, Nick Redfern, and other well-known names of the genre. We were all on stage, and George Noory posed a question to the audience.

"How many of you believe in life on other planets?" *Every hand in the room went up.*

Then he asked, "Is there anyone here who doesn't believe that life exists outside of earth?"

I raised my hand, and as I did so, I looked around the room and realized I was alone in my position. George was taken aback by this, and asked me why I held to this belief.

I present the following diatribe at most of my conferences that deal with the UFO phenomenon.

If the universe is analogous to the United States, where is planet

Earth? Is it in Duluth? Walla Walla? Dallas? Orlando? You see what I mean? We have no idea where Earth is in the expanse of universe.

The argument presented that we are not alone in the universe goes something like this. With the universe containing thousands of galaxies and innumerable planets, we would be arrogant to think we are the only life or creation.

At first this seems to make perfect, rational sense. But what if the universe as we see it and know it is a hologram?[1] If that is a true statement, it would explain a lot of what we see in regard to the UFO phenomenon.

Here are some of the reasons I hold to my position regarding the plurality of worlds.

1. Jesus incarnates here on Earth. Even though C. S. Lewis posits this with his incredible series *Out of the Silent Planet*, *Perelandra*, and *That Hideous Strength*, in the end Jesus came here, not to some other planet in a galaxy far away.

2. We have scriptures that tell us God will roll up the heavens like a scroll (Isa. 34:4; Rev. 6:14) and create a new heaven and a new earth (Isa. 65:17; Rev. 21:1). Do we take this literally? I do; I have no problem believing in the literal meaning of rolling up the heavens.

3. Finally, the New Jerusalem descends (Rev. 21:2) into the atmosphere of Zeta Reticuli, right? Of course not! The huge flying craft that descends from another dimension into ours arrives at, you guessed it, planet Earth.

With all of this on our intellectual plates from the biblical narrative, it sums up why I do not believe there is life elsewhere in the universe.

But who and what are these intruders, as Gary Stearman likes to call them? They are, in my opinion, interdimensional entities. They are the fallen ones, the watchers, the ones who left their first estates, the rebels. They can move in and out of our dimension, and they have created the technology to do this.

Former Defense Department official Christopher Mellon appeared with James Fox on *Tucker Carlson Tonight* to discuss Fox's new documentary, *The Phenomenon*. Mellon stated that the metal from crashed UFOs was tested. The results showed the "materials were engineered at an atomic level" and that they were *not* found on planet Earth.[2]

The implications of Mellon's statement change everything—we have scientific proof that the metal did not originate on planet Earth. This immediately raises all sorts of questions: Where did the metal come from? Who are the beings that created the metal? Can we duplicate this metal?

Now that we have this information, *we know that we are not alone*. But this still doesn't mean we are being visited from entities from another world. They are the ancient ones that we read about in Genesis 6.

CHRISTOPHER MELLON

According to the biography on History:

> A descendant of the founder of the Mellon Bank, Chris Mellon served as the Deputy Assistant Secretary of Defense for Intelligence during the Bill Clinton and George W. Bush administrations. For over a dozen years, Chris worked on national security issues on Capitol Hill, including many years on the Senate Intelligence Committee, where he ultimately served as the Minority Staff Director. Chris is the team's government liaison, using his access and relationships with high-level officials to prompt the government to take action on what he believes is a serious threat to national security.[3]

In 2020 Phil Owen wrote an article, published on *The Wrap*, covering the episode of *Tucker Carlson Tonight* where Tucker interviewed Fox and Mellon. Ufologist Jacques Vallee is referenced in regard to the metal that was retrieved from "crashed" UFOs. Quoting the documentary as well as the interview, the article says:

> "Dr. Jacque [*sic*] Vallee has collected purported metal debris from UFO cases dating as far back as 1947 that experts are analyzing in a state-of-the-art laboratory. He was astonished to find their composition was unlike any known metal."
>
> Then we see Dr. Vallee claim that the materials he has were "manufactured" by someone—but the problem is that the materials are "not natural to the materials that we have around us in the lab on the Earth."...
>
> "In terms of the materials, there are private researchers, Jacques, perhaps foremost among them," Mellon said. "Jacques is a meticulous scientist, so he's sending it to peer review and multiple labs. But the gist of it is that those materials were engineered at an atomic level. *It's a capability that we don't even possess.* If they can prove that, demonstrate that, that'll raise a lot of interesting questions."[4]

CONCLUSION

What is really interesting to me about this rung on the UFO ladder of disclosure is the fact that scientists have looked at the metal that was retrieved from crashed UFOs and stated on the record that the signature doesn't match anything that we have on earth, like the metal we found on the Roswell debris site. As Mellon said, this raises a lot of questions. Where was this metal created? Who created it? I am amazed that with the data released by the government, information documented in the film *The Phenomenon*, and the fact that Tucker Carlson has been covering this, Americans remain so unfazed. You would think that there would be a groundswell of people all across our country demanding answers. Yet, as Tucker stated in the interview, people were more concerned about the fly on Mike Pence's forehead during the 2016 presidential debates than they were about these jaw-dropping revelations.[5]

As we continue to climb up the rungs of the UFO ladder of disclosure, we will see that the information being released on the UFO/ UAP subject affects literally every single person on this planet. This is why it's imperative that we come to terms with the phenomenon from a biblical standpoint.

Chapter 5

THE FOURTH RUNG: "OFF-WORLD VEHICLES NOT MADE ON THIS EARTH"

D R. ERIC DAVIS revealed the information in the title of this chapter in an interview with the *New York Times*.[1] Think about it. This is an astounding statement and one that essentially affects every man, woman, and child on this planet. Its implications are staggering. This statement changes everything, and yet nothing changed with the vast majority of people. People got up and went to work. People went out to dinner and the movies, played golf, cheered their favorite sports team, hunted, fished, went camping, and a thousand other activities that humans engage in. It was business as usual! And yet this statement is anything but business as usual.

The first question we must ask is this: How long has the Pentagon had these so-called vehicles that were not made on this earth? Did this happen in the 1950s when then President Eisenhower went to Holloman Air Force Base?[2] The story that was circulated to the American people was that President Eisenhower had emergency dental surgery. However, for those of us in the field of ufology, this claim seemed to be a cover for what really went down.

Here's the summary of it: Eisenhower was, at some point, briefed about the crash at Roswell and the retrieved bodies, as well as parts of the wreckage. He may have seen pictures or actual film of the retrieval of both the wreckage and the corpses. He may have been told that the "aliens" were interested in making a treaty of some sort with us, and that they were willing to give us the technology for access to the human population. This may have been done under the lie that these were extraterrestrials from a dying planet who were incapable of reproduction due to the degradation of their DNA, meaning they needed fresh DNA from us to continue their species.[3] I have heard this theory for decades and used it in my first book, *Nephilim: The Truth is Here.*

At any rate, there are many of us who believe that Ike was whisked away to Holloman Air Force Base, met with the aliens, and signed a treaty with them.

In our second film in the *UFO Disclosure* series,[4] I sat down with researcher and author Preston Dennett. We both agreed that this was the case—that Ike did sign the treaty at Holloman, and this led to the U.S. acquiring the *vehicles not made on this earth!*

It is interesting that this mirrors what happened so long ago, in the days of Noah, when the sons of God (i.e., the watchers) landed on Mount Hermon and then made sort of a contract with the men, which was essentially this: *We'll give you this technology, and in return you give us access to the women.*

Was the same type of quid pro quo exchanged between Ike and the so-called extraterrestrials? Many of us believe the answer to this is a resounding yes. This happened before the Flood, and the results will be just as catastrophic now as they were in the days of Noah.

Remember, Jesus warned us that *it will be like the days of Noah when the Son of Man returns* (Matt. 24:37; Luke 17:26). Out of all the books in the Tanakh that He could reference, He pointed back to the Genesis 6 narrative. Why did He do this? What was He trying to tell us?

I do believe that two thousand years ago the Jews who followed Jesus knew exactly what He was referring to. At that time, there was no Sethite theory, which states that the *sons of God* in Genesis 6 are the godly line of Seth and the women mentioned in the text are the ungodly line of Cain. This theory came about hundreds of years later.[5] Yet this exegesis of Genesis 6—that I believe is deficient—is now the prevailing position of most seminaries. That being the case, the people sitting in the pews never understand the implications and warnings of Genesis 3:15. I will bring the reader to this scripture once again, because I don't think I can repeat it often enough. I think it's paramount to our understanding of *the seed war*, which is, in my opinion, the essence of the biblical prophetic narrative. It's that important. The summary of the scripture is this: *The offspring of the Dragon will be at war with the offspring of the woman. The Messiah will crush the Dragon's head, and the Dragon will bruise His heel.*

This is the first prophecy in the Bible. It is the first mention of the *protoevangelium*, the first mention of the Messiah and the first promise of redemption in Scripture. Genesis 3:15 essentially contains God's plan of salvation, as Jesus is the Seed of the woman who would one day crush the head of the serpent (Satan). In the process of conquering the Dragon, Jesus would bruise His heel on the cross, being wounded as He achieved victory over sin.[6] In my opinion this one scripture encapsulates the entire biblical prophetic narrative; it sets up everything else we read in our Bibles. If we don't get this right, then we have no understanding of *the seed war*, its implications, and its consequences for humanity from the time of Moses until the present day.

Back to the Pentagon having "*off-world vehicles not made on this earth.*" The American people had no say in any of this. We were not represented at Holloman Air Force Base. We were not privy to the discussion. In fact, what happened at Holloman—if the stories are true—remains hidden from us, but we can go back to the Roswell crash of 1947. I think there was a retrieved disc, and the army had it right with the first report. But the story was changed, and the *big* lie was told to the American people, I assume under the ever-changing pretext of national security. In reality the American people were kept in the dark for decades. Shadow government anyone?

WHAT ARE THESE VEHICLES?

This is a big question for me. And how do they work? What materials are used in their construction?

I have heard all sorts of stories about these craft, these UFOs/UAPs. I have no idea whether any of them are true. Witnesses who go inside the craft sometimes say that the craft is the size of a football field inside, yet the outside diameter is only around sixty feet! How is that possible?

Then we have the reports from the Roswell event about the so-called mystery metal.[7] According to some witnesses, the metal had very strange properties. It was very light, and you could roll it up into a ball, but when you let it out of your hand, it would return to its original shape without a crease or wrinkle in it. Reports stated technicians that hit the metal with a hammer to try to dent it were unsuccessful. In other words, the metal was almost indestructible, yet when the Roswell crash happened, the craft disintegrated into perhaps thousands of pieces.

As we show in our films on Roswell, and as I already mentioned, we found two pieces of the metal in the Roswell debris field. We too had it professionally tested in a respected lab, and the results were shocking.

Bob Lazar talks about working with the propulsion system. He allegedly was hired to back engineer what made the craft go. Years ago Lazar talked about a gravity wave that pulled the craft along using the mysterious element 115.[8] He stated that this gravity wave bent time and space as we know it and *pulled* the craft, so essentially there were no g-forces like pilots experience when they accelerate or make a sharp dive. This would account for the right angle turns that we see these craft do. It also would account for the "jumping" through space, as Norio Hayakawa and Gary Shultz recorded at Area 51 decades ago.[9]

This may also explain what Commander David Fravor stated on Tucker Carlson's show, when he said the Tic Tac–shaped object shot away from him like *a bullet from a gun*. This also corroborates the testimony of a man we refer to simply as Dennis, the pilot I interviewed in our first UFO film. He stated, on the record, that the craft moved about fifty miles in two seconds.[10]

Who Made Them?

Of course, the questions that every researcher asks are: Who is making these craft? Where are they constructed? For those who hold to a biblical worldview, some have a problem when it comes to this because many of us have, in my opinion, a truncated view of the supernatural. This is why I research supernatural technology in the Bible. There is technology throughout the pages of our Bibles. I'll give you one example, and it's one of my favorites: the *flaming sword* that turns every which way in the Garden of Eden! What is that? A heavenly laser-sword?

Some folks will immediately state that angels, both on the side of the Lord and the fallen ones, don't need a craft of any kind. But how do we know this?

At this point we need to go to 2 Kings and read this important text because I think it demonstrates to us that there are vehicles that are used by the heavenly hosts.

> Once when the king of Syria was warring against Israel, he took counsel with his servants, saying, "At such and such a place shall be my camp." But the man of God sent word to the king of Israel, "Beware that you do not pass this place, for the Syrians are going down there." And the king of Israel sent to the place about which the man of God told him. Thus he used

to warn him, so that he saved himself there more than once or twice.

And the mind of the king of Syria was greatly troubled because of this thing, and he called his servants and said to them, "Will you not show me who of us is for the king of Israel?" And one of his servants said, "None, my lord, O king; but Elisha, the prophet who is in Israel, tells the king of Israel the words that you speak in your bedroom." And he said, "Go and see where he is, that I may send and seize him." It was told him, "Behold, he is in Dothan." So he sent there horses and chariots and a great army, and they came by night and surrounded the city.

When the servant of the man of God rose early in the morning and went out, behold, an army with horses and chariots was all around the city. And the servant said, "Alas, my master! What shall we do?" He said, "Do not be afraid, for those who are with us are more than those who are with them." Then Elisha prayed and said, "O LORD, please open his eyes that he may see." So the LORD opened the eyes of the young man, and he saw, and behold, the mountain was full of horses and *chariots of fire* all around Elisha.
—2 KINGS 6:8–17, ESV, EMPHASIS ADDED

What were these chariots of fire that the text refers too? Remember that Gehazi was witnessing something that was first and foremost supernatural; he had never seen anything like them. Second, he had no words in his vocabulary to communicate what he was seeing. At the time of 2 Kings, the mode of transportation was a chariot. So Gehazi was using something that he knew and was familiar with to explain what he was seeing. Fire, torchlight, and cooking fires with glowing hot coals were common to Gehazi. Putting the two together, *chariots of fire,* we get some kind of vehicle that is *not from this earth.* I realize that for some of you this might be a stretch, but there are other passages in the *Guidebook to the Supernatural* (a term I coined referring to our Bibles) that point to this. One passage is found in Ezekiel. Many commentators have attempted to describe what Ezekiel was seeing. I remember talking with a guy who called Ezekiel's description "Father God taking a spin in his '57 Chevy."

To wrap this up, I might add that no one has all the answers to the mysteries that surround us; I am not claiming to have all the answers either. However, it seems reasonable to me that craft are used by both sides in the heavenly war that we find ourselves in.

WHERE ARE THEY STORED?

In our two films on Roswell, which are episodes 7 and 8 in the *UFO Disclosure* series, Jim and Carolyn Rankin give an on-camera testimony regarding Colonel Hill.[11] Hill was Office of Strategic Services (OSS), which was the forerunner of the CIA. He had several degrees and was fluent in multiple languages. Hill stated that the wreckage from the Roswell crash in 1947 was flown to Wright Field in Ohio. There is also the possibility that some of it was moved to Area 51 outside Las Vegas, Nevada.

Bob Lazar stated that he had worked on back engineering the propulsion system of the craft. He said he was working with element 115. He stated that our government had more than one UFO disc in their possession, and he allegedly saw one craft, which he called the sport model, hovering outside a hangar.

When did the Pentagon come into the possession of these vehicles? Who gave these off-world vehicles to the Pentagon?

WHERE ARE THEY FROM?

This is the big question for many people: Are we alone in the universe? Some insist that with the billions of stars and galaxies we now know make up the *known* universe, surely we would be remiss to think that we are the only life in the vast expanse. I have mentioned this before, so I won't belabor this here. But as you know, I do not believe in the plurality of worlds; I think we're it.

I realize this goes against what many people now think; however, we don't know what this—the universe—is and how it was created. We don't know. More importantly, as Christians we believe that Jesus spoke everything into existence.

> In the beginning was the Word, and the Word was with God,
> and the Word was God. He was in the beginning with God.
> All things were made through him, and without him was not
> any thing made that was made.
>
> —JOHN 1:1–3, ESV

I hold onto this with both intellectual hands. This is my anchor, my reality, my hope, the answers to life's most puzzling questions.

Are these intruders, as elder brother Gary Stearman likes to call them, really from Zeta Reticuli or Epsilon Eridani? Are they our space brothers, our progenitors, who seeded us here millennia ago? Or are they nefarious entities with a dark, malevolent agenda? Of course you know what I think; it is the latter—they are indeed nefarious entities.

They abduct children, which is kidnapping; they implant them with metallic objects; they violate or rape them as they take sperm from men and ova from the women. They have no regard for humans and seem to enjoy our fear.

I have been studying and researching this phenomenon for decades. I have spent time with abductees. And in our film *UFO Disclosure: The Coming UFO Invasion*, which examines the abduction phenomenon, I think Al Matthews says it best when he states, "These are not our space brothers."[12]

WHY DIDN'T YOU TELL US YEARS AGO?

We are left with nagging questions. Why didn't our government tell us the reality of contact decades ago? They knew, but they deliberately obfuscated the truth from the American people. And why are they discussing this now? Why change the vernacular from UFOs to UAPs? Why reveal that our government has in its possession vehicles not made on this earth? Why now? I can only imagine what the powers that be actually know. However, to repeat myself, this is at best a Faustian bargain; in the end it will destroy those who are tied to it.

Chapter 6

THE FIFTH RUNG: THE "OFFICIAL REPORT"

UNCLASSIFIED

OFFICE OF THE DIRECTOR OF NATIONAL INTELLIGENCE

**Preliminary Assessment:
Unidentified Aerial Phenomena**

25 June 2021

T HE IMAGE ABOVE says it all: this was the government's "assessment" of UAPs. We dare not utter the verboten acronym UFO!

This report came out on June 25, 2021, and is about nine pages long.[1] So, what may be the greatest event in all human history—other than the resurrection of Jesus—is the acknowledgment of the truth of the so-called extraterrestrial presence. Guess what? We get about nine pages! Seriously? I about fell out of my chair I was laughing so hard. Nothing to see here, folks, keep moving! This is another example of our hard-earned tax dollars at work for us!

I'm from the government, and I'm here to help!

In short, this report was one big nothing burger.

Out of the 144 UFO sightings in the report that are supposedly investigated, only one was "solved"—the other 143 remain unsolved mysteries! Isn't that the name of a television show?

And of course our government doesn't tell us anything about where the craft may be from, who is piloting the craft, if we made contact with these entities who are flying in our skies with impunity, and on and on it goes.

You will also notice, as I mentioned earlier, that the powers that be have replaced the standard nomenclature. Instead of referring to unidentified flying objects *in the assessment,* the weasels use the new and sanctioned term *unidentified aerial phenomena*! For decades the phenomena have been referred to as UFOs. End of story. Period.

I remember when I was in Peru around 2017, UFO researcher Chase Kloetzke told me that "they" were about to change the term *UFOs* to *UAPs.*

How can they do that? I thought.

Sure enough it happened, and here we are in 2024. Now it is perfectly acceptable to use the term *UAPs* and not get laughed at or get the deer in the headlights look from our fellow Americans when talking about the burgeoning phenomenon.

What a lot of hooey!

As the late Chuck Missler would say, *this is a managed agenda.*

Folks, it is a carefully crafted narrative. I would posit that our government has known about the details of the UFO phenomenon for decades, and in fact, we have reverse engineered certain aspects of the craft.

Remember Colonel Philip Corso's book, *The Day After Roswell?* Corso revealed that he was involved in the distribution of materials that were recovered from crashed UFOs. This was an astounding admission on his part. Researchers like Stanton Friedman and others didn't buy Corso's book at first, and they gave it negative reviews.[2] I went with what Corso was telling us because it jibed with what whistleblower Bob Lazar had stated years earlier. Lazar stated that he was involved in the back engineering of the propulsion system of UFOs, so when Corso came out with his book, it backed up what Lazar had stated. By the way, Stanton Friedman didn't think too highly of Bob Lazar either.[3]

Think about it. According to Corso's book, he was given parts of the wreckage to disseminate to private industry for back engineering purposes, so his superiors knew about it. How high did this order to disseminate the wreckage go? Surely the Joint Chiefs of Staff must have known about what was going on. How much was Corso allowed to tell, let's say, Raytheon or Skunk Works?

According to Corso, he knew exactly where the wreckage came from. There was no mystery. Circling back to his higher-ups, was this order apart from the workings of Congress? Was there any congressional oversight to what Corso and his superiors were up to? Was this all a militarily controlled dissemination of "off-world" materials? If it was, then we no longer have transparency in our government, and in fact, I would posit there is a rogue element that is using black budgets to fund secret programs.

Recently this lack of oversight has come to the attention of Congress. But is it just a dog and pony show? Will the American people ever find out what's really going on?

I would posit that Corso was giving this wreckage out to private industry because the military-industrial complex wanted the end results for weaponry. The problem is, as I have stated above, there is no oversight. I am reminded of the words of President Eisenhower just before he left office. Here is a portion of his speech that is germane to our discussion:

> A vital element in keeping the peace is our military establishment. Our arms must be mighty, ready for instant action, so that no potential aggressor may be tempted to risk his own destruction.
>
> Our military organization today bears little relation to that known by any of my predecessors in peace time, or indeed by the fighting men of World War II or Korea.
>
> Until the latest of our world conflicts, the United States had no armaments industry. American makers of plowshares could, with time and as required, make swords as well. But now we can no longer risk emergency improvisation of national defense; we have been compelled to create a permanent armaments industry of vast proportions. Added to this, three and a half million men and women are directly engaged in the defense establishment. We annually spend on military security more than the net income of all United State corporations.
>
> This conjunction of an immense military establishment and a large arms industry is new in the American experience. The total influence—economic, political, even spiritual—is felt in every city, every state house, every office of the Federal government. We recognize the imperative need for this development. Yet we must not fail to comprehend its grave implications. Our toil, resources and livelihood are all involved; so is the very structure of our society.
>
> *In the councils of government, we must guard against the acquisition of unwarranted influence, whether sought or unsought, by the military-industrial complex. The potential for the disastrous rise of misplaced power exists and will persist.*
>
> We must never let the weight of this combination endanger

our liberties or democratic processes. We should take nothing for granted. Only an alert and knowledgeable citizenry can compel the proper meshing of the huge industrial and military machinery of defense with our peaceful methods and goals, so that security and liberty may prosper together.

Akin to, and largely responsible for the sweeping changes in our industrial-military posture, has been the technological revolution during recent decades.

In this revolution, research has become central; it also becomes more formalized, complex, and costly. A steadily increasing share is conducted for, by, or at the direction of, the Federal government.

Today, the solitary inventor, tinkering in his shop, has been over shadowed by task forces of scientists in laboratories and testing fields. In the same fashion, the free university, historically the fountainhead of free ideas and scientific discovery, has experienced a revolution in the conduct of research. Partly because of the huge costs involved, a government contract becomes virtually a substitute for intellectual curiosity. For every old blackboard there are now hundreds of new electronic computers.

The prospect of domination of the nation's scholars by Federal employment, project allocations, and the power of money is ever present and is gravely to be regarded.

Yet, in holding scientific research and discovery in respect, as we should, we must also be alert to the equal and opposite danger that public policy could itself become the captive of a scientific-technological elite.

It is the task of statesmanship to mold, to balance, and to integrate these and other forces, new and old, within the principles of our democratic system—ever aiming toward the supreme goals of our free society.[4]

Regarding the previous quote, is it safe to say the military-industrial complex remains powerful and unaccountable to the American people? I would say yes, and this is demonstrated by

Colonel Corso contacting private industry and giving them parts of the wreckage from crashed UFOs to back engineer.

And this wasn't the first time, as we shall see.

THE NAZIS AND PEENEMUNDE

In 1936 a UFO allegedly crashed in the Black Forest of Germany. Many people believe this is the stuff of conspiracy theory, and we will most likely never know for certain whether it really happened. But what we do know is this: the Nazis had rockets, the V-1 and the V-2, that were created at the top-secret Peenemünde Army Research Center. The rockets were real and were fired over the English Channel at London and other cities in Great Britain.

What remains apocryphal is these *wunderwaffe (wonder weapons)*, as the Germans called them, seemed to appear out of nowhere. There is a quote that allegedly comes from Wernher von Braun. There's no way of vetting it, but I bring it to our attention because it may have a link to our discussion. I'll leave it to your discernment as to whether you believe it or not.

UFO researcher Allen Greenfield said he met Nazi rocket engineer Wernher von Braun at Wright-Patterson Air Force Base in Ohio while reviewing declassified files.

> And I said to him, "How did you develop that much technology so fast?" And he looked down the rows of UFO files. And he said, "We had help from them." And I said, "You mean, them?" Meaning the aliens. He said, "Yeah, we had help. We all got help from them." And that was, like, the eye-opening moment.[5]

Researcher Jim Marrs, author of *The Rise of the Fourth Reich* and *Alien Agenda*, made this comment:

The evidence that the Nazis were aware of nonhuman technology is simply the fact of the existence of this incredible technology that they had by the end of the war.[6]

To those of us who have studied the UFO phenomenon for decades this is old news, and frankly, these stories may be just that, stories. The entire affair can't be vetted. Like the Roswell event, which can't be proven either, they cannot be vetted and may not be based in truth. Welcome to the murky world of UFO research.

Now let's examine what we have that is "official," the "Preliminary Assessment: Unidentified Aerial Phenomena" report that first appeared in 2021. I include quotes from the report, and following each quote, I will comment.

DEFINITION OF KEY TERMS

This report and UAPTF databases use the following defining terms:

- **Unidentified Aerial Phenomena (UAP):** Airborne objects not immediately identifiable. The acronym UAP represents the broadest category of airborne objects reviewed for analysis.
- **UAP Event:** A holistic description of an occurrence during which a pilot or aircrew witnessed (or detected) a UAP.
- **UAP Incident:** A specific part of the event.
- **UAP Report:** Documentation of a UAP event, to include verified chains of custody and basic information such as the time, date, location, and description of the UAP. UAP reports include Range Fouler reports and other reporting.[7]

So with a magic wave of the pen, the decades-old term *UFO* is magically changed to *UAP*—and now it would seem we have permission to talk about it! As I mentioned earlier, a fellow UFO researcher, Chase Kloetzke, told me this was about to happen. In my opinion this is part of the ongoing managed agenda that is being run by the military-industrial complex. Why am I so insistent on this? I will address it in a later chapter. But know this: so far everyone who has been trotted out before the public is tied in some way to the military-industrial complex.

- Luis Elizondo—senior leader of AATIP
- Christopher Mellon—deputy assistant secretary of defense for intelligence
- Nick Pope—British ministry of defence
- David Grusch—military whistleblower
- David Fravor—F/A-18 pilot

The list goes on, but I think you get my point.

EXECUTIVE SUMMARY

The limited amount of high-quality reporting on unidentified aerial phenomena (UAP) hampers our ability to draw firm conclusions about the nature or intent of UAP. The Unidentified Aerial Phenomena Task Force (UAPTF) considered a range of information on UAP described in U.S. military and IC (Intelligence Community) reporting, but because the reporting lacked sufficient specificity, ultimately recognized that a unique, tailored reporting process was required to provide sufficient data for analysis of UAP events.[8]

First off, there is the incredible Kumburgaz UFO footage taken in Turkey in 2009 while Dr. Roger Leir was there.[9] I have stated numerous times that it is the best UFO footage I have ever seen. We broke this story in our *Watchers* series. I have used the footage, as well as a subsequent interview I did with Dr. Leir in his office, in our ongoing *UFO Disclosure* series.

This executive summary falls of its own weight when you consider that we have film that clearly shows both the craft and the occupants. Furthermore, the video is hours long, and it shows the craft moving in the night sky and then in the early dawn. We also witness certain parts of the ship opening up. We see a heat signature from the craft. We clearly see entities in the ship moving about. We see the ship move and turn. There also seems to be someone in the prone position in front of what has become known as the Grays. Richard Shaw, who directed and edited the segment in our *Watchers* series,[10] believes, as I do, that we might be looking at an abduction taking place.

The bottom line is this: there are many good videos, photos, and other evidence that show the veracity of the craft.

BUT SOME POTENTIAL PATTERNS DO EMERGE

Although there was wide variability in the reports and the dataset is currently too limited to allow for detailed trend or pattern analysis, there was some clustering of UAP observations regarding shape, size, and, particularly, propulsion. UAP sightings also tended to cluster around U.S. training and testing grounds, but we assess that this may result from a collection bias as a result of focused attention, greater numbers of latest-generation sensors operating in those areas, unit expectations, and guidance to report anomalies.

AND A HANDFUL OF UAP APPEAR TO
DEMONSTRATE ADVANCED TECHNOLOGY

In **18** incidents, described in **21** reports, observers reported *unusual UAP movement patterns or flight characteristics.*

Some UAP appeared to remain stationary in winds aloft, move against the wind, maneuver abruptly, or move at considerable speed, without discernable means of propulsion. In a small number of cases, military aircraft systems processed radio frequency (RF) energy associated with UAP sightings.[11]

For decades eyewitnesses have reported the incredible movements of UFOs. We see right angle turns, craft jumping through space, and other incredible aeronautical feats that defy our physics.

In 1990 Gary Schultz and Norio Hayakawa brought a Japanese film crew out to what has become almost household term—Area 51. When Schultz and Hayakawa were engaged in this, they were perched on what has become known as *the Mailbox*, which, by the way, was purchased by the powers that be at Area 51 to make sure prying eyes didn't pry.

The film clearly shows what I would call a UFO jumping through space.[12] A link is in the endnote so you can see this for yourself. The reason I bring this up is because the government's claim that these phenomena don't exist is, in my opinion, so disingenuous as to be laughable—unless, of course, the people who are engaged in this official investigation financed by our tax dollars really don't have access to the huge amount of data, photos, and videos that show these craft.

———

UAP PROBABLY LACK A SINGLE EXPLANATION

The UAP documented in this limited dataset demonstrate an array of aerial behaviors, reinforcing the possibility there are multiple types of UAP requiring different explanations. Our analysis of the data supports the construct that if and when individual UAP incidents are resolved they will fall into one of five potential explanatory categories: airborne clutter, natural atmospheric phenomena, USG or industry developmental programs, foreign adversary systems, and a catchall "other" bin. With the exception of the one instance where we determined with high confidence that the reported UAP was airborne clutter, specifically a deflating balloon, we currently lack sufficient information in our dataset to attribute incidents to specific explanations.

Airborne Clutter: These objects include birds, balloons, recreational unmanned aerial vehicles (UAV), or airborne debris like plastic bags that muddle a scene and affect an operator's ability to identify true targets, such as enemy aircraft.

Natural Atmospheric Phenomena: Natural atmospheric phenomena includes ice crystals, moisture, and thermal fluctuations that may register on some infrared and radar systems.

USG or Industry Developmental Programs: Some UAP observations could be attributable to developments and classified programs by U.S. entities. We were unable to confirm, however, that these systems accounted for any of the UAP reports we collected.[13]

In my opinion the above statements are necessary because it makes clear that the report is being conducted in a very scientific way. However, as I maintain, I believe the powers that be know exactly who and what they are dealing with. I pointed earlier to Colonel Corso's book, *The Day After Roswell.* We have several choices to consider when regarding Corso's account.

1. Corso is a disinformation agent, and everything he writes is intended to lead serious researchers into the world of the dreaded red herring.

2. Corso is delusional and a narcissist who is only interested in letting everyone know how great and important he is.

3. Corso is telling half-truths. In other words, Corso is being allowed to reveal certain aspects of the UFO phenomenon in order to get the public ready for disclosure. This may be a real possibility. Corso passed away in 1998, so this was years before we began to see what I would call the revealing of the so-called extraterrestrial presence.

4. Corso is telling us the truth as he sees it, as he experienced it. He is not exaggerating in any way. He is spilling the beans, as it were, because he realizes his days are numbered and he feels burdened after the long years of silence. He wants to set the record straight.

In some ways, choice four mirrors what I discussed in an earlier chapter about Colonel Hill and the Roswell event. Hill came clean to Carolyn Rankin, and she recounts this in our *UFO Disclosure* series.[14] Being a student of body language, I believe the report of Carolyn and her husband, Jim, is accurate and true. Along the same line, in my opinion, Corso's book is both true and accurate. Corso is giving us an inside look into the way everything worked decades ago. In other words, what we glean from this is that our government had the wreckage from Roswell, and they systemically and deliberately gave the wreckage to certain sections of the military-industrial complex, *who then back engineered the technology.*

There is a link to the Kumburgaz UFO footage in the endnote.[15] Dr. Roger Lier gave the footage to us to use, and now it is being copied by bootleggers who act like it's their footage. This is how the game is played.

Foreign Adversary Systems: Some UAP may be technologies deployed by China, Russia, another nation, or a non-governmental entity.[16]

I'll be brief here. I do not believe for one second that the Russians or the Chinese have developed the kind of mind-blowing technology that is associated with the phenomenon. End of story.

CONCLUSION

The whole affair is in, my opinion, one big nothing burger—without the pickles and lettuce to boot!

Chapter 7

THE SIXTH RUNG: NASA HIRING PRIESTS, PREPARING FOR CONTACT

WHEN I SAW the following headline, I was astounded: "Nasa Is Hiring Priests to Prepare Humans for Contact With Aliens."[1] This theme was also picked up by other news outlets.[2] This is the sixth rung on the ladder.

Here's a quote from an article in *The Hill*:

> "The most significant question there is is probably whether one would respond theologically to the prospect of life elsewhere in terms of there having been many incarnations, or only the one theologians talk about in Jesus," [Rev. Dr. Andrew Davison] wrote at the time. "I have also been thinking about the doctrine of creation, especially in terms of how it deals with themes of multiplicity and diversity."[3]

The previous quote reminds me of the late C. S. Lewis' classic trilogy that deals with this subject. I read the trilogy in my early twenties and then reread them a few months later. Here is the basic premise:

> Published in 1938, *Out of the Silent Planet* is a science fiction novel by author C. S. Lewis, best known for his bestselling fantasy children's series, *The Chronicles of Narnia*. It is the first book in Lewis's *Space Trilogy*, followed by *Perelandra* (1943) and *That Hideous Strength* (1945). With *Out of the Silent Planet*, Lewis sought to write a narrative that differed from contemporary popular science fiction, which he believed promoted harmful ideas like human supremacy and xenophobia. *Out of the Silent Planet* explores themes of morality, theology, and humanity's place in the universe through the intergalactic journey of protagonist Dr. Elwin Ransom.[4]

Of course, Lewis was positing that there is life on other planets. I want to make this really clear because recently I came under attack from a well-known Christian ministry for my supposed belief in the existence of aliens or beings from other worlds. Here is my statement, read publicly at the 2023 Prophecy Watchers Conference in Norman, Oklahoma:

> I do not believe in the plurality of worlds. The UFO phenomenon with all its complexity is, in my opinion the handiwork of FALLEN ANGELS! In other words, these "intruders" are, what I have come to call, the major players in The Coming Great Deception or as 2 Thessalonians tells us, this is the strong delusion sent to mankind because they did not believe the truth.

I did this to make it really clear that I did not believe in the plurality of worlds—in other words, life on other planets.

Back to NASA and the Priests

The headline "NASA Is Hiring Priests to Prepare Humans for Contact With Aliens" has vast repercussions for every person of faith. Notice NASA chose priests. Are there any evangelicals in the mix? I think not. Why priests? Is it because the Vatican has changed their perspective on so-called extraterrestrials?

I have several books in my library that essentially promote the plurality of worlds. Please remember that the Vatican did not hold to this position just a few hundred years ago. My, how much has changed.

The Pope went on the record, stating that if ET does show up, he will "baptize" him.[5] Wow, what a change from excommunicating people who believed in life on other planets. Here's a quote from the article:

> ["]That was unthinkable. If[—for example—]tomorrow an expedition of Martians came, and some of them came to us, here...Martians, right? Green, with that long nose and big ears, just like children paint them...And one says, 'But I want to be baptized!' What would happen?"
>
> What would happen? They'd get baptized, that's what would happen. He goes on:
>
> "When the Lord shows us the way, who are we to say, 'No, Lord, it is not prudent! No, let's do it this way'...Who are we to close doors? In the early Church, even today, there is the ministry of the ostiary [usher]. And what did the ostiary do? He opened the door, received the people, allowed them to pass. But it was never the ministry of the closed door, never."[6]

This is a far cry from what the Catholic Church did when Galileo stated that the earth revolved around the sun, not the sun around the earth. Galileo was charged with heresy and placed under house arrest for the rest of his life. You will also notice that it is the Vatican who holds sway at NASA. At the very least, NASA reached out to the Vatican because Catholicism is the largest Christian denomination in the world—as well as the oldest, although some would debate my later statement. Catholicism boasts upwards of 1.3 billion followers, which is by far the largest Christian denomination on the planet.[7] With 8 billion people on the globe, that is about 15 percent of the global population. There is also this to consider: Catholics make up about 23 percent of the U.S. population, with Protestants making up about 49 percent.[8]

One reason NASA is connecting with the Catholic Church is this: ETs, as you must know by now, are *not* extraterrestrials but interdimensional entities, in other words, fallen angels and the disembodied spirits of the Nephilim, which, in my opinion, are now demons.[9] If ET shows up, how will this impact the church at large? Did NASA pick the Catholic Church because of the 1.3 *billion* followers? Perhaps.

What did NASA discuss with the priests? The headline at the beginning of this chapter speaks volumes: to prepare us for contact! I have to ask the question, Why now? Does NASA know something we the people don't? Or are they just having a nice catered lunch with the good fathers and playing bingo? In other words, what would be the theological implications of contact with a group of entities or extraterrestrials who were more advanced than us? How would Jesus and our redemption fit into the mix? Remember this, that the Catholic religion holds to an *amillennial* position, meaning there is no literal, physical thousand-year (millennial) reign of Jesus on earth. Let's call these space intruders what I think they are—impostors! So if these impostors, posing as a race of advanced extraterrestrials, do appear in the skies above earth, it changes everything. How does it affect Joe and Beth in the pew? I think it would blow them out of their theological water, and thus the priests are talking to NASA to figure out a way of couching all of this, squaring it all, with the Catholic faith.

I will present to you a fictional account of what may happen when these intruders show up. But before I do that, I want to present you with another account that happened just over one hundred years ago that greatly affected the people who witnessed it. I'm referring to 1917 and the so-called Fátima apparitions.

Fátima—Harbinger of Deception

Fátima! In 1917 something happened on the moors of Fátima, Portugal, that would change that sleepy, tiny village for all time. Three children—Lúcia, age ten, Francisco, age nine, and Jacinta, age seven—were illiterate shepherds. They were out tending their sheep on the moors of Fátima when suddenly there appeared a figure above the treetops. The female figure was small and wore a short dress that fell to just below her knees.

It is important to understand that women in 1917 wore dresses that fell to just above their shoes; a knee-length dress would have been scandalous, to say the least. She communicated with the three children telepathically; they never saw her mouth move. She gave each child something to eat and drink—both Lúcia and Jacinta ate and drank, but Francisco only ate. After this was done, Lúcia and Jacinta could both see and hear the entity, while Francisco could only see the entity. At this point in the story, Lúcia asked, "Where are you from?" The entity told her, "I am from the sky," then instructed the children to come back a month later. This happened in May of 1917.

However, there is a backstory to this that few people know about. World War I was raging, the Communists had seized power in Russia, and the world stage was incredibly unstable. At this moment in history, a group of psychics got together in Portugal and conducted a séance. Through the use of *automatic writing*, a message appeared.

Before I talk about the message, I need to address the technique that was being used. *Automatic writing is an occult technique*, and essentially the person who is going into a trance is allowing an entity—which I would state emphatically is a demonic entity that lies and does so habitually—to take over the person's writing. The writing appeared from right to left, similar to what Leonardo da Vinci used in his writings, and could only be read by looking at the text's reflection in a mirror.

The message stated that something wondrous was going to happen on May 13, 1917. The group of psychics published their message in a paper in Portugal. I have actually been to what amounts to a museum of this group of psychics. This group still meets from time to time, although it is in a different building than the one used to conduct the séance back in 1917. I have also seen the original handwritten document stating that something wondrous would happen in May of that year. What is interesting to me is that the letter was signed with the name of Stella Matutina, which, incredibly, translates as "morning star." Guess who that is? The Dragon himself personally signed the letter.

Interestingly, there was a separate group of psychics that met, and they received the same message as the first group; they, too, published the message they received. So there were two documents with the same message by two different groups of psychics. Let me make something perfectly clear—the God of the Bible, the God of eternity, does not need a group of psychics to inform people what is going to happen. The Dragon uses these people, who are steeped in occult practices, to mislead the masses. Thus the false message that came from the Dragon and was published in papers really was the touchstone for the entire Fátima event.

Now let's go back to the three children in the field at Fátima, tending their sheep. They saw this entity appear above the treetop. It was only found out much later, in fact decades later through the work of researcher Fina D'Armada, who had access to the records, that there were important papers documenting the incident in remarkable detail—handwritten at the time of the event by the parish priest, Father Ferreira. These documents were in the archives, and they recorded numerous eyewitness testimonies of what happened.

Fina D'Armada was at the archives doing research for a paper she was writing about influential twentieth-century women in Portugal; she chose Lúcia, one of the children from the Fátima apparitions. Fina D'Armada had access to the handwritten records by Father Ferreira. She was shocked to discover that the account she read was completely different from what she had been told as a small child. It was different from the approved narrative that is now accepted and promulgated by the Vatican and the people of Portugal themselves. She was taken aback by what she was reading. She discovered in the carefully written documents a witness who had gone unrecognized for decades, Carolina Carreira.

Fina D'Armada searched for Carolina and found her, and by this time, of course, she was an old woman. Fina interviewed her and, to her astonishment, discovered that Carolina too had an encounter with a strange being just a few weeks prior to the event involving Lúcia, Francisco, and Jacinta. The being that Carolina encountered was an androgynous-looking child, with shoulder-length blonde hair, and it was singing and dancing under the same tree where Lúcia, Francisco, and Jacinta later encountered their female entity, which, in my opinion, was a much different entity than the one that appeared to Carolina.

Carolina looked at the sheep, and they were seemingly frozen in position, paralyzed; she was taken aback by this. When she looked toward the child again, the child with blonde hair was now floating above the treetop. Needless to say, this was a supernatural event that defies any natural explanation. What is interesting about this is, according to the handwritten documents produced by Father Ferreira, this was the same tree where Lúcia, Francisco, and Jacinta would see the female entity.[10]

After the three children had their first encounter with the entity who stated that she was from the sky, they told their parents and the parish priest, Father Ferreira. Father Ferreira, right from the get-go, believed that the entire affair was demonic. Cheers for him! The next month the crowds began to swell as word got around that something supernatural was occurring.

Please remember that these were illiterate peasant children who did not know how to read or write. When July came around, there were even more people gathered because the story had spread.

Combined with the rumors of the children seeing the apparition, there were also strange aerial phenomena happening in the sky above. People were seeing what they described as flying hats. Remember, in 1917 the terms *UFO* and *flying saucer* were not part of the lexicon; that would not happen until the mid-twentieth century. So people were looking up and trying to frame what they were seeing within their grid system, or what they knew—thus, flying hats.

When August rolled around, the children were in jail because the entire affair had really blown up. So even though the crowds were much larger now, the children were *not* present. According to the handwritten records that we have from Father Ferreira, there were still very strange atmospheric conditions happening directly over and around the so-called apparition site.

September came, and the children were free to go to look at the apparition; however, they had been given a task by the powers that be to ask the apparition for some sort of a sign. Once again, the children had contact with the entity, who communicated with them telepathically. According to the handwritten documents, the entity was only about three feet tall. The skirt she wore fell just below the knees. This was alarming because the Mary of the Bible would never appear that way, and women in 1917 did not wear short skirts. What were they looking at? The children went to the site, the apparition appeared, they communicated with it, and they asked for some sort of a sign. The apparition informed them that there would be a sign on October 13, 1917.

A month went by, and word had spread like wildfire. Thousands of people gathered in Fátima. According to some tallies, there may have been as many as seventy thousand people in the field that day. It had been raining all night. There is one photograph taken by Joshua Benoliel that shows a sea of black umbrellas spread out over the moors of Fátima. Here's where the story took another very unusual turn. This is why our two films on Fátima draw exclusively from the 1917 handwritten records of the eyewitness accounts of the event. We do not include Lúcia's memoirs from ten years later when she was a nun under the watchful and controlling powers of the Jesuits.

It had been raining, and the ground was sopping wet. All of a sudden the rain stopped, and a few minutes later the sun came out. A large cloud moved in front of the sun, and out of that cloud came a spinning disc. Eyewitnesses to the event said they looked up and saw a *large, spinning disc-like object.* Others saw the disc throwing off multiple colors. The disc fell like a leaf to the ground and then whisked back up to the sky. That happened three different times. Then it did what we have come to call the *flyby,* where the disc-like object—essentially a UFO—flies low directly over a crowd of people. Alarmingly, according to the eyewitnesses, car windshields exploded, and some of the cars spontaneously combusted. People who were directly underneath the craft as it flew by, whose clothes were wet from all the rain, were suddenly dry. How is that possible? Some people had what I can only describe as radiation burns. Although at the time, people did not know about radiation burns, the skin effects looked like bad sunburns. The ground became dry, and some people saw beings waving at them through the windows of the craft. All of this to get to this point: the handwritten records from Father Ferreira specifically show that, in my opinion, what happened in Fátima in 1917 was, in fact, a UFO event. It was later dressed up in Catholic clothes, and the entity became Mary of the Bible. But as you can see from the above information, it most certainly was not Mary of the Bible as we know her. What flew over the crowd that day was not the so-called "miracle of the sun."

I need to address the "miracle of the sun" before closing this section. Eyewitnesses to the event stated that the sun left its place in the solar system and came down over the crowd; clearly, that is not what happened. There was a disc-like object that came out of a cloud and moved in front of the sun; that disc-like object was the object that people saw. My point is, in my opinion, many people that were in the field at Fátima that day were deceived. This is why we call our film *Fatima 1: Miracle of the Sun or Harbinger of Deception.*[11]

CONCLUSION

The events of 1917 that were foretold by a group of psychics were, in fact, a UFO event. Many people even today believe in the official version of the story, which claims Mary of the Bible appeared to the children, and the sun left its place in the solar system and fell to earth. In my opinion, based on the handwritten letters and documentation from Father Ferreira, this is not what happened. Over one hundred years later this is still how the Catholic Church deals with the phenomenon. Fátima is a carefully managed, ongoing affair.

One last word: Pope Benedict distanced himself from the Fátima operations and stated, on the record, that Fátima was for another time.[12] I am speculating here, but did he do that because he actually knew the truth of the matter? Jesus warned us that even the elect would be deceived. It is perhaps one of the direst warnings in the entire biblical narrative. As many as seventy thousand people were in the fields of Fátima that day. Many were confused as to what they were looking at. And the official version was promulgated repeatedly until the truth was completely obfuscated. After my research, I firmly believe that this was a harbinger of deception—a UFO event.

We will talk more about the Vatican's position on so-called extraterrestrials in a later chapter, where I circle back a few years to discuss the interview we did with author Chris Putnam for our *Watchers* series. You can watch the full-length interview with Chris by going to the special site we created just for this book, rungsofdisclosure.com.

Chapter 8

THE SEVENTH RUNG: ALIEN ABDUCTIONS

THE ALIEN ABDUCTION phenomenon is very strange and disturbing. I am going to open this chapter with the narrative I created for the fourth film in our ongoing *UFO Disclosure* series, which deals with the abduction phenomena in depth. This is what the film opens with:

> Something very dark and disturbing is happening. It is a global phenomenon that knows no boundaries, and it adheres to no cultural mores. The ones who are engaged in this nefarious activity do so with impunity. People are being taken against their will, in the cover of darkness, in the dead of night. They are subjected to bizarre examinations that are often sexual in nature. These people are terrified, violated, and confused, with no place to turn. Who would believe them? This is their story.[1]

On Fox News, Bret Baier ran a very bizarre story stating that some women who are taken aboard UFOs find themselves pregnant.[2] In some ways this is an incredibly profound statement, and I was shocked when I read it. Remember, this is the conservative Fox News network, not *Coast to Coast AM* with George Noory. In order for us to fully grasp what is happening, we need to go back to the beginning and understand Genesis 3:15. I cannot reiterate this enough because the importance of it is paramount to our understanding of the entire UFO phenomenon. The Genesis 3:15 narrative took place directly after Adam and Eve had sinned. The scene opens with the preincarnate Christ in the Garden, and He declared what I believe is the touchstone for the rest of the biblical prophetic narrative. We see Jesus declaring to the serpent and Adam and Eve this incredible statement. *If we do not understand the Genesis 3:15 narrative, then we don't understand what is really going on in the rest of the biblical prophetic narrative.*

> I will put enmity between you and the woman, and between your offspring and her offspring; he shall bruise your head, and you shall bruise his heel.
> —Genesis 3:15, esv

There it is! Jesus' statement is describing the *seed war*: it's the *offspring* of the Dragon against the *offspring* of the woman. It erupted only three chapters later in Genesis chapter 6. Then throughout the rest of the biblical narrative we see the seed war manifest in different passages. Perhaps one of the most poignant examples of this is the conquest of Canaan thousands of years after Jesus' proclamation in the Garden. For there, at the threshold of the Promised Land, the seed of Abraham had grown to the twelve tribes of Israel, and in the Promised Land were many different Nephilim tribes. The *Promised Land* was literally the seat of the Dragon, and his offspring were placed strategically in the land that God called His own. At the entrance to Canaan were the twelve tribes who would take it from the Dragon and drive the Nephilim out.

The abduction phenomenon is not new; we have heard about it for decades now. Harvard professor John E. Mack wrote a bestselling book on the subject.[3] Whitley Strieber's book *Communion* was a number one bestseller.[4] In these tomes are accounts of people who were taken against their will. In our *Watchers* film series we interviewed Dr. David Jacobs, who was trained under Dr. Mack. In the book *Further Evidence of Close Encounters,* I quoted Dr. David Jacobs from a written interview I conducted with him. Jacobs stated that when he realized that this was not fantasy or psychosis or imagination or schizophrenia, he walked around for six months saying, "Oh my gosh. Oh my gosh. Oh my gosh."[5]

A classic abduction goes something like this. A person is lying in bed. They are awakened from their sleep. They can be either male or female. Suddenly they are overcome with fear as they realize something, someone, is in their room. They find themselves completely paralyzed and unable to move except for their eyes, which frantically dart around the room, landing on what we have come to call the Grays, the small, four-foot-high, so-called aliens with large heads and large black almond shaped eyes. To the person being abducted, this is terrifying, and rightfully so. They are unable to scream or do anything for that matter except look.

The fear level is through the roof. These people are utterly terrified. Then they find themselves levitated off the bed, then floating through the air, usually toward the window, which is locked. As they notice they stop moving and are hovering in front of the locked window, they wonder to themselves if the window is going to open. The window does not open; instead the victim goes right through the closed and locked window. We know that this is an impossibility, at least from our point of view. But these entities that are abducting people are manipulating space, time, matter, and energy in ways that defy our known physics. I have asked some abductees what it feels like, and they say their body is tingling all over as they go through the window.

Next, many of them find themselves bathed in a brilliant white light as they are sucked into the ship. Not all abductees experience this. Sometimes abductees go unconscious and don't come to until they are inside the ship on a metal table, where sadistic tests, for lack of a better word, are being conducted on them. Often one of the Grays will put their face in the abductee's face, and images will suddenly appear in the victim's mind. These entities can and do communicate with the abductees telepathically. The Grays seem to be the worker bees. As you know, I believe the Grays are nothing more than avatars, "meat suits" to house the spirits of the Nephilim that became the demons that roam the earth after the Flood of Noah.

It seems like these entities feed off the fear. Remember, fear is always the calling card of the *kingdom of darkness*.

Sometimes very painful procedures are done to these people. Sperm is taken from the men, and ova from the women. Other times the men are forced to copulate with what appears to be a female hybrid, a mix of alien and human. The women find themselves raped by male hybrids or worse, what appears to be a reptilian creature.

As Al Matthews (one of the abductees in our film whom I have interviewed numerous times) states, "These are not our friendly space brothers; these entities kidnap and rape people."[6]

In short, there's absolutely nothing good about it.

CASE STUDY: AL MATTHEWS

My first introduction to Al Matthews came in a phone call from Vancouver, Canada. A mutual Christian friend, Gordy Tong, called me up and said that a friend of his had an encounter and was terrified. We covered this in our very first *UFO Disclosure* film. Al, who is a professional mover, met up with a new client, Diane. She was a very pretty woman and dressed very nicely. But she was wearing unusual dark glasses that wrapped around her head, almost like swimmers' goggles. Al didn't say anything; he just figured she had sensitive eyes. He'd never met or seen the woman before. They got on the freight elevator to go up to the warehouse where her belongings were. Diane leaned forward and whispered in Al's ear,

"They're listening, Al." In Al's words, he was creeped out by this; frankly, who wouldn't be?

Al turned to her and said, "Who's listening?"

Diane replied, "You know, the Grays. I know that you've been taken many times, and we were supposed to meet on the ship."

To cut the chase, Al gave Diane his phone number, and she pestered him for weeks, trying to meet up with him. Finally, one day after work, Al decided to meet with her at her friend's apartment. The two women were drinking wine out of large goblets. Al sat down and joined them. He noticed a large fly, like a deerfly, on the edge of Diane's glass. He said, "I'll get it for you."

Diane said, "No need to do that; I'll get it." Diane reached out but didn't grab the fly between her fingers—instead the fly just stuck to her index finger alone. How did that happen? She brought it near her mouth, and when it was about six inches away, she somehow sucked it in, which is also an impossibility. She ingested the fly. She then took off her unusual glasses, got up, went over to Al, and got on his lap facing him.

At this point in the interview, I stopped Al and asked him, "You have a girlfriend; why are you allowing this?"

Al had never been asked that question, so he stammered and said, "I don't know."

Diane lifted up his shirt, rubbed his chest, and said, "My, you're well preserved." Then she leaned forward to kiss him. At that point, Al pushed Diane off him, and she fell to the floor. When she hit the floor, her eyes shape-shifted, changing into what I would call reptilian. Then she let out the evilest laugh you've ever heard.

Al, completely freaked out, fled the scene and ran to Gordy Tong's home. At this point, Gordy picked up the phone and called me. I prayed with Al over the phone, and I promised to send him materials. Several weeks later, Al gave his life to the Lord. *That action of coming to Christ stopped his lifelong abductions.*

Al later informed me that he was taken at the age of six, and he had been abducted all throughout his life. One of the most chilling encounters was when he was driving home from work, and he somehow knew he was about to be taken. Sure enough, he woke up hours later, hundreds of miles away from where he last was. It was now dark, and the car was being lowered in the most brilliant white light you have ever seen. Al's body was vibrating, and he knew he had been violated—raped. The car touched down on the road and began to drive itself—yet another impossible action. Al finally took the steering wheel, got home, crawled into a fetal position in his bed, and wondered, Why me.[7] Again, all of this—the lifelong abductions—stopped when Al accepted Jesus.

CASE STUDY: EMILE

I first met Emile while making our *Watchers* series. The late Richard Shaw had just moved into a beautiful townhouse, and a tall ex-basketball player entered the room to change the smoke alarms and inspect them. At the time, Rick was working on one of our films, and after Emile introduced himself, he asked Rick what he was working on. Rick replied he was working on a film about UFOs. Without hesitation Emile stated, "I have an implant."

At that point, we had been working with Dr. Roger Leir for years, so Rick and I were familiar with Dr. Roger's work regarding so-called alien implants. Rick called Dr. Roger, and he also called me. Perhaps a week later we all met at Dr. Roger's office with Emile. Roger had a protocol set up to weed out those seeking publicity from those who genuinely wanted to get rid of their implants. Emile filled out the paperwork. Emile was taken from the time he was a small child. He was raped repeatedly, sperm was taken from him, and he was implanted.

We then took an X-ray. Sure enough, right below Emile's right knee was a metallic object—with no sign of an entrance wound. We also conducted other tests on this object, including a CT scan and later an ultrasound. There are those in the Christian community who state—I believe incredibly disingenuously—that these implants do not exist. What do they base this on, wishful thinking? I will not disparage anyone by mentioning their names here, but I ask: Have you done the scientific research? Have you been in the lab? Have you operated on and removed an implant? Have you looked at the images of an alleged implant from a scanning electron microscope? The answer, I would think for the most part, is a resounding no.

We followed Dr. Roger Leir's protocols to the letter. Using an ultrasound machine at Dr. Matrisciano's office, we found the implant within minutes. We scheduled a surgery to remove the implant, and finally the day of the extraction came. We had cameras rolling and witnesses watching the proceedings on a large HD monitor in another room. There were nurses and assistants. Dr. Matrisciano was the surgeon who would remove the implant, and Dr. Roger Leir would assist. At this point, I figured it would take twenty minutes or so to do the whole thing. But after an hour and twenty minutes they were unable to find the implant! Dr. Matrisciano turned to Dr. Roger Leir and suggested that we might need to get another X-ray. Dr. Leir didn't think that was necessary, saying that they knew where it was, as they had seen it before.

At this point, the Holy Spirit tapped me on the shoulder and said, "You need to take authority over this now!"

I was in a room full of nonbelievers, except for Richard Shaw. I stated very quickly, "Hey guys, this might sound really strange, but I'm going to pray, and I'm going to do it now." My prayer was short and simple: "Father, if there are forces which are hiding this implant, I pray that You would break their power and do it soon."

The room went quiet. About two minutes later the implant suddenly zoomed up into view on the monitor! Everyone was in shock. What is really sobering to me is this: "they" knew exactly what we were up to and did not want that implant removed. End of story. We then successfully removed the implant, and two days later we were at a lab, looking at it under a scanning electron microscope. So naysayers who want to tell us that the abduction phenomenon is not real, that it's all in the head, and that implants are not what they seem to be are blowing a lot of smoke, and they know not of what they speak.

Emile was taken numerous times. In our film on abduction, the fourth in our *UFO Disclosure* series, there is a clip where Emile talks about winding up outside his room on the front lawn as a small child. His parents found that, needless to say, extremely alarming. So they put locks on the windows and doors. Nevertheless, the next morning Emile was out on the lawn.[8] How is that possible?

I try to meet with Emile at least once a month, and we talk about the Lord, salvation, and the Bible. As far as I know, Emile has not had another encounter. Please make sure you go to our interactive link and check out the video clips featuring Emile.

Case Study: Karin

Karin emailed me several years ago, and I met up with her in Dallas. She went on the record for our film on abductions. Karin's testimony is one of the most riveting I have ever heard. We recently published her book *Stolen Seed, Evil Harvest*.[9] Karin was taken against her parents' will and against her own will beginning at about five or six years old. During the abductions, she found herself with other children. She was probed, and bizarre "medical" experiments were done on her. This went on all throughout her young life, and at one point, when she tried to tell people what was going on, these nefarious entities placed images in her mind, showing her parents being decapitated. They threatened her that they would do this unless she shut up.

When Karin reached puberty, the abductions became more frequent. After she was married, she found herself pregnant with her first child. What I am going to tell you next is a deep dive into the abduction phenomenon and links directly back to Bret Baier's story on Fox News. *Some women who are taken aboard UFOs find themselves pregnant.* But Baier stopped there and didn't really drill down into what was going on. In other words, there wasn't a lot of detail. This is *my* wheelhouse and essentially my life's work, so I interviewed Karin, and her story was extremely disturbing. Karin became the center of the entire film.

Karin found herself pregnant and was delighted that she and her husband were about to have their first child. However, in the third month of her first trimester Karin was abducted, but she was not aware that she had been abducted. The next morning, when she awoke, she had pain in her abdomen and knew something was wrong. She went to the ER and told them she was pregnant. They examined her, and she had no fetal tissue and no fetal heartbeat. The doctors looked at Karen and said, "Are you sure you were pregnant, ma'am?"

Karin replied, "Talk to my OB/GYN. We saw the heartbeat."

What you just read is classic. This is what they do. They do it over and over and over again. It's a very closely guarded secret, and only in recent years have a few of us dared to probe into the evil underbelly that surrounds this phenomenon. What is really disturbing in the film is Karin's body language. I am a student of body language, so when I interview someone, I watch them like a hawk. Karin was telling the truth. Her body language showed the distress of something that happened many years ago. Her face contorted with pain when she told me the story in Dallas just a few years ago. Unfortunately, she was impregnated by "them" another two times, and like the first pregnancy, "they" returned and took what I would call the hybrid fetus.

She divorced her husband a short time later. Karin also informed me that her first husband never seemed upset about losing the babies, which makes me wonder.

Karin got back on track with the Lord, and the abductions stopped. She remarried and had other children, but the medical complications of being abducted this many times were in some way overwhelming—Karin was recently diagnosed with a brain tumor, and the doctors were extremely concerned.

Karin and her husband, David, met up with me at a conference.

We prayed earnestly for her, and the Lord healed her! Greater is He that is in us than he that is in the world (1 John 4:4).

To see more videos, please go to our interactive website.

THE PHYSICALITY OF THESE ABDUCTIONS

As I stated earlier, there are some people in the Christian community who insist that none of this is really taking place. What evidence do they offer that the abduction phenomenon is all in a person's head or demonic delusion? After decades of being in the field and doing research, that kind of a statement to me is so disingenuous; it maligns the witnesses, which is exactly what the Christian community does not need. The abduction phenomenon is all too real, and it links directly back to the Genesis 3:15 narrative, which talks about the *seed war.*

All of the abductees that we interviewed in our film were able to stop their abductions by coming to Jesus and calling out to Him. This is the way to get out of the phenomenon. I will tell you another story that is chilling.

There was an elder in a church who called me several years ago. He was a standup guy, a real straight shooter, walking where he should be walking with the Lord. One night he was awakened and found himself paralyzed, and just like every other abductee I have ever spoken to, he was levitated and was moving toward the wall of his bedroom. He was between the bed and the wall, floating about three feet above the floor. He knew he was about to get sucked through the wall. He cried out to Jesus, and instantaneously, like a rubber band being snapped back, he found himself back in the bed. His experience was not delusional. He called me the next day in great distress, wondering why this had happened to him. I talked with this man for several hours and came to the conclusion that there was nothing in his life that would've opened the door to this dark-side activity. But these entities came in anyway to try to take him. They were unsuccessful because this man cried out to Jesus, and it stopped the abduction.

What did Jesus say about the last days? Jesus warned us that it would be like the days of Noah when He returns. This is why the correct interpretation of Genesis 3:15 is absolutely critical. I cannot stress this enough; I cannot repeat it enough here and elsewhere in this book. It is that paramount to what is going on in today's world. Why would Jesus warn us that it would be like the days of Noah? What differentiates the days of Noah from every other time in history is, in my opinion, the presence of the fallen angels mixing their seed with the seed of men and creating a hybrid entity known as the Nephilim. Fallen angels came and took wives, plural; I wrote about this in my book *Countermove: How the Nephilim Returned After the Flood.*

They—the fallen angels—do it over and over and over again. Why? They are trying to corrupt the seed. They are trying to corrupt the bloodline. In Noah's day, they were trying to make sure the seed coming from the woman—the Messiah, the protoevangelium— did not manifest, so they could control the earth.

Then we get a very enigmatic scripture in the Book of Daniel. But before I tell you the scripture, remember the angel who appeared to Daniel told him to seal up the words in the book until the time of the end.

If we were to trace world history from that time, which is roughly 2,500 years ago, civilization made little progress until Gutenberg's printing press. This paradigm-shifting invention meant that—for the first time—the common man could read the Bible for himself. But the angel that appeared to Daniel told him this: many will run to and fro over the face of the earth, and knowledge will increase (Dan. 12:4). Until Gutenberg's printing press, progress was pretty much flatlined. From the days of Gutenberg until the industrial revolution, it was a slow, steady, upward curve. Finally knowledge did explode. As I write this, people are roaming to and fro over the face of the earth via jet airliners, and now knowledge increases exponentially.

Daniel 2:43 says, "'They will mingle with the seed of men; but they will not adhere to one another.'" Who are "they"? Obviously it's not the seed of men; it has to be something else. When I asked the late Chuck Missler this question on camera in our *Watchers* series, he stated without hesitation that the Dragon, Satan, is outnumbered two to one, and he is creating an army.[10] Why is it so hard for Christians to wrap their heads around what is really going on? It's right there in our Bibles. All we need to do is open its pages and realize that there is a supernatural dynamic to the biblical prophetic narrative. It warned us about exactly what we are seeing in modernity—the abduction phenomenon and consequent breeding program.

Chapter 9

THE EIGHTH RUNG: CATTLE MUTILATIONS

THE SIXTH INSTALLMENT in our *UFO Disclosure* series explores the bizarre and unsettling subject of cattle mutilations. Gil Zimmerman and I flew to Colorado and met up with the guru of cattle mutilations, Chuck Zukowski. Chuck has been immersed in the cattle mutilation phenomenon for decades and, in fact, gave the late Richard Shaw and me footage on the subject for our first film in the *Watchers* series.[1]

If you're not familiar with this grizzly phenomenon, let me give you a brief thumbnail sketch using the following fictional account.

———————

Roy is a rancher with a 1,500-acre spread in southern Colorado. He has worked the land all his life and, in fact, is in the fourth generation of ranchers on the property. His great grandfather homesteaded the acreage in the late 1890s, so his family has deep ties to the territory.

In 1997 something strange and disturbing occurred on Roy's ranch. Around sunset Roy was checking his herd of 176 head because he had just moved them into a new pasture. Roy noticed some funny lights in the sky, darting about in the distance, but didn't pay too much attention to them. He surveyed the herd, saw that they were grazing on the lush grass in the pasture, and then closed the gate and headed back to the ranch house to meet up with his wife, Darlene, for some tasty dinner. Life was good, predictable, steady, and sure.

The next morning, Roy went to check on the herd, as he did every morning. When he arrived at the pasture, he noticed that the herd had moved to the far side of it. He thought that strange. Roy then noticed a cow laying on her side at the opposite end of the pasture, away from the herd. He turned off the engine on his four-wheeler, opened the gate, and made his way over to what he thought might be a sick cow. As he got closer, he was taken aback and shocked to the core—the udder and sex organs of the cow were missing. They had been somehow cored out with a strange surgical perfection. Roy ran the rest of the way to the cow and circled the animal.

He scanned the ground, carefully looking for signs of predator tracks. There were none. He also noticed that there were no signs of struggle—the animal looked as if it had been placed there carefully, deliberately. Then he noticed that the flesh around the animal's jaw had been completely stripped all the way down to the bone.

Roy had never seen anything like this before. He backed away from the carcass, took his flip phone from the front pocket of his worn jeans, and dialed the veterinarian he had known for years. In fact they had met in first grade, had become good friends through high school, and remained so now.

"Bob, you need to get out the ranch and look at this dead cow. I've never seen anything like it...ever. Something happened here last night after I tucked the herd in, and I can't get my head around it."

"What happened, Roy?" Bob asked cautiously.

"Something took the cow's udder and scraped away all the flesh around the animal's jaw."

"Coyote? Mountain lion?"

"Nope. There's not a track around the dead cow. Nothing. No signs of a struggle. And here's the odd part—there doesn't seem to be any blood left in the animal."

"I'll be right over. I'll leave in about ten minutes."

———◦•◦———

While this is 100 percent fiction, it is based on the many reports and interviews that I have read and conducted over the years.

For this film, *UFO Disclosure Episode 6: Cattle Mutilations,*[2] we flew to Denver, rented a car, and made our way to Colorado Springs, Colorado. There we met up with Chuck Zukowski, who is, in my opinion, one of the leading investigators of the ongoing cattle mutilation phenomenon. We filmed Chuck in his office, which is packed with UFO posters and memorabilia. Chuck is the mainstay of our film.

As I stated, Chuck has been investigating the cattle mutilation phenomenon for decades. Since Chuck began his investigations, there have been thousands of mutilations, and so far, no one has ever been charged with a crime or brought to justice—no one.

The FBI investigated the phenomenon and concluded that whoever or whatever was mutilating the cows, it was not the work of predators or some satanic cult. Others who have examined the carcasses attest to the fact that the incisions on the cow's bodies were done with surgical precision. Then there's the very disturbing fact that these animals were drained of all blood.

The animal is always placed back in the field, as if it were dropped from the sky. The other cows won't go near it. Scavengers won't touch the carcass. It just doesn't add up.

Most of the investigators who delve into this grisly phenomenon are not Christians. They do not know of the prophetic words that tell of a seed war between the Dragon and the Most High God. They are, for the most part, ignorant of the giants that are found in passages of our Bibles, specifically the Nephilim, which were the unholy offspring of fallen angels and the women of earth. And they certainly never connect it back to Genesis 3:15, where we find the protocols dictated by Jesus—the preincarnate Christ in the Garden of Eden—that will, in my opinion, frame the rest of the biblical narrative.

> I will put enmity between you and the woman, and between your offspring and her offspring; he shall bruise your head, and you shall bruise his heel.
>
> —GENESIS 3:15, ESV

Your seed, your *offspring*, will be at war, at enmity, with the seed, the *offspring* of the woman. He, the Messiah, the protoevangelium, will crush your head, and you will bruise His heel.

Most of the investigators have no idea of the *seed war*, so they will never come to grips with what is really happening regarding the mutilations of animals and the draining of blood. Many of these researchers seek to find excuses for what is taking place. They acknowledge that the phenomenon is deliberate and ongoing, but they make excuses for whoever is doing this.

Comments I have heard over and over again go something like this: "Well, maybe whoever is doing this just doesn't understand what they are doing," or "The fact that they are returning the cow to the farmer's field shows that they care." The bottom line is that these lame excuses seek to vindicate the perpetrators' grisly deeds. In no way am I buying this for a minute.

Here's what I think is happening.

1. Cattle mutilations are deliberate. Whoever is doing this (I'll get to this in a bit) knows exactly what they are doing; it is very deliberate.

2. There is an agenda, a goal, a protocol that has been set in place for decades. Material is taken from the animal, whether sex organs, eyes, udders, hearts,

lungs, or other parts of the animal. They—the perpetrators—know what they want, and they take it deliberately and with impunity.

3. The cuts on the animals are done with surgical precision, as if surgical instruments and a surgeon's skill
are used. The animal is not torn apart, which would
indicate that a predator was involved in the killing
and mutilation. The cuts on the animal are deliberate,
clean, and executed with great precision, almost like
the animal was operated on at a veterinarian's office.

4. The animals are drained of blood. This is the signature of literally every mutilation to date—no blood
left in the animal. How is this accomplished? How is
it that the cow is drained of blood? Chuck Zukowski
believes that the animal is drained of blood *after* it is
removed from the field, which immediately begs the
question, How does the animal leave the field? There
have been reports of lights in the sky as well as witnesses who recount seeing a cow being lifted into the
bottom of a UFO in a beam of light. I believe this is
how the cow is taken alive into the ship, where the
blood is then drained from the animal and material is taken. Zukowski believes the animal is killed
before any of this occurs, but we don't know for certain. I will weigh in on what the blood is used for
toward the end of this chapter.

5. There is no sign of struggle around the animal. It's
almost like they are just lifted off the ground by an
unseen force that renders them immobile, which is
where the beam of light may come into play. The
beam of light seems to have powers of levitation that
we do not yet understand.

6. There is no sign of natural predators, and scavengers won't touch the carcass. When law enforcement investigates the scene of a cattle mutilation, they sometimes attempt to blame mountain lions or other common predators; the problem with this is an utter lack of supporting evidence. In other words, there are *no* footprints around the animal—not one. Coyotes and vultures, who will eat just about anything, won't touch the carcass.

7. Whoever is doing this drops the carcass back in the rancher's or farmer's field. This is very deliberate, and in my opinion, this act alone tells me that whoever is doing this—and I believe I know who it is—conducts the grisly affair with complete impunity. They know nothing can stop them.

The entire phenomenon creates fear!

The currency of the kingdom of heaven is one of faith. Faith is the substance of things not seen but hoped for (Heb. 11:1).

The kingdom of the Dragon is one of fear. Fear is always, and I mean always, his calling card. With that in mind, to think that these entities, these perpetrators, these intruders, don't know what they are doing is, in my opinion, void of critical thinking. Here's why.

Dropping the mutilated animal back on the rancher's or farmer's field is bound to create fear. I've interviewed ranchers who stated, on the record, that they became fearful when they saw their mutilated cow. Frankly, who wouldn't be? When the rancher's wife and family look at the mutilation, they become afraid. Word gets out to other ranchers, and they, too, become unsettled and fearful. The vet is afraid, as well as law enforcement. Then the local newspaper does a story on it, complete with photos, and the local townspeople are gripped in fear. And so the Dragon and his cohorts win the day, at least temporarily.

The endgame here is this, and it ties into the biblical prophetic narrative. We know from prophecy that the seed of the Dragon will war against the seed of the woman. That manifested two thousand years ago with the advent of the promised Messiah, Jesus—the Dragon's head was crushed; he was defeated at Calvary. But not so fast, citizen. The Dragon will not give up easily. Even though he lost his right to rule the earth at the cross, where Jesus poured out His life for all of mankind, he wants to drag as many humans as he can away from the good news of the gospel, from the salvation and true freedom that await those who accept it.

So now we come to the prophecy that we find in Daniel chapter 2. Here's what it states.

> And whereas thou sawest iron mixed with miry clay, they shall mingle themselves with the seed of men: but they shall not cleave one to another, even as iron is not mixed with clay.
>
> —DANIEL 2:43, KJV

Without a grasp of the Genesis 3:15 narrative (thank you, Elder Brother Gary Stearman, for teaching on this years ago; it changed my life), when we arrive at this enigmatic passage, we are left wondering what it means.

Remember, the Book of Daniel is a sealed book. The angel instructed Daniel:

> But you, Daniel, shut up the words, and seal the book until the time of the end; many shall run to and fro, and knowledge shall increase.
>
> —DANIEL 12:4

Remember, until the industrial revolution of the nineteenth century, progress was pretty much flatlined. Now knowledge doubles within a matter of months!

As I write this in an airplane at thirty-seven thousand feet above the earth, I am now one of those who are running to and fro over the face of the earth. We are here at the end of days. So the seed of the Dragon is mingling with the seed of men. In other words, *they*, the Dragon's kingdom, are creating hybrids.

Remember Jesus' warning to us:

> For the coming of the Son of Man will be just like the days of Noah.
>
> —Matthew 24:37, NASB

We are in the days of Noah, the days of Lot. It's happening—the present-day manifestation of the seed war.

So, you may wonder, what does all of this have to do with cattle mutilations?

Here's what I think is happening. First, the phenomenon is fear-based. Secondly, the animal is always drained of blood. But did you know that *bovine blood products* can be used in human transfusions?[3] Let that sink in for a minute. United States military programs have used and researched this for decades, including the Letterman Army Institute of Research (LAIR), which "carried out investigations in such spheres as laser physics and artificial blood."[4]

Thirdly, we now know that there is a breeding program that has been ongoing for decades. Authors like Dr. David Jacobs, John Mack, and others have stated as much and have written numerous books on the subject.

In our film on the abduction phenomenon, Karin told of being taken from early childhood, and then when she was a young woman being impregnated by "them."[6] In the third month of her pregnancies, she was abducted again, and the fetus was taken from her. What happened to the fetus that was taken from Karin, and what about the thousands of others?

The fetus cannot survive outside the womb, so I propose that the fallen ones, the Dragon's forces, *use the material and blood of the animals to create an artificial womb!*

While this is speculation on my part, it is based on the many testimonies of unfortunate people who have been taken aboard these craft and have seen rooms full of containers, something like jars, with hybrids in them at different stages of development.

CONCLUSION

Tens of thousands of cattle have been taken and mutilated. The phenomenon is ongoing with no end in sight. If what I stated above is true, that the material and blood is being used to create artificial wombs for the hybrids, then it becomes very clear as to what the endgame of the phenomenon is. This is extremely disturbing.

The first time I stated this publicly was in Ohio at the 2023 Go Therefore Conference, which was put on by Pastor Mike Spaulding. There was a woman seated about five rows back in the audience. When I was connecting all the dots for the audience regarding how the blood and genetic material from the cattle are used to create artificial wombs for the hybrids, she burst into tears.

I realize that some of you who are reading this will have a lot of trouble getting your heads around this; I can't blame you. Our film on the cattle mutilation phenomenon is not for the faint of heart, and as I have warned people, there's no happy ending. There is nothing good about what happens with these cows.

My final word is this. The cattle mutilation phenomenon is part of the ongoing breeding program, which is creating hybrid beings that will be used by the Dragon in the last days.

These are the days of Noah.

THE NINTH RUNG: CONGRESS HOLDS ITS FIRST UFO DISCUSSION IN FIFTY YEARS

A s I have mentioned throughout this book, the subject of UFOs or UAPs has been, up until recently, reserved for tinfoil-hat-wearing people, the stuff of conspiracy theorists, a subject that intelligent and reasonable people just didn't discuss. With Congress holding its first discussion on the subject in more than fifty years, what are we to think?

I correspond with someone who is employed by our government. I think he is with one of the three-letter agencies, although I have no idea of which one. He could also be an independent contractor. When we first began to correspond, we were texting each other to discuss the possible outcomes this congressional hearing might bring to we the people. I will call this person *Osprey*. An osprey flies high in the sky and can see events unfolding clearer and farther out than someone just standing on the ground. They have keen eyesight, so the name is more than fitting for this contact. I will post our conversation in this chapter. Just to clarify, I am the one standing on the ground, and Osprey is the one flying overhead with a bird's-eye view.

Here's what *TIME* magazine had to say about the hearings:

> The House Intelligence Committee's Counterterrorism, Counterintelligence, and Counterproliferation subcommittee would like to make one thing very clear: They did not spend 90 minutes this morning conducting public hearings into the existence of UFOs. Yes, they were discussing unidentified objects, and yes those objects were seen to be flying, but the term for them today is "unidentified aerial phenomena" (UAP)—which means exactly the same thing but carries less whiff of tin foil hat conspiracies than the old UFO designation did.[1]

What I love about this statement is the assertion that we are now going to call these ongoing phenomena UAPs instead of UFOs. So, as I have stated before, with a wave of the hand, somehow, it's now OK to discuss UFOs! Oops, I mean UAPs.

In essence the hearing was exactly what I expected, a dog and pony show, one big nothing burger. Nothing of any significance was accomplished, the public didn't learn anything new about the ongoing phenomenon, and no new information was released. This brings me back to our discussion of the so-called *shadow government*.

When I was threatened by the guy from the deep state in 2016, he warned me that my work on the Giant of Kandahar was what put me on their radar. I suppose at this point I'll have to digress and at least offer a brief explanation of the Kandahar giant; otherwise you will be in the dark.

THE GIANT OF KANDAHAR

Years ago, when Richard Shaw and I were making the *Watchers* series, Richard was on a podcast talking about his film focused on the Torah codes. The host of the show was taking live-on-air calls, and at the end of the show one of the callers remained on the line. The show went off air, and the host, the caller, and Richard struck up a conversation. The conversation shifted to the Nephilim—the offspring of the fallen angels and the human women of earth. The caller stated that he had been in Afghanistan, and he had been part of a company of soldiers that brought down a giant! Rick was astonished, and after listening to the caller's story, he got his phone number and email. When Richard got off the podcast, he immediately called me and relayed the story. I was, needless to say, taken aback.

The next day I called the number Richard gave me, and the caller answered. We talked for a good while, and in that conversation the caller relayed the events that had taken place in Afghanistan years before. They went something like this: There was a patrol that was dispatched in the Kandahar province of Afghanistan, and they were looking for high-value targets. They missed their rally point and never checked in with base command. The following day, a platoon was dropped off in the same location of the first patrol. The caller was in this platoon, and they began to follow the trail created by the patrol that had gone missing. They travelled for some time and then found themselves on a large terrace-like outcropping that overlooked the valley below. This is where the caller, whom I now will call the shooter, began to see bone fragments and pieces of what looked like material from the missing patrol. There was also blood on the ground. Above the platoon was a large cave. Suddenly, without any warning, a "nightmare" came out from the cave. It was a fourteen-foot giant with flaming red hair!

The giant was brandishing a large lance. His voice was terrible to the hearing,[2] and the shooter and everyone else in the platoon were frozen in their tracks. One soldier's training kicked in, and he began to run toward the giant, firing his weapon. According to the shooter, the giant moved with such incredible speed and agility that the men in the platoon were taken aback. Before anyone could react, the giant impaled the soldier and lifted him above his head, all the while emitting a deafening roar from his huge throat.

The shooter yelled, "Shoot him in the head!" The platoon began to fire their weapons at the giant, and the firefight lasted perhaps thirty seconds. The giant fell to the ground, essentially decapitated. The soldier who had been impaled was still alive but in dire condition. One of the soldiers in the platoon radioed for a medivac and related what had just gone down. The chopper arrived, but it was too late—the soldier succumbed to his wounds. Later a large helicopter arrived, the platoon secured the body of the giant in a cargo net, and the giant was whisked away. The giant had six fingers and six toes on each hand and foot. He also had double rows of teeth. According to the shooter, the stench coming from the creature was so foul and nauseating that some of the men actually threw up. When the platoon returned to base and wrote out their reports, they were told to rewrite them and never talk about it again.

In our *Watchers* film series, we broke the Giant of Kandahar story. Since then I have talked with corroborating witnesses. One of these is a man from special forces, who went to the same cave with a company of men and allegedly had a firefight with three of the remaining giants. They managed to kill one, but the other two dematerialized, disappeared. I realize this might sound incredible, but I have heard the same story from other witnesses. Just months ago, I interviewed a man whose grandmother lived in the Kandahar province and was a witch. She would actually bring live animals to the cave and leave them there as an offering to the giants to make sure they did not raid the village.[3]

FROM OSPREY

I sent Osprey the David Flynn assessment on the 1947 Roswell incident. This is his feedback after he read Flynn's incredible insight. I will include what I deem are pertinent parts of our conversation.

> Osprey: Sent it out to two 32nd-degree Masons to read. The math is interesting to say the least. I'm not aware of the matrix he used, as I don't do that kind of work. But it lays bare the argument of visitors from another planet. The entire premise

is tied to this earth and the fallen watchers intervening to secure mankind. An earthbound epic.

The players are intertwined with human endeavor. And for the modern age, Roswell, positioned as it is, mathematically kicks it off. Two thousand twelve I've noted elsewhere was the catalyst year that began the decline or attack on Western civilization or, better put, Christianity. Little wonder we marvel at the rapidity of the decline. Roswell was a manifestation of the age-old forces that have plagued mankind since the fall. Tim Alberino says, "I can accept the interdimensional argument." I appreciate that. Jesus moved through space and time at will upon His resurrection in front of His disciples. He went to Sheol upon His death. Stephen was allowed a glimpse of the other or another dimension at his death. I suspect Paul and the prophets were seeing the same in their visions. Eden witnessed interdimensional travel. Abraham and Lot witnessed it. They were not traveling to or from another planet. It is not about interstellar travel to another planet. Now were the planets once different? Very possible. But that is long past.

Roswell, it appears, was the reemergence of the Dragon's minions to unseat Christianity and take mankind into their grasp. Roswell was prepositioned in space and time for a specific purpose. Satan always uses secret knowledge and societies to lock away and protect his wares on earth. Every society has experienced some form of this. It's the same pitch he made to Eve: eat and you'll be wise, know things, be like God. Last, you said it, it's about the earth. Man's destiny and home. Jesus died for man. No higher honor could He bestow on us. That alone put Satan's plan in perspective. Eisenhower was by all accounts, from what I've read and from conversations with the old guys, led by Allen Dulles in creating a strata of government out of public view. He simply knew from World War II we cannot fight a modern conflict in public view. But Dulles took that and went way, way beyond Ike's intentions. So much so, he realized later he had created a beast. Roswell fit into Dulles and Bill Donovan's narrative.

LA: What are your thoughts on the alleged whistleblower, David Grusch?

Osprey: Grusch is the reason the government goes to such length to bury things in the private sector. He and others like him have some level of conscience. They do not want that. Money buys a great deal of silence, compromise. And disposable people.

David Flynn connected the dots. It is orchestrated at the highest level. The agenda is the same today even if new players come out. In DC the CFR [Council on Foreign Relations] and their likes (national agenda) remain decade after decade, in government, then out to a consulting group, if you're worthy. They never go away. Just change seats. Presidents are bought and sold.

LA: What about Grusch?

Osprey: Leslie Kean told Fox that the WB [whistleblower] was not the only one who told her about alien craft. She said there were multiple sources—off the record of course.

She said bodies in those cases were not mentioned.

A quick google will bring up Kean. She is well respected. She says the WB has impeccable credentials. He was on the [UFO] task force. As part of his job to gather information, he hit a wall. Congress approved the task force and funded it. It had a legal mandate. This is his point; information was withheld from Congress illegally. He took his complaints to the IG for the intelligence community, IC IG [intelligence community inspector general], who found his complaint valid and creditable. He spoke with DOD [Department of Defense] approval. That simply means air your complaint, but cross no line in releasing classified information.

He has not. He stated a fact. The fact that something exists is not the same as explaining full operational details. Retrieval teams exist. Stop. The full spectrum of what they do was not exposed. But they exist for a reason.

I highly suspect the wall he hit was not DOD or any government agency. It was private sector who could not care less about congressional mandates regarding intelligence gathering and are not under their jurisdiction.

[Senator Lindsey] Graham and others get paid to run the interference.

If I am correct, it's going to be [a] contest between congressional oversight and some very powerful corporations who will curtail and line up their elected friends very quickly.

Let me give you another perspective on the UAP situation and others classified issues.

As a contractor you have money and power. But not total control. You work for the government. Do their bidding up to a point where your expertise kicks in.

Congressmen sleep with Chinese intelligence [operatives].

Biden and family are well linked to China. The FBI has more espionage cases than agents to work them. Our best universities are Chinese technical schools. The military is filling up with woke staffers.

Congress will hold hearings to determine if alien technology and pilot bodies were recovered. Stashed and hidden away. And they may well have been. Stashed to be reverse engineered. Not insignificant.

They will posture and bellow about deception and honesty and right to know.

But every contractor knows they can't be trusted. They are liars who can't keep a secret. Sell their country and souls to the highest bidder. And there is plenty of evidence of that.

The fact that they don't know means the contractors have done their job well. Too well it seems; the top intelligence agencies were lost to it.

So, the contractors and their supporters on the Hill will circle the wagons. Throw up smoke and mirrors to create an image of compliance, while a convoy of trucks and a squadron of heavy aircraft will be shuttling any sensitive material and artifacts to some back site God knows where. So that nothing remains even if sites are identified.

I don't think anyone in this business remotely trusts the government to have any merit in holding this equipment. A few old used-up pieces may be tossed out as a bone to the persistent hounds. Truth is that can't be trusted. Ample evidence of that. Nor does the public need to know. No legal right exists for that.

I may be wrong and that is always a reality. I live with it. But I don't expect anything more than minimal disclosure at best. Why would there be in the current corrupt environment? Trust me, there are elected officials who have integrity, and they know the consequences as well as anyone and will block a full disclosure.

LA: However, the monkey wrench in the whole affair are the fallen ones themselves. It's they who just may reveal themselves without the consent of the powers that be. They will call the shots, when it's time. Most likely after a nuke goes off either in the Middle East or Ukraine. The fact that these idiots are saber-rattling with tactical nukes even if it's all bluster is certainly alarming and something that we haven't seen since the Cold War. A nuke goes off...they show up.

Osprey: I would agree. It is evident from all I see and hear that Washington is going to stay the political course. WB has met with the House Select Committee on Intelligence in [a] closed session. He briefed them thoroughly. He briefed the ranking members privately. So, they are fully on board. He was supported by the testimony of others who hold similar positions but will not go on record. Press sources have ten hours of WB interviews.

I know the contractor side has a lot to lose on this. Huge amount of money riding on any back-engineering programs. It also appears that the U.S. was the first to capture the technology.

But it is a global pursuit. I suspect way more to that than we [can] see at the moment. So, giving up access to this technology is not going to happen without a fight. And as I said, contractors have support on the Hill regarding maintaining their status. This weekend was interesting as I found out how little people care. One of the media students did a profile of this story, and it ranked well below Trump's indictment. In fact, it was given very little airtime. Barely three-minute segments.

People simply don't take it seriously or don't care. The networks dismiss it for the most part.

Russia could nuke tactically. But the bet in intelligence is on Iran. They absolutely will and their program is accelerating. N Korea stepped up their missile program by a huge leap. Israel is clearly the target.

As for Christians who are informed and care, the story validates their belief system. The majority don't seem to care. In fact, it's dismissed locally. But I would agree behind the curtain the entities who control the technology, control the narrative. I thought this might be a soft disclosure. Now I'm not so sure. It may be a soft protracted rollout. Also found out as I said the 32nd-degree Masons are social political networkers. The have read little of their icons' actual beliefs. If they have, they mask it well.

At least your conferences are on the edge and timely.

LA: Do you think Congress would be interested in talking with me?

Osprey: I had a conversation with the Congressman's office. They have your contact information.

You are now one of many who are willing to offer an assessment of the UAP/ UFO phenomenon. The current revelations lay open the past two recent denials by NASA and DOD.

Getting all of the essential witnesses on board is a priority. Giving them legal protection is essential. And no small feat. The contractors are already there pitching. They were on it.

So, outsiders are welcome but not a priority.

"The truth will set you free" only applies to Jesus and salvation. Elsewhere it does not work so well. In fact, it's perilous at times. And serves no higher purpose. Truth will not come out, I suspect. At least not as the UFOLOGIST sees it. We shall see.

LA: What's the latest on the hearings?

Osprey: The Burchett hearings are closed door right now. A long line of witnesses are coming through to give favorable testimony to the WB allegations. The climate is tense, as it appears that information was both hidden and well-protected.

Once this is finished and collated, then the contractors will be called. They will have shields up for them, as this is not what many with security concerns want released. They have an elected group who fear letting go of it. And I think wisely so. While mainstream media does not cover it, the lesser ones are and doing a decent job. I'm sure leaks are forming.

Very few have sufficient clearance to even attend this hearing. You can imagine that only a mere handful even knew it existed. *It cast great doubt on the NASA and previous UAP hearings that are in full contradiction. Did they lie?? Some did as is the norm. But for the most part they knew absolutely nothing. How could they? This was buried deep. And still is.*

Christian prophecy pundits still claim a government coverup. Well, that's a half truth. You can't cover up what you know nothing of and are completely secure from ever knowing. NASA was at the fringe. And few of them. DOD same. CIA same. There was no need to write them in. Geospatial simply was data collecting and hit a wall. If he had not broken silence, [I] doubt anything would have ever been revealed willingly. Curious as to the extent.

I hold him in high regard. Just unclear. Reading up on the spider web of contracting. Mind boggling. And black. Very intricate system. You would not know them. Nothing familiar.[4]

CONCLUSION

Recently, as of January 2024, Representative Anna Paulina Luna made a startling statement: The whistleblower David Grusch told Congress that the UFO phenomenon is *interdimensional!*[5] This statement is a dramatic departure from the ongoing narrative that we have been hearing for years promulgated on such shows as *Ancient Aliens* and in countless films. In my book *UFO Disclosure* I included a list of films and TV shows that have conditioned the populace. Is this predictive programming? Perhaps. I do think it's very deliberate and has far-reaching consequences, especially when we consider that the under-thirty crowd has grown up with this reality. For them there is no Roswell event or Kenneth Arnold calling the phenomenon *flying saucers* or a threatening armada of UFOs over Washington, DC. I would posit that the under-thirty crowd believes in the plurality of worlds, in life on other planets. Essentially they have been conditioned to accept it.

As Osprey stated, *"It cast great doubt on the NASA and previous UAP hearings that are in full contradiction. Did they lie?? Some did as is the norm. But for the most part they knew absolutely nothing. How could they? This was buried deep. And still is."*

So while Congress chips away at the secrecy, we the people have to realize that this information is buried deep, it's compartmentalized, and deliberate obfuscation is the norm. As one congressman recently stated, "This is one more example that this isn't our government. We just get to live here in America, and the government doesn't answer to us."[6] This statement speaks volumes. The American people are distracted by all sorts of things that, in the long run, don't matter. Taylor Swift is a prime example. Here is a mediocre singer who is all over the media and essentially just serves to distract. King Charles and the royals are always in our news. Why? Lull the people to sleep, and give them bread and circuses.

Chapter 11

THE TENTH RUNG: "PENTAGON FINDS 'NO EVIDENCE' OF ALIEN TECHNOLOGY IN NEW UFO REPORT"

Nothing to see here! Keep moving!

My email inbox blew up the other day with a news article, "Pentagon Finds 'No Evidence' of Alien Technology in New UFO Report."[1] Folks were asking me why the report appeared to contradict the ongoing disclosure that we had seen since Commander David Fravor appeared on Tucker Carlson's show.[2] When asked about the Tic Tac–shaped object he had encountered and photographed, Fravor stated, on the record, "It was something not from this world."[3]

This profound statement by a credible air force commander was, as we discussed in the early chapters of this book, the first rung on the *ladder of disclosure*.

So now, in 2024, we have Air Force Major General Patrick Ryder telling us essentially, "There's nothing to see here. Keep moving!" Let's look at some articles about the Pentagon report, and I'll break it down.

A lengthy Defense Department review of U.S. government activities related to "unidentified anomalous phenomena," more commonly known as UFOs, has found no evidence that extraterrestrial intelligence has visited Earth or that authorities have recovered crashed alien spacecraft and are hiding them from the public.[4]

Taking this statement at face value makes one wonder how the Pentagon can dismiss the statement and report by Commander Fravor.

An NPR article described the sixty-three-page document as

the most comprehensive report the Pentagon has produced on the topic, and yet another instance in which it has batted down claims of alien spaceships.[5]

How can this document be the most comprehensive report the Pentagon has produced when it ignores the testimonies of credible, trained witnesses who have come into the public eye after 2017? Are Pentagon officials deliberately avoiding the testimony of Commander Fravor? Are they living on another planet? Sorry, but here's what I think is going on; see the endnote for a UFO update on my YouTube channel.[6]

There is a term I started using a few years ago in regard to the cover-up and deliberate obfuscation of the UFO phenomenon: *the old guard*. Let me explain.

In 1947 the Roswell event established the paradigm to which our military-industrial complex would adhere until recently (referring to the statement by Commander Fravor in 2017). The face of the old guard was and is General Ramey and those in the deep state, the shadow government, the military-industrial complex, who are not elected officials and yet dictate policy.

It was Ramey who floated the cover story of the weather balloon—created by the deep state or the military-industrial complex—and that *there was nothing to see, so forget about it.* It was Ramey who stated *the "excitement is not justified."*[7] Where did General Ramey get his orders from? Who or what group of people decided how this information would be disseminated to the American public? This behind-the-curtain group of men, who rule by secrecy and remain in the shadows, set in motion the way the public would deal with the UFO phenomenon and specifically what crashed in Roswell in late June of 1947. The original story published by the *Roswell Daily Record* had it right from the get-go; they told the truth. Later, in my opinion, the *old guard* took control and gave Ramey his marching orders. Then Ramey ran with the cover story, while Jesse Marcel Sr. became the patsy. I call Jesse Marcel Sr. *the Lee Harvey Oswald of ufology*!

Here's a question: Who is checking the fact-checkers? The NPR article states, *"[The Pentagon] has batted down claims of alien spaceships."*[8] What? Batted down claims? From my point of view that statement at this point in time is laughable! As I mentioned, we have a series of whistleblowers who have come out since Commander Fravor's groundbreaking interview in 2017 on Tucker Carlson's show. We also have Luis Elizondo, Christopher Mellon, and even Nick Pope, who was with the British government and worked on documenting sightings of UFOs. Are we to dismiss all of them? Just throw their testimonies under the bus? Negate their stories and information? Of course not. We have, for one, the Roswell incident, where the same powers that be proclaimed that what crashed in Roswell was a weather balloon. In addition we have the testimony of Dan Wilmot, who was an eyewitness to the craft in the skies over Roswell; he had this to say in the July 8, 1947, edition of the *Roswell Daily Record*:

> Mr. and Mrs. Dan Wilmot apparently were the only persons in Roswell who have seen what they thought was a flying disk.

They were sitting on their porch at 105 South Penn. last Wednesday night at about ten minutes before ten o'clock when a large glowing object zoomed out of the sky from the south-east, going in a northwesterly direction at a high rate of speed.

Wilmot called Mrs. Wilmot's attention to it and both ran down into the yard to watch. It was in sight less than a minute, perhaps 40 or 50 seconds, Wilmot estimated.

Wilmot said that it appeared to him to be about 1,500 feet high and going fast. He estimated between *400 and 500 miles per hour.*

In appearance it looked *oval in shape like two inverted sau-cers,* faced mouth to mouth, or like two old type washbowls placed together in the same fashion. The entire body glowed as though light were showing through from inside, though not like it would be if a light were merely underneath.

From where he stood Wilmot said that the object looked to be about 5 feet in size, and making allowance for the distance it was from town he figured that it must have been 15 or 20 feet in diameter, though this was just a guess.

Wilmot said that he heard no sound but that Mrs. Wilmot said she heard a swishing sound for a very short time.

The object came into view from the southeast and disap-peared over the treetops in the general vicinity of six-mile hill.

Wilmot, who is one of the most respected and reliable citi-zens in town, kept the story to himself hoping that someone else would come out and tell about having seen one, but finally today decided that he would go ahead and tell about seeing it. The announcement that the RAAF was in possession of one came only a few minutes after he decided to release the details of what he had seen.[9]

------·------

Here's the bottom line. Weather balloons do not look like inverted saucers, and they most certainly do not travel at four hundred miles an hour. Case closed! But I'm getting ahead of myself. Did the Pentagon take into consideration this statement? Most likely not.

Then we have a book that came out in 1997, *The Roswell Report: Case Closed,* another laughable moment brought to you by the same folks who are telling us, yet again, that there's nothing to see here.[10]

Dr. Stanton Friedman blew this book apart, and I'll include some of what he stated here. *The Roswell Report: Case Closed* is another attempt by *the powers that be* to steer the narrative, to obfuscate the truth, to create a false report that goes against the facts of the case. Talk about propaganda! Deliberate obfuscation! Who are these people, and why do they insist on creating a false narrative?

Dr. Friedman was a pioneer in ufology. He knew something was going on and the American people were not being told the truth.

I include for you here excerpts from an article by Dr. Friedman with my comments interspersed:

"Frankly I am sick and tired of the U.S. Air Force lying to the public, the press, and members of Congress about UFOs," said nuclear physicist Stanton T. Friedman at a public lecture "Flying Saucers ARE Real" in Albuquerque. "I have had a serious interest in UFOs for 39 years, lectured in a dozen countries, and visited seventeen document archives," he continued. "For 50 years there has been massive misrepresentation about UFOs in general, and in recent years the Roswell Incident in particular. The Air Force has come up with four different answers for Roswell:

1. A flying saucer

2. A radar reflector and weather balloon

3. A Mogul balloon train over 500 feet long with 23 balloons, sonobuoys, etc.,

4. And most recently, a Mogul balloon train plus crash test dummies dropped at least six years AFTER the 1947 crashes Southeast of Corona and West of Magdalena.

..."The Mogul explanation doesn't fit. There are gross differences among the testimony of their witnesses, and they ignore the testimony they don't want to consider while claiming falsely that they have talked to all the original witnesses still alive who handled material totally different from the Mogul explanation."[11]

Friedman is addressing the official government explanation, the MOGUL balloon story, in regard to what happened at Roswell.

The fact is in 1978 I was the first to talk to a key witness, Major Jesse Marcel the intelligence officer for the only atomic bombing group in the world in 1947. I was referred to him by an old ham radio buddy of his who had seen the press stories in 1947. Jesse never sought publicity. I discussed many of these false charges in my book TOP SECRET MAJIC.[12]

Notice that Dr. Friedman stated a fact, that he was the first to talk with *the* key witness in the entire affair, Major Jesse Marcel Sr. Once again, we must note that Major Marcel was true to his oath of secrecy until late in his life. He decided to break his silence, and I can only thank him for doing so. It led to our film *Revisiting Roswell: Exoneration*.[13]

One of the silliest official USAF stories is the crash test dummy nonsense. I spoke in person with Colonel Madson, whose picture is in the *Case Closed* volume and was heavily involved in the research program. He is adamant that the explanation doesn't fit. Remember that the dummies had to be the same height and weight as air force pilots. *None were dropped anywhere near the two crash sites and none were dropped earlier than 6 years AFTER the 1947 events.*[14]

When I first read this years ago, I shouted a loud *yes*! Friedman did it again! He debunked the debunkers. He beat them at their own game. These people had egg on their faces big-time. They lied.

They concocted a bogus story. They thought no one would check their data. They thought, in their hubris, they were smarter than the public and those of us who have closely followed the UFO phenomenon, like Dr. Friedman. They were flat out wrong, and they were caught with their hands in the cookie jar! Notice that in *The Roswell Report: Case Closed*, the author made the claim that what crashed was a MOGUL weather balloon and the so-called bodies were nothing more than crash test dummies.[15] Dr. Friedman did the research on this and found that the crash test dummies were not used until 1953, six years after the events in Roswell. As I stated in our UFO film *The Experts Weigh In*, unless the government had access to a time machine, this is highly improbable.[16]

In my opinion *The Roswell Report: Case Closed* is nothing more than another attempt by *the powers that be* to create confusion, disinformation, and a false narrative.

———·———

Going back to the Pentagon report. In a statement, General Ryder said:

> AARO [All-Domain Anomaly Resolution Office] has found no evidence that any U.S. government investigation, academic-sponsored research, or official review panel has confirmed that any sighting of a UAP represented extraterrestrial technology. All investigative efforts concluded that most sightings were ordinary objects and the result of misidentification.[17]

The key words here are "any sighting of a UAP represented extraterrestrial technology." This is where the whole concept of confirm/deny comes into play. In other words, Ryder can just use the standard phrase: "I can neither confirm nor deny."

Here's how it works. AARO is given information; however, it is compartmentalized and truncated at best. They don't have access to all the information. That is how they can make blanket statements like this. Furthermore, when Ryder made the statement that nothing extraterrestrial was found, he may have been telling the truth as he knows it.

Recently, Representative Anna Paulina Luna, a member of the House Oversight Subcommittee on UAPs, stated that we need to pay special attention to what David Grusch was saying. Grusch stated, on the record, that these are *interdimensional*, not extraterrestrial. With that in mind, Ryder could be stating the truth *as he knows it*.

This is my wheelhouse. The entities, or intruders, are interdimensional beings. They are the fallen ones, the watchers of old, Satan's legions; they are *messengers of deception*. They lie and do so habitually. They are dark entities and have a nefarious agenda.

> Some [UAPs] have later been attributed to foreign aircraft, surveillance balloons, atmospheric anomalies or simply debris floating in the air. [18]

How convenient! My late business partner, Richard Shaw, and I used to laugh about statements like this. In the film *Men in Black*, the men in black state, "Swamp gas from a weather balloon was trapped in a thermal pocket and reflected the light from Venus."[19] Rick and I would laugh ourselves silly over this, and yet here it is again in 2024, and we're supposed to believe this!

While it is true that some UFOs can be explained with natural phenomenon, what does General Ryder do with the Kumburgaz UFO footage? Richard Shaw and I broke this story in our *Watchers* series. Dr. Roger Leir gave us the footage. As I said before, in my opinion, it is the best UFO footage to date. People steal our work—and the Kumburgaz footage—and never give Rick or me credit. However, we were the ones who broke the story. I would love to see General Ryder's face and body language as he watches this incredible footage.

The Kumburgaz UFO footage is the real deal. The Tic Tac–shaped

UFO caught in the gunsights of Commander Fravor's F/A-18 is the real deal. The endless reports and photos that come across my desk on a weekly basis are the real deal. The numerous witnesses that I have interviewed for our UFO films are telling the truth. With all due respect, General Ryder is either completely incompetent or a shill for the shadow government.

> AARO's report goes on to state that, despite widely publicized claims made in a July 2023 congressional hearing that included testimony from former U.S. military and intelligence community personnel, the office found no evidence suggesting the U.S. government is in possession of crashed or reverse-engineered alien technology, nor that any hidden "UAP reverse-engineering programs" actually exist, either in the U.S. government or in private industry.[20]

Whom do we believe? The article is referencing David Grusch, a former Air Force intelligence officer who claimed before Congress that for years the government has operated a covert program in which it reverse engineers recovered UFO aircraft. Why would Grusch lie under oath? Why would he risk everything by coming forward with what I believe is the truth? This is the *countermove* by the powers that be, and Admiral Ryder is the mouthpiece. They are once again trying to steer the narrative, to keep the truth from the American people. Shame on all of them.

I'll tell you a story.

A few years ago at a conference, a woman told me about her father, who was a Navy SEAL. According to her testimony, his team was deployed to a site where there was a crashed UFO. They set up a perimeter around the craft so the *retrieval unit* could remove it. They essentially secured the area. This woman told me that her father and the other men who were with him looked into the vehicle and saw the bodies. *The biologics were not human.*

So is Grusch lying? Or is Ryder telling the truth from only what he knows and what he's been told, which is not the whole picture?

Ryder is, in my opinion, nothing more than another disinformation agent telling us that there's nothing to see here. Shame on him.

The UFO phenomenon is real, burgeoning, and *not* going away, but these are not advanced vehicles carrying our space brothers from another galaxy—they are nefarious entities that are part of the *coming great deception*. Ryder said:

> To date, AARO has found no verifiable evidence for claims that the U.S. government and private companies have access to or have been reverse-engineering extraterrestrial technology.[21]

This statement goes against the book written by the late Colonel Corso, *The Day After Roswell*, which stated exactly the opposite of what Ryder is saying. Corso claimed that he distributed material recovered from crashed UFOs to different companies in the private sector for back engineering purposes. Once again, whom do we believe?

CONCLUSION

The Pentagon report is full of disinformation, lies, and deliberate obfuscation. It is nothing more than another attempt by the old guard to manage the agenda. Ryder is just another General Ramey, who will say what he has to say in order to appease those who are controlling him and those to whom he is beholden. In the end the truth will prevail.

We are being visited but not by extraterrestrials. These are fallen ones, beings that are depraved in every way. They have lost or abandoned their first estate. They have a nefarious agenda, and it is linked back to Genesis 3:15.

In short, despite what General Ryder insists upon, UFOs are real, burgeoning, and *not* going away. This is the coming great deception.

Chapter 12

THE ELEVENTH RUNG: UFO INTERFERENCE SYNDROME

D R. GARRY NOLAN is a professor in the pathology department at Stanford University School of Medicine. His faculty page says:

> He trained with Leonard Herzenberg (for his Ph.D.) and Nobelist Dr. David Baltimore (for postdoctoral work for the first cloning/characterization of NF-κB p65/RelA and the development of rapid retroviral production systems). He has published over 330 research articles and is the holder of 50 U.S. patents, and has been honored as one of the top 25 inventors at Stanford University.[1]

I had the privilege of speaking with Dr. Nolan in regard to the extensive DNA research we did on the elongated skulls. We had several meaningful discussions on the subject, and while Dr. Nolan remained skeptical, our discussions were cordial. In August of 2022 I was surprised to see Dr. Nolan on the *Tucker Carlson Today* show discussing the biological effects UFO encounters and that the CIA had come to his office to ask for help with people who had been injured from exposure to these vehicles, something known as interference syndrome.[2]

Most of us remember Steven Spielberg's Oscar-winning film *Close Encounters of the Third Kind*. The humble hero, *Roy*, played by Richard Dreyfuss, has a close encounter with a UFO where the craft sneaks up behind him while he's in his truck. Not yet aware of what is happening, only knowing that lights came up behind him, *Roy* motions for what he thinks is a car to go around him. Then strange things start to happen, and Roy is wondering what is going on. The UFO is now hovering directly overhead with lights blazing. *Roy* cranes his neck out the window, looks up to get a better view of the craft, and is suddenly hit with a burst of light. In a classic scene, *Roy* looks in the bathroom mirror the morning after the encounter and sees that half of his face is sunburned.[3]

The sunburn effect depicted in the film is common among real-life UFO experiencers, like the people in Fátima who reported sunburns on their faces after the flyby. In fact, people have been photographed after seeing a UFO up close to document this phenomenon. By the way, when the UFO is that close, it is classified as a *close encounter of the second kind*, or *CE2*. I suppose this would be a great time to discuss J. Allen Hynek's classification system used when reporting UFOs.

- CE1: "Sightings where the UFO, whatever its appearance, comes near enough to a witness—typically within about 500 feet—that details of the UFO can be readily observed. There is no interaction with the witness or the environment."[4]

- CE2: "Sightings where the UFO causes an effect on the environment, or the witnesses or animals. This can vary from marks on the ground, or damaged vegetation, to interference with electronic equipment, vehicles, or mobile phones, to burns or ill health for witnesses. These sightings have been the most important because there was evidence that could be studied after the event."[5]

- CE3: "Sightings where an entity of some type, whatever the appearance, was seen in or near a UFO. Often the UFO landed, and sometimes there was also an effect on the witness, such as paralysis."[6]

- CE4: "Sightings where a witness reports being taken against their will into a UFO, or at least removed from their normal environment to somewhere else. The witnesses may undergo examinations and sometimes be given information. This category was added in later years to separate abduction reports from Close Encounters of the Third Kind."[7]

- CE5: "An alien abductee receives some manner of physical effect from their close encounter, typically either injury or healing." The witness is shown how the craft works and is flown to other parts of the universe. Some also refer to "human-initiated contact with extraterrestrial life forms or advanced interstellar civilizations, claiming direct communication between aliens and humans."[8]

Now back to *Roy*. His character had a sunburn on only part of his face. I want to digress here for just a moment. Spielberg definitely *did his homework* in that he wove the sunburned face into the storyline. When I saw the blockbuster film in 1977, I was twenty-seven years old. Even though I had seen a UFO when I was twelve, I didn't start researching the phenomenon until many years later. And I was a New Ager all the way. I even wrote a song after seeing the movie.

> As you sit in silence waiting for the space alliance
> Listening to the ringing in your ears
> And you know you want to go…

At that point in my life, I was all in with our supposed space brothers. At the end of the film *Roy* was the one that the aliens selected to take with them,[9] and in 1977 I wished that I was the lucky one to be taken! Decades later, Spielberg produced what I believe may be the best TV miniseries ever created on the subject. The ten-episode series was called *Taken*. By the time the series came out, I had been walking with the Lord for years, was Spirit-filled, and had newfound discernment regarding what I was seeing. The series explores everything from foo fighters in WWII to the abduction phenomenon and even the creation of hybrids.

The last two episodes of *Taken* show a girl who is the end product of *mixing the seed* of these so-called extraterrestrials. She is, in fact, a hybrid—the show makes this very clear. The hybrid girl is also able to stop time![10] Is this a foreshadowing of what the Antichrist might be able to do? It certainly is possible.

It's amazing the difference being born again and Spirit-filled can make in a person's life. At age twenty-seven I was sold out to the space brothers—I wanted to go with them! But years later I was able to see the *deception* that was being touted in the film. To wrap this up, I'll go down another rabbit trail. While Spielberg produced a fantastic series, the series, in my opinion, is far from the truth.[11] He is promulgating the same deception that the History Channel has pushed now for over a decade through shows such as *Ancient Aliens*.

I'll say it once again here to make things perfectly clear. These intruders are *not* our space brothers—they are, in fact, interdimensional entities with a nefarious agenda. All of this hails back to the *seed war*, and specifically the prophetic warning that we read in Daniel 2:43: "They shall mingle themselves with the seed of men: but they shall not cleave one to another" (KJV). This scripture, in my opinion, is a direct reference for what is happening now in modernity.

KARIN'S STORY

Garry Nolan stated that people who are exposed to close encounters with UFOs have brain anomalies. Earlier in the book I introduced you to Karin Wilkinson. I am honored to say we published Karin's book, *Stolen Seed, Evil Harvest*. Karin was an abductee—taken from the time she was five or six years old—and she was impregnated by "them" three times. As I mentioned earlier, Karin was a main pillar of our film on abductions. In her book, Karin discusses what happened to her as a result of being in close proximity to UFOs for years. Here is her story in an excerpt from her book.

———

I will say of the [LORD], He is my refuge and my fortress: my God; in him will I trust. Surely he shall deliver thee from the snare of the fowler, and from the noisome pestilence.

—PSALM 91:2–3[, KJV]

"Anomalous Acute and Subacute Field Effects on Human Biological Tissues"—this is the name of a U.S. Government report released in 2022. It sounds complicated, scientific, and official, and it is. But to me, it is the sound of confirmation. It is the confirmation I needed that a lifetime of physical anomalies, pain, and trauma finally has an explanation. I can finally say that the government confirms that my decades of strange and unusual and sometimes terrifying and often life-threatening health issues were caused by my lifelong exposure to otherworldly beings and their vehicles of conveyance, in other words, aliens and UFOs.

On April 6, 2022, Bret Baier aired a report in which he stated, "I feel like we should have the *X-Files* music here, but they say the truth is out there and it might be terrifying. A just-uncovered defense department summary of UFO-induced effects ranging from abduction and paralysis to electrical shocks and even sexual encounters is shocking the world tonight."

On August 2, 2020, Tucker Carlson interviewed Garry Nolan on Fox Nation. Nolan talked about serious brain injuries suffered by military personnel who had been exposed to UFOs, known as *Interference Syndrome*. Referring back to the official report…page six lists the following:

Amongst the most important pathophysiological effects are:

- Heating and burn injuries ionizing and non-ionizing
- Thermally-induced neurological effects
- Cognitive/central nervous system
- Neuromuscular/central and autonomic nervous systems
- Sensory/peripheral nervous system
- Neuropsychiatric/neuroendocrine—Auditory/cranial nerves VII & VIII
- Communication and disabling effects
- Noise and central neurocognitive

Page nine of the report goes on to explain that acute high-strength electromagnetic fields, ionizing radiation, intense lasers, et al., can have harmful effects on human physiology.

The report also includes Appendix A, which lists physiological effects reported through the Mutual UFO Network (MUFON) from 1873 to 1994. The catalog comprises a summary of 356 selected cases of UFO-induced physiological effects on humans during close encounters. The catalog thus constitutes a useful database from which it is anticipated that certain physical source causes may be inferred.

This list is decades old. It doesn't include any recent cases and I would posit that a much more comprehensive list could be compiled from further research. I was going to highlight the number of items on the list that I have personally experienced, but instead, I will just summarize that out of the 77 physiological effects listed, I have experienced all but fifteen of them—and I could add a few to the list. I am not a hypochondriac, but I have experienced very real medical issues for no apparent reason. It is my opinion, based on the above reports, my personal experiences, and the experiences of other UFO abductees

I have spoken with, that these medical issues are directly related to and caused by the UFO abduction phenomenon.

TABLE OF EFFECTS
Apparent abductions

Electromagnetic effects on vehicle(s)

Paralysis

Perceived time loss

Light beam effects

Eye injuries

Heat

Medical exam

Burns

Unconsciousness

Marks left on the body

Significant sound effects

Electrical shock

Physiological/ emotional shock, intense fear

Pricking, tingling sensations

Pain

Skin sores, rash

Induced headaches, migraines

Force field impact

Nausea, vomiting

Sensation of cold

Disorientation, confusion

Ground traces

Weakness, fatigue

Amnesia

Apparent experience of telepathy

Numbness

Significant odors

Voice loss

Appetite loss

Insomnia

Perceived time suspension

Dehydration

Swelling of tissues

Dizziness

Weightlessness, levitation

Healing

Sexual encounters

Deaths

Diarrhea

Hair loss

Nightmares

Claimed ESP development

Nose bleeds

Tastes

Ringing in ears

Weight loss

Breathing problems

Urination problems

Gynecological problems

Claimed implant

Perceived teleportation

Stunned

Itching

Loss of taste

Loss of hearing

Induced feeling of calm, serenity

EM effects on power system

Involuntary muscle movement

Induced body odor

Wart growth

Sooty deposit

Mental enhancement

Mental degradation

Swallowing difficulty

Teeth vibration

Fillings crumbled

Hair precipitously turned white

Time sped up

Unaccounted-for pregnancy

Cancer

Fever

Stomach sickness

Physiological energization

Loss of smell

External control of a vehicle

Material evidence

Mine is a long and grisly medical history, so I will not elaborate, but I will provide a brief, abridged summary of some of the more significant issues I have faced. I have included my pictures not for shock value but rather to provide further evidence.

The first oddity I encountered was when, at the age of about five or six years old, I woke up with a burn under my right shoulder blade. I still have a mark there today. Here is a photo of the scar.

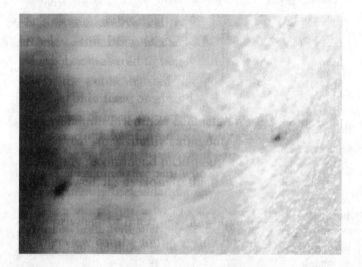

At the age of thirteen, I was diagnosed with scoliosis. That is not the real oddity, although it is unusual that no one else in my family had ever had it, so there was no medical history. The real abnormality was that they began measuring my growth through various tests. I was informed that my body's physical age was not aging at the same rate as others, so my physical age was younger than my chronological age. I was aging more slowly than the average person.

When I was seventeen, the rate of bone growth in my spine was out of control to the degree that the doctors decided I needed spinal fusion surgery. They wired rods to my spine and with the help of a bone graft from my hip, lessened the degree of curvature in my spine enough to prevent my internal organs from being damaged and other life-threatening symptoms. The surgery was a success, although quite risky and very painful.

Throughout my twenties, I had three confirmed unaccounted-for pregnancy losses. There were other pregnancies where I would perform a home pregnancy test, get several positive results, and then the pregnancies would be gone before I could get in to see my doctor. I have no idea how many times I might have been impregnated by these non-human entities, but I am quite certain that there were at least three.

In my thirties, the tumors started growing. The first one grew so large and so fast that the doctors prepared me for a mastectomy. They were almost certain it was a malignant tumor. The tumor, although large and unexplainable, was benign. It was the first of three breast tumors I would have removed over the years.

In my late thirties through my mid-forties, the uterine issues surfaced. I had many unusual masses removed, unexplained tissue growth going from the inside through to the external uterine walls, and a collection of issues that eventually led to a hysterectomy.

From the mid-forties to today, bone and spinal issues have become more significant. I have had seven more spinal surgeries in the past seven years. My discs are degenerating, my spinal bones are growing spurs, my spine is growing bone that is squeezing my spinal cord, my vertebrae are twisting and arching, and bone growth is happening in my joints—osteoarthritis—and in my circulatory system. It is a massive list of problems and an army of dedicated doctors keeping me alive and keeping me moving. But no one in the medical industry can tell me why any of this is happening.

See the pictures below.

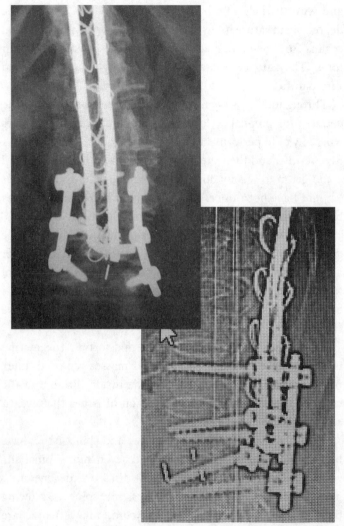

Hardware put into my spine (2 angles)

And even though the government admits to the injuries caused by non-human entities and their UFOs, there is no one for me to contact for help. There is no financial restitution for my physical and emotional pain. No one wants to believe me. Even the scars on my body and the metals used to rebuild it aren't enough to get the attention of anyone. I have known that I am in this on my own from the very beginning. From the moment the alien entities threatened to kill my family when I was only six years old, I knew. But God was and is always with me and my family, and before the next unexplained illness would take hold, God sent me another supporter.

MIRACLES

L. A. Marzulli was the first person I shared my story with. I met up with L. A. at a conference in Dallas, Texas. After exchanging emails, I agreed to go on the record with my experiences in a filmed interview. I sat in a simple chair in front of the cameras, and I recounted my life story. For the first time. I cannot even remember what questions L. A. asked me or what I said. An hour flew by in what seemed like seconds. As L. A. walked me to the door after the interview, I felt like I was going to collapse. I struggled to find my way back to my room. I had released the pain and agony that was living inside me, eating me alive day after day. It was finally time to start healing. Someone listened to me after fifty-five years of hiding my past. Someone believed me. It was a miracle.

Over the next few months, the pain in my back came back worse than ever. Just six months after a major spinal surgery, I was going in for yet another major spinal surgery. I recovered from my surgery and continued to believe that I would hear something from L. A. I refused to lose faith. I knew L. A. believed me. I just did not know what to do next. Then, I received an email from L. A. informing me that he was going to use the footage of our interview and that he was looking forward to getting the four abductees from his movie together to meet on a Zoom call. If you saw the fourth *UFO Disclosure* movie in the series, "The Coming UFO Invasion," then you know what happened next. Suddenly, I wasn't alone anymore. I had support and a community of people who had experiences just like mine. I had people to talk to! Christian people! Another miracle.

The UFO movie was finally released in December 2022, and I was terrified about going public with my life experiences, but the more I talked about my life, the easier it was to share. I had been conditioned since early childhood to keep the abductions quiet. But now, God sent L. A. to help set me free. I kept writing, and then what I considered to be miracle number three happened. L. A. asked me to write something for him and he liked what I wrote. I have never felt good enough at anything because of the damage done to me by the evil, non-human alien entities. I can be painfully insecure at times, so I was thrilled that something I did was good enough. I continued to write, and I was wielding off constant satanic attacks. What happened next was an attack, unlike anything I could have imagined.

I had a headache that started in November 2022 and did not stop. It wasn't a migraine; I get those often. This was different. In January, my neurologist noticed something strange about one of my eyes and sent me for an MRI. Then several CT scans. I had a cluster of abnormal cells in my brain—a brain tumor. Now, doctors don't like to cut through your skull until they have all the information, so I was scheduled for blood tests, a lumbar puncture, more specialists, and more MRIs to verify what we were dealing with. I was terrified.

It just so happened that L. A. was visiting a nearby church that weekend, so I went to say hello and hear him speak. At the end of the evening, my husband and I went quietly to leave, and I heard someone call my name. I turned around to see L. A. asking that we pray together. He somehow knew that I was terrified and prayed for God to take away the fear.

The next day was a full speaking day for L. A. at the church. He said that he would like to pray over me at lunch. I felt so unworthy. There were too many others there who wanted and needed prayer. Peggy, L. A.'s wife, and I were sitting and chatting and getting to know one another better, and she prayed with me while he was giving his presentation. I felt quite blessed after her beautiful prayer and I did not want to bother L. A. further with my health issues. After lunch, L. A.'s friend found me and walked my husband and me back to a little prayer room. It was there that L. A. and his friends, my husband, and members of the church prayed for my healing. I felt the Holy Spirit in that room. I felt incredible love. I felt healed.

The medical industry moves very slowly. It took weeks to get all the tests run and find out what, if anything, was growing in my head. My peripheral vision was gone on one side, my eye was bulging out more and more, and I was more exhausted than at any time in my life. My headaches were getting worse, I was dizzy, and I could not drive. I was barely functioning. I felt like I was dying.

During a particularly difficult, sleepless night of pain, I felt like I could not go on anymore. I wanted to end it. I prayed for God to please take me home. I continued to pray. I didn't even know what to pray for; I just prayed and praised God. Suddenly, I felt different. I felt a small jolt of energy coursing through me, and I could hear God telling me that I had received healing, and I just needed to accept the healing gift.

The next week, I finally had another MRI of my brain. I felt an eerie sense of calm about it, and that is when it happened. They said the tumor was gone! No explanation, just gone. I had been healed by the grace of God. Yet another miracle.

This is my little thank you note. Thank you, God, for believing in me. Thank you, God, for rescuing me when I feel hopeless and helpless. Thank you, God, for bringing L. A. and Peggy into my life. I am blessed to call them friends.

See, miracles do happen. Sometimes several of them.

A picture of L. A. and me at the conference

I believe that miracles do happen, so I am not worried anymore about these anomalous acute and subacute effects that have plagued me; I am protected by a higher power, by my Lord and Savior Jesus Christ. God is healing my physical and psychological wounds. But the fact remains that these non-human, alien entities are continuing to cause harm to others, and I believe that this is just the beginning of a much larger, much darker, much more sinister plan to destroy humanity and it is looming on the horizon.[12]

CONCLUSION

There are some researchers who state that there is no *physicality* to the UFO phenomenon, that all of this is nothing more than demonic delusion. I couldn't disagree more. We have scientific proof that there is physicality. We have hundreds of cases of people being physically abducted. We have metal from the 1947 craft that we recovered in the debris field. We have whistleblowers who testified before Congress that we have in our possession not only crashed craft but nonhuman biologics! To say that people like Karin are delusional is an injustice to the countless people who have been *taken.* Dr. Nolan put all of this to rest. The UFO phenomenon with all of its complexity is real. People are taken. People are implanted, women become pregnant, and the fetus is then removed at the third month of pregnancy.

Karin's testimony is very disturbing, but it is all too real. The side effects from being exposed to UFOs is now a scientific reality. Time for those who say this is all delusion and that there is no physicality to the phenomenon to stop maligning those who have had their lives interrupted by these nefarious intruders.

Chapter 13

THE TWELFTH RUNG: FOX NATION'S SHOW *ALIEN ABDUCTIONS*

I HAVE ALREADY COVERED the abduction phenomenon in great detail, so I will approach it from a slightly different perspective here.

In 2022 Fox Nation, Fox News's streaming service, aired a new program, *Alien Abductions*, hosted by Abby Hornacek. It aired for only one season with six episodes. I will explore some of what Abby Hornacek's shows cover. Here's what the description on the Fox site says.

> Abby Hornacek travels the country engaging people and places connected to mysterious reports of alien abduction.[1]

Well, bully for Abby! Abby, I hope you have your armor of God on and are walking close to Jesus, because this kind of research is not for the faint of heart. It's not another episode of *The X-Files* where the actors go home at the end of the day and relax! This research is rife with attacks from the enemy of our souls, the fallen one. I hope Abby knows about putting on the armor of God described in Ephesians 6.

I will cover some of the episodes Hornacek hosted and take a look at Fox, which can have significant budgets for their shows that could run in the tens of thousands of dollars per episode.

I've selected a few of the episode titles and will comment on each one. For a ufologist like me, all of this is old news. I have to wonder why Fox would spend this kind of money rehashing what I would call *Ufology 101*. I would posit that these types of shows are created to bring the layperson up to speed. In order to access the series and the episodes' descriptions, I would have to pay for them, so I will use Wikipedia for source material, then I will comment afterward.

THE BARNEY AND BETTY HILL INCIDENT

According to a variety of reports given by the Hills, the alleged UFO sighting happened about 10:30 p.m. September 19, 1961. The Hills were driving back to Portsmouth [New Hampshire] from a vacation in Niagara Falls and Montreal. Just south of Lancaster, New Hampshire, Betty claimed to have observed a bright point of light in the sky that moved from below the Moon and the planet Jupiter, upward to the west of the Moon. While Barney navigated U.S. Route 3, Betty reasoned that she was observing a falling star, only it moved upward. Because it moved erratically and grew bigger and brighter, Betty urged Barney to stop the car for a closer look, as well as to walk their dog, Delsey. Barney stopped at a scenic picnic area just south of Twin Mountain.

Betty, looking through binoculars, observed an "odd-shaped" craft flashing multicolored lights travel across the face of the Moon. Because her sister had several years earlier said she had seen a flying saucer, Betty thought it might be what she was observing. Through binoculars, Barney observed what he reasoned was a commercial airliner traveling toward Vermont on its way to Montreal. However, he soon changed his mind, because without looking as if it had turned, the craft rapidly descended in his direction. This observation caused Barney to realize, "this object that was a plane was *not* a plane."

The Hills said they continued driving on the quiet and isolated road, moving very slowly through Franconia Notch in order to observe the object as it came even closer. At one point, the object passed above a restaurant and signal tower on top of Cannon Mountain and came out near the Old Man of the Mountain. Betty testified that it was at least one and a half times the length of the granite cliff profile, which was 40 feet (12 m) long, and that it seemed to be rotating. The couple watched as the silent, illuminated craft moved erratically and bounced back and forth in the night sky.

About one mile south of Indian Head, they said, the object rapidly descended toward their vehicle, causing Barney to stop in the middle of the highway. The huge, silent craft hovered about 80 to 100 feet (24 to 30 m) above the Hills' 1957 Chevrolet Bel Air and filled the entire field of view in the windshield. It reminded Barney of a huge pancake. Carrying his pistol in his pocket, he stepped away from the vehicle and moved closer to the object. Using the binoculars, Barney claimed to have seen eight to eleven humanoid figures, who were peering out of the craft's windows, seeming to look at him. In unison, all but one figure moved to what appeared to be a panel on the rear wall of the hallway that encircled the front portion of the craft. The one remaining figure continued to look at Barney and communicated a message telling him to "stay where you are and keep looking." Barney had a recollection of observing the humanoid forms wearing glossy black uniforms and black caps. Red lights on what appeared to be bat-wing fins began to telescope out of the sides of the craft, and a long structure descended from the bottom of the craft. The silent craft approached to what Barney estimated was within 50 to 80 feet (15 to 24 m) overhead and 300 feet (91 m) away from him. On Oct. 21, 1961, Barney reported to National Investigations Committee On Aerial Phenomena

(NICAP) investigator Walter Webb that the "beings were somehow not human."[2]

The Hills' story was covered in the third episode of *Alien Abductions*. What makes this story so interesting is that, as far as I know, the Hills were the first abduction case that was recorded and publicized in America. I have read and reread their account numerous times, and I believe they were taken. In the Wikipedia article the so-called debunkers tried to deconstruct what the Hills experienced and downplay the reality of it. Jason Colavito, quoted in the section "Influence from *The Outer Limits*,"[3] is the modern equivalent of Philip Klass, who made his living by being a professional debunker. No matter what a witness saw, Klass would always disparage what the witness was saying and, in the end, state *there was nothing to see here!*

Colavito has written several pieces on my work, so it makes me wonder why he is so adamant in his stance. Is he a paid shill like Klass? Only time will tell. However, much of what the Hills state in their testimony has been recapitulated by virtually every abductee I have talked to. There is also a dynamic that may be present here. These entities do have the ability of planting false memories in those who are taken. This dynamic further obfuscates researchers getting to the truth. This is why Karin Wilkinson's book, *Stolen Seed, Evil Harvest*, is so vital to the ongoing abduction phenomena research.

If we only had Betty and Barney Hill's story and nothing else, then debunkers like Klass and Colavito would have a strong case. However, in our film on abductions, *The Coming UFO Invasion*, we have four people who have been taken. The debunkers, by their insistence that these stories are fabricated, disparage the people who are bold enough to come on the record. The question I have is this: Are the four people in our abduction film lying, mentally unstable, concocting stories to get attention, and/or delusional, or are they victims of an event that has traumatized them and left them ashamed as well as groping for answers? The abduction phenomenon is real, and every aspect of it hails back to the Genesis 3:15 narrative that I have repeatedly called to your attention throughout the pages of this book.

INCIDENT AT PASCAGOULA

On the evening of October 11, 1973, 42-year-old Charles Hickson and 19-year-old Calvin Parker told the Jackson County, Mississippi, sheriff's office they were fishing off a pier on the west bank of the Pascagoula River in Mississippi when they heard a whirring/whizzing sound, saw two flashing blue lights, and observed an oval shaped object 30–40 feet (9–12 m) across and 8–10 feet (2–3 m) high. Parker and Hickson claimed they were "conscious but paralyzed" while three "creatures" with "robotic slit-mouths" and "crab-like pincers" took them aboard the object and subjected them to an examination.[4]

I spoke with Calvin Parker a few years before he died. He was supposed to do a sit-down interview with me the next morning at a conference we were both speaking at, but he suddenly left the conference, and we never connected. I attended his lecture and found him credible and not sensationalistic. I talked with him one-on-one and told him my position in regard to the whole UFO phenomenon. He was with his wife when this conversation took place, and to the best of my recollection, they both acknowledged the biblical worldview regarding abductions and UFO encounters. Parker was caught up in something that he didn't ask for, and that experience deeply affected him throughout his life. In my opinion what happened at Pascagoula is another classic case of abduction, combined with screen memories to alter the truth. In almost every case I have ever read about regarding this phenomenon, there is a sexual component to it—sperm is taken from the men and ova from the women.

> They shall mingle themselves with the seed of men: but they
> shall not cleave one to another.
> —Daniel 2:43, kjv

As of this writing, another witness to the abduction of Calvin Parker has just come forward. After all these years she has finally decided to go on the record. She stated that she saw the so-called alien beings, and that they match the description of what Calvin Parker saw.[5] Can you imagine what Calvin Parker endured the rest of his life? Can you imagine the ridicule, the skepticism, the shunning from people and perhaps relatives? Parker endured all of this and much more for the duration of his life as he lived with the memories of being taken *against his will*. This is the opening monologue to our film on abduction, and I think it's pertinent to insert it here.

> Something very dark and disturbing is happening. It is a global
> phenomenon that knows no boundaries, and it adheres to no
> cultural mores. The ones who are engaged in this nefarious
> activity do so with impunity. People are being taken against
> their will, in the cover of darkness, in the dead of night. They
> are subjected to bizarre examinations that are often sexual
> in nature. These people are terrified, violated, and confused,
> with no place to turn. Who would believe them? This is their
> story.[6]

Implanting Terry Lovelace

This is an excerpt from an article first published by *The Guardian* in 2021.

> Despite the debunkers and proliferation of more mundane
> explanations for UFOs, reports of close encounters have per-
> sisted for decades. Terry Lovelace, a retired assistant attorney
> general in Vermont, USA, and author of *Incident at Devil's
> Den*, kept his abduction to himself for 40 years due to fear of

losing his job. He had a close encounter in 1977 while serving in the U.S. air force.

Lovelace, now 67, was on a camping trip in Devil's Den state park in northern Arkansas with a friend and colleague named Toby when things got strange. They were sitting around a fire, struggling to chat over the din of buzzing crickets and croaking tree frogs before everything went quiet. "That sounds kind of clichéd—out of a movie—but that is exactly what happened to us," he says.

Three bright lights appeared on the horizon and moved in their direction. When the lights were overhead, they could see that they were emanating from a black triangular prism as wide as two city blocks.[7]

The *Northwest Arkansas Democrat Gazette* said it's hard to dismiss Lovelace as "a crazy man."[8] An EMT and medic in the air force, he enlisted at age eighteen then served from 1973 to 1979. Part of that time he was stationed at Whiteman Air Force Base in western Missouri, the 509th Bomb Wing, which during his time there had B-52s and nuclear capabilities. A lifelong defense attorney, he has been married to the same woman for more than forty-five years.[9] With his education, military service, and government position, he comes across as professional, communicates well, and is calm and detailed when sharing the story—the very opposite of the caricature the career debunkers often describe.

Here is a summary of his experience as he described it in February 2024.

The center of the craft emitted a bright white column of light straight down into the center of the campers' campfire, and after a few seconds it was shut off. Something similar to a laser beam shot down at various spots in their camp for several seconds at a time and then would shut off and focus on another target. This beam hit

Lovelace directly in the chest three times. He and Toby did not talk during all of this.

As if critical thinking had been shut down, Toby said, "Show's over," and they silently picked up their air mattresses and went into their tent. I call this UFO brain fog, an induced condition where the human ability to respond to the events happening around them seems dulled or shut down. Lovelace tried to describe a strange feeling that presented from the moment this all started. He said it felt as if they were observing the events, not really experiencing them.

At that point, Lovelace said he went from feeling sedated—which began when the beams of light started—to feeling very drowsy. He specified that he never removed his army boots, and he lay down in the tent. He believes he went to sleep instantly but then woke up a few hours later. He saw a flash of lights, yellow, greenish, and white, for a millisecond but didn't have "his wits" about him. Then he wondered what the lights were. He sat up and immediately saw that both his boots had been unlaced. "I don't do that," he said. "It's army training to keep your boots on and laced."

He started to take his boots off to put them on correctly and noticed that his socks were on wrong as well. He put his socks and boots on correctly, then noticed Toby looking out of the tent. As the flashes of light hit Toby's face, Lovelace saw a single tear go down his right cheek. "This is what alarmed me," Lovelace said. "I'd worked with him for three years. This was very out of character." He looked out his side of the tent and saw that the craft was now only about thirty feet above them. He also saw about twelve to fifteen little beings that looked like the classic Grays "walking around like tourists." He had a feeling they weren't sentient beings but rather more like "worker bees."

As he described the craft, he said the exterior looked like a "medical building," but inside it looked like a "football stadium."

Only later did he begin to recall what had happened. When he woke up inside the craft, he was paralyzed except for his eyes. To his right, he saw a row of humans: men, women, children, all naked as he was, all holding their clothes in the same manner. "And," he noted, "they were all crying."

Then Lovelace saw a group of about six men and one woman roughly the same age as he at the time—eighteen to twenty-two—with military-type hairstyles. Dressed in tan-colored flight suits, they were silent but seemed "very nonchalant."

Lovelace saw a being he estimated to be about six feet tall; this one was not like the Grays; his skin color was "pinkish." The three-foot-tall Grays were scurrying around doing tasks. It felt to Lovelace like the tall one was in charge.

Then Lovelace described the "most frightening thing that happened." He strained his eyes as far to the left as he could to see this tall being. When the being turned around and locked its eyes on Lovelace's, it was as if it instantly knew everything about him. This tall being seemed to be nothing but a raw intellect, and Lovelace said, "I felt like the [animal] in the experiment."[10]

The *Guardian* article adds:

> Lovelace has suffered enormously since that night. "I've had 40 years' [sic] of nightmares. I still have a phobia of crossing open ground. I still sleep with a light on and a gun beside my bed." But he feels vindicated by acknowledgments made by the U.S. government, military personnel and Obama. "I've got a long list of people that I'm going to email and say, 'I told you so.'"[11]

Like all abduction accounts, the stories are chilling, troubling, and almost beyond belief, yet they are all too real. There is also the fact that Lovelace was implanted.[12] As I mentioned before, Richard Shaw and I removed an implant from Emile, who also appeared in our *UFO Disclosure* series in episode 4 on the abduction phenomenon. We are the only Christian team who has ever removed an implant. We took the implant to a lab in Los Angeles and looked at it under a scanning electron microscope. All of this is in our film.[13]

This is *real investigative journalism*. I have gone on the record and will do so again here with the proclamation that these implants are the prototypes of the *mark of the beast* that we read about in the Book of Revelation. Whoever is doing this has spent a great deal of time and resources to create these implants. Their structure is complex, and unlike any earthly foreign object that gets into the body, the nervous system does not reject them but seems to integrate with them. And in many cases, there is *no* entrance wound. Sometimes they "travel" through a person's body from one location to another, as witnessed by Dr. Roger Lier who removed seventeen of these implants. Emile's was the last implant that Dr. Lier removed.

CONCLUSION

I have to ask the question why the Fox network is spending so much money on shows about alien abductions when the subject matter was already covered decades ago by many researchers. *Coast to Coast AM* with George Noory and his predecessor, Art Bell, was and still is in many ways the tip of the spear. They have talked about the abduction phenomenon as well as all other aspects of ufology for many years. I do find it interesting that Fox is now covering parts of the phenomenon, but as I stated earlier, it's old news.

Abductions are real. There is *physicality* to the phenomenon—it is not merely demonic delusion. It's all too real, and the implants prove it; we have the metal that was removed from Emile in an operating room, and all of it was recorded on film. Debunkers and skeptics can whine and moan and tell us there's nothing to see here—but there is. People who have gone through this have had a life-altering experience. Instead of ridicule, they need healing. Instead of being shunned, they need to be embraced and cared for. All of this bears the fingerprints of the fallen one. He comes to rob, kill, and destroy. He is mixing the *seed* that we read about in the Genesis 3:15 narrative. He is trying to build an army because he's outnumbered two to one. He will be defeated by the rider on the white horse. This is the future, but what was written will come to pass; *what was foretold is unfolding.*

In the meantime we need to understand how all of this fits together—that is the driving force behind what I do and the purpose in writing this book.

Chapter 14

THE THIRTEENTH RUNG: ROBERT SALAS—UFO ENCOUNTER OVER MALMSTROM AIR FORCE BASE

ROBERT SALAS WAS a lieutenant at Malmstrom Air Force Base in 1967. The base housed ten intercontinental ballistic missiles that were stored in silos underground. The control center was deep underground, and that is where Salas would spend his time during his watch. The control center was where the firing mechanisms for the missiles were housed, as well as the silos where the missiles were stored.

In 1967 the cold war with the former Soviet Union was still going on, and the threat of nuclear exchange was a real concern. The missiles stored at Malmstrom were able to travel to Russia and deliver their payload, which were nuclear warheads many times more powerful than the atomic bombs dropped at Hiroshima and Nagasaki during WWII.

On March 24, 1967, one of the guards topside reported a sixty-foot, glowing orange-red UFO hovering over the gate. The man was petrified; he had never encountered anything like this. The object was a solid craft—a UFO. Suddenly, without warning, all ten intercontinental ballistic missiles went offline. In other words, the UFO had somehow been able to shut off all the missiles *remotely*. From Salas's perspective this was impossible, yet the UFO had been able to do so.

Robert Salas (pictured left, and as a young man, right) encountered a glowing orange-red flying disc that turned off ten ballistic missiles at Malmstrom Air Force Base in Montana in 1967, when he was serving as a launch officer.

In our *Watchers* series Richard Shaw and I interviewed Robert Salas. We were the first film company that Salas agreed to do an interview with because none of the other film companies would allow Salas's input in post-production. In other words, they would not allow Salas to give the final approval of the interview. Rick and I discussed this and told Lieutenant Salas that we had no problem showing him the final cut for his approval, and if he wanted to change something, that would be fine. Rick showed him the finished segment, and Salas approved it without any changes. Rick was a great director and film editor. We made a great team.

By the way, *Watchers* broke the story. We were the first production company to put this information out. Since then, Salas has written a book on what happened and has appeared across all media, telling the story of the events that happened to him in 1967. The following is a transcript of the interview I conducted with Robert Salas.

ROBERT SALAS INTERVIEW

LA: What was your position in the military? What did you do in the army?

RS: I was a missile launch officer. And what we do is we have to go out to the launch control facilities, we called them. The one I went out to was Oscar Flight on this particular occasion that we're going to talk about. It's about a hundred miles east of Great Falls, sixty feet underground, a hardened capsule, meaning supposedly it would survive a nuclear blast overhead. State of the art, it was a very reliable system. I was in this capacity for about three years, and we never had any serious incidents in that time except this one particular accident.

LA: Tell us what happened on March 24th.

RS: OK. March 24th I was the one that was on alert status in the evening. My commander was taking a rest break. We had a little cot down there. I get a call from the topside guard. We had six guards upstairs, security people that would protect the facility and also go out and check the launch facilities where the missiles are actually located. The action, so to speak, was all underground. We had all the control systems for the missiles underground, and this was an enclosed and very secure facility. At that time, we had the ability to launch nuclear weapons, but just the two of us. We could have launched ten nuclear missiles. And each missile was independent, by the way. The missiles were not interconnected in a way where if one failed, they would all fail—they were independent. We could have launched them independently or launched them in salvo, meaning all ten at the same time.

LA: Wow.

RS: So on this particular evening, I get a call from the topside guard. They're saying strange lights in the sky are making unusual maneuvers, flying at high speeds, reversing direction, turning on a dime, and making ninety-degree turns.

LA: And Montana is called Big Sky Country. And it's called that for a reason, because of the view. You can see for miles, correct?

RS: Exactly. It's very clear; the sky is very clear. Obviously, just wheat fields and nothing else basically. I didn't think much of that call, although I thought it was strange because these guys are very professional. They did not engage in joking around. Anyway, I said, "Thank you for the information," and basically hung up. Then five minutes later they called back, and this time the guard is screaming into the phone. He's just ultra-excited, frightened; I could tell by his voice he was very frightened. They're looking at the front gate, he says, and seeing this glowing red object hovering just above the front gate of the facility.

LA: Did he tell you how big the object was?

RS: Later I asked him; he said it was maybe forty, fifty feet long. Something like that. But he had trouble describing the structure of the object. What he described was just a glowing, red light, pulsating, silent. They could hear no engine noise or anything like that. He wanted me to tell him what to do next. I had all the guards out there with their weapons. This was a shocker. I didn't quite know what to say, except I told him to make sure nothing comes into the fenced area.

So then he hung up. I went to my commander to wake him up and start telling him about the phone calls. I looked over at my board; I had a display panel showing the status of the missiles. And I had this strange feeling that something was going to happen to those missiles. It was just a feeling. I woke up my commander and started to tell him about these phone calls, and all of a sudden, missiles started shutting down or being disabled. We get bells and whistles, screwing up claxons, and things like that. The lights go from green to red. So all ten of them went down within seconds.

LA: What do you attribute that to?

RS: Well, I had just hung up the phone with this guard, this object was still up there, and those missiles went down. So yeah, I've concluded that object disabled our missiles. The Air Force did a preliminary investigation, although they were never to explain completely what happened. They concluded—this was in one of the documents that I received under the freedom of information act—that this was highly improbable.

LA: Highly improbable?

RS: It used words to that effect—highly improbable that this could have happened. Because of what I just described to you and [because] all the missiles went down or disabled because of guidance and control system failure. So there was a particular piece of equipment on a missile that was related to the guidance system that had to be upset or fail in a certain way in order for this to happen.

LA: Forty- to fifty-foot something, I don't want to use the word *craft*, glowing orb over the front gate. Did anyone fire a weapon at it?

RS: I'm not sure in my case; however, I have reports from other cases where something similar happened and weapons were fired at it without any impact.

LA: In your research you've uncovered, no pun intended, something we find extraordinary. They're apparently on top of the silo; there are these concrete doors.

RS: This is very well-documented, [a] well-supported case. This happened at an air force base in 1968. This man was named Bradford Runyan, and told [me] the cover, which was twenty tons—about a twenty-tons cover—over the launch facility had been removed during the UFO incident....

RS [regarding UFO abduction]: Well, that's what I recall, going through the window. The next thing I remember...I don't remember being outside or seeing a craft of any sort, at that point. The next thing I remember is being on a table and being shown....They made a point of showing me this large what looked like a needle. By large, I mean almost a football.

So, they were gonna insert it into my private area, let's put it that way. And they did, and they told me it was not going to be painful. But as they started to insert this needle or whatever it was, it was excruciating pain. And that's point number two, as to why this was a real incident, because I recall the pain. I recall how bad the pain was.

LA: Did you attempt to fight them at this point at all?

RS: I was...I think I was struggling, because I yelled out that this is very painful. And as soon as I did that, as soon as I expressed that, the pain went away. It was just like magic. As soon as I expressed the idea that this was very painful, the pain went away; it was gone. And they continued with the procedure, whatever they were doing. What I just told you is what I derived from my own memories and also the hypnotherapy sessions I've had.

Now, aside from that, I have had dreams, which I think are related. So this is in the box that I call "May Have Happened." One of these dreams, I see a large black oval-shaped eye right next to me, and I can see the glassy appearance of the eyeball. I can actually see some of the skin, I guess, around the eye. And its right here.

LA: Dr. Jacobs believes, and I know you know who he is.

RS: Yes, David Jacobs.

LA: Dr. David Jacobs believes there is a breeding program going on, a very vigorous breeding program. There's an agenda that hybrid beings are being created. Now when you were on board that ship, did you see any evidence of a hybrid being?

RS: I don't recall seeing any evidence of a hybrid being; however, I think they did take a sample of my semen. So we can derive from that why they did that, sure. But, no, I didn't see any evidence of a hybrid program myself.

LA: With everything you have seen, and I realize it's a complex issue. On one hand, it seems like, gee, they're shutting down the silos; they don't want nuclear war on the planet. On the other hand, they're taking you against your will, shutting your wife down against her will, kidnapping you, because that's what it is, and doing things which you don't really want to have done to you. So, with that in mind, do you think the phenomenon's intentions are good, or something more sinister? Or don't you know yet?

RS: Well, I would not even want to speculate on that. I can rationalize the idea that they want us to get rid of our nuclear weapons. That's a good thing. That's a good thing for civilization.[1]

CONCLUSION

What I love about this interview, which can be found in video form in *The Best of Watchers*, is that it overlaps other areas of investigation that we cover in our films. What we have with the Salas interview is a close encounter of the second kind, as the craft was directly over the base. Then years later Salas was abducted, which brings us into the breeding program. It's all connected. There is a nefarious agenda that is hidden from the peoples of the world, and yet the agenda has been going on for millennia. It is the seed war! In a later chapter I will address the focus on our nukes. This is important and ties into the saying I coined a few years back: *We go up; they show up.*

Chapter 15

THE FOURTEENTH RUNG: "UFOS ARE 'DEMONIC' ALIENS VISITING FROM OTHER DIMENSIONS IN LATEST THEORY"

T HE SUBTITLE OF the article in the chapter title is "With talk of parallel dimensions and visions of 'Doom' in people's minds, UFOs have taken a turn for the traditionally evil."[1] What if this rung on the ladder of disclosure is actually the truth? What if they are demonic entities? What if there is a nefarious agenda regarding these entities? What if ancient prophetic texts warn of these entities in the last days? What if these other dimensions are actually listed in our Bibles? I'll take each of these what-ifs and expound on them.

WHAT IF THESE ENTITIES ARE DEMONIC?

You are a five-year-old boy, and you are being visited by entities that scare the daylights out of you. You are taken by these entities; you are helpless against them. They do to you what they wish. You find yourself on a cold, metal table. There are Grays all around you. They are cold and emotionless. You have been here before—many times—so it is unsettlingly familiar. You are distressed, and you realize your bladder has released from terror. One of the Grays leans over your face, and you are forced to stare into its eyes. Your mind explodes with images and scenes that are unfamiliar and disturbing. You want to scream, but you can't; you find that you are immobilized. Then you feel something being put into your leg. You open your mouth to scream, but nothing comes out. Then you black out.

The above narrative is an example of what Emile may have experienced when he was a five-year-old boy. As I mentioned before, Richard Shaw and I watched as Dr. Roger Lier and Dr. Matrisciano removed the implant. But there was something I didn't mention.

Dr. Roger Leir was Jewish, pretty much an atheist, and in some ways anti-Christian. I'll give you one example of the exchanges Dr. Roger Leir and I had. We were at lunch one day. I was biting into my sandwich at a deli when Roger looked at me and asked, "What about the nuns who killed their babies?"

I looked at Roger and said, "Well, that's indefensible." He shrugged his shoulders and went back to eating.

But the day of Emile's implant removal, Roger had his world turned upside down in that operating theater.

Two days later Richard Shaw, Dr. Roger Leir, and yours truly were at SEAL Labs (now known as EAG Labs) in Los Angeles. We were with the experts examining the implant under a scanning electron microscope. The implant was about forty years old when we removed it from Emile, and we were able to cut it in half with a razor knife. The implant that Dr. Leir had taken out before this one, which was number sixteen, could not be cut with a diamond saw. He had to take it to a laboratory and have it cut with a laser beam. This implant had double-walled carbon nanotubes in it and was much different from the implant taken from Emile. This shows that there seemed to be an evolution of the implant technology.

I looked at Roger and said, "Hey, can I talk to you privately out in the hallway?" So Roger and I went out in the hallway, and I said,

"I hope you realize what happened in that operating theater a couple of days ago."

Roger looked at me, and his eyes got really big. He said, "LA, I firmly believe that there is a supernatural dynamic to the abduction phenomena, and I am going to tell Whitley Strieber about it." For Roger to admit something like this to me privately was unprecedented for him. He realized that he had witnessed something that was outside his realm of experience. That was the last time I ever saw Roger alive. He died a few months later of a massive heart attack.

What If There Is a Nefarious Agenda Regarding These Entities?

I am always amazed when I talk to ufologists who insist that the phenomenon is benevolent, that these beings are really our space brothers who have come to rescue us. When I'm speaking at UFO conferences (which has recently become a rarity because people think I'm religious), I will usually start out my presentation by asking the audience this question: "How many of you think it's OK to abduct a five-year-old child and implant him?" Not one hand goes up—ever. Everyone in the audience, regardless of their paradigm or their belief system, knows instinctively, viscerally, that it's wrong to abduct five-year-old boys and implant them. And yet these are the same people who want to be taken, want to have contact, want to see our so-called space brothers return.

I will call your attention once again to the *Ancient Aliens* show on the History Channel, which has been going on for over a decade now.[2] I was on the first two seasons of the show, which led Richard Shaw and me to create the *Watchers* series, which now has eleven documentaries.[3] Your kids and your grandkids watch *Ancient Aliens*; they're internet savvy, and they spend more time on their cell phones than they do talking to you or their grandparents. They have been indoctrinated—and the church is asleep, afraid to talk about UFOs or the Nephilim or any of the important points of discussion found in the *Guidebook to the Supernatural*, the Bible.

It is imperative to understand that we are at war here. There are two ideologies being promulgated. The ancient-alien paradigm tells us that we were created here, seeded here, by an advanced race of extraterrestrials. The biblical prophetic narrative states that God, Jesus specifically, spoke everything into existence. Jesus is not an extraterrestrial. He is not an alien. He is fully God and fully man. He spoke, and the universe was formed. His word is true, and He will return soon. So these two paradigms cannot exist together; they are completely contradictory to one another. In the last two films of our *UFO Disclosure* series, titled *What Is the Truth?*, Gil Zimmerman and I delve into this in detail,[4] and I'll comment more in an upcoming chapter.

Unfortunately, much of the church is afraid to even discuss this, yet all the kids in the youth group know about it. It's time for the church to understand that this is *the coming great deception*. It is a calculated, nefarious agenda. The late Chuck Missler used to say he believed that the Antichrist would boast of some sort of alien connection. I couldn't agree with him more. It's happening right in front of us. Every week there are new reports, new videos, new eyewitnesses to the UFO phenomenon. This is, in my opinion, the coming great deception, or as 2 Thessalonians calls it, the strong delusion.

WHAT IF ANCIENT PROPHETIC TEXTS WARN OF THESE ENTITIES IN THE LAST DAYS?

Once again, I call your attention to Genesis 3:15 (NASB): "And I will put enmity between you and the woman, and between your seed and her seed." Three chapters later, in Genesis chapter 6, in the days of Noah, the sons of God did the unthinkable and mixed the seed. Remember, Jesus warned us in the Gospels of Matthew and

Luke that the end of days would be like the days of Noah. Out of all the places in Scripture He could point to, He chose that.

Remember, at the time Jesus warned us, there was no New Testament. There were a handful of followers that were hanging on His every word. Jesus assumed, rightfully so, that they understood what He was talking about. Josephus, the first century Jewish historian, stated in the *Antiquities of the Jews* that the bones of the Nephilim were on display in Jerusalem before AD 70, when Titus and the Roman army destroyed Jerusalem.[5] In other words, the skeletons were displayed to show countless generations after the conquest of Canaan the reality of Genesis 3:15. It was, I believe, a fact that every Jew knew. It was not something that they had to be taught. Hundreds of years later, Augustine and others would rewrite the Genesis 6 narrative and create what I have come to call the bogus Sethite theory, which states that the sons of God are the godly line of Seth, and the women of earth are the ungodly line of Cain. But the biblical texts do not say this.

My mentor, Dr. I. D. E. Thomas, penned *Omega Conspiracy*, which has become a classic.[6] Within its pages he set the record straight. It was a book that many of us cut our teeth on. I received my honorary doctorate from Dr. Thomas, and it was one of the most incredible days of my seventy-three years. I will never forget it. Until I read Dr. Thomas's book, I was completely confused about Noah's flood, the tower of Babel, Abraham and the kings, the destruction of Sodom and Gomorrah, and finally the conquest of Canaan, which, unless a person understands about the Nephilim and the seed war, is genocide.

Jesus also warned us to not be deceived. He then said that men will faint from fear from what is coming upon the earth. (See Luke 21:7–28.) Was He talking about a mile-wide asteroid? Or was He talking about a mile-wide mothership? In my opinion it's not an asteroid. It's something that's been cooked up in hell's kitchen for perhaps thousands of years. It is the endgame of the Dragon. It is the great deception. Paul warned us that the Dragon, Satan, will come with all signs and lying wonders (2 Thess. 2:9). The theory of evolution has cut Christianity off at the knees, and it is now the prevailing paradigm in both the scientific community and academia. Darwinism states that we evolved over millions or billions of years to what we see now. This is in direct contradiction to the biblical narrative, which tells us that Jesus spoke everything into existence.

> In the beginning was the Word, and the Word was with God, and the Word was God. He was in the beginning with God. All things were made through Him, and without Him nothing was made that was made. In Him was life, and the life was the light of men. And the light shines in the darkness, and the darkness did not comprehend it.
>
> —JOHN 1:1–5

Ufologists do not hold to a biblical paradigm; *Ancient Aliens* is a perfect example of this. They never come to the truth. It's like a dog chasing its tail around and around and around. Once we plug the biblical paradigm into the UFO phenomenon, everything makes perfect sense. It has taken me years of study and research to connect all the dots. I truly believe that we are in the last of the last days and that the UFO phenomenon is *the coming great deception.* Millions of people will believe the lie. Remember, Paul admonished us that because they did not believe the truth, God will send them strong delusion (2 Thess. 2:10–11). This is where we are. The strong delusion is manifesting in ways that I have never seen.

WHAT IF THESE OTHER DIMENSIONS ARE ACTUALLY DESCRIBED IN OUR BIBLES?

The biblical narrative says that there are three heavens. The first heaven is the earth and the atmosphere just directly above us. The second heaven, in my opinion, is the universe around us. The third heaven is where the Most High God dwells. We know from the Book of Revelation that Michael and his angels will fight with the devil and his angels—the devil will lose that battle. The devil will be cast to earth along with all the fallen ones. I have come to call this the *great eviction* because this area of the second heaven will finally be cleared of all these foul and unclean spirits.

People who take the drug ayahuasca often report seeing the Grays when they pop up into what I call the second heaven. I remember reading in Graham Hancock's book *Supernatural: Meetings With the Ancient Teachers of Mankind* that he was perplexed after taking ayahuasca; he saw the Grays and wondered what they were doing there.[7] Unfortunately for Mr. Hancock, he completely dismissed the Bible, and thus, in my opinion, he can never come to the truth. Every shaman, witch doctor, and occultist knows about the second heaven—it is the place where they get their power from. They all know who it is that they serve and where that power they want comes from. It is from the Dragon himself—he will bestow this power on those who give their souls to him. There's always a price.

After Michael and his angels boot the devil and all his fallen angels and unclean spirits from the second heaven, a loud voice from heaven will say, "'Woe to the inhabitants of the earth and the sea! For the devil has come down to you, having great wrath, because he knows that he has a short time'" (Rev. 12:12). Those two sentences are pregnant with meaning. How does the devil know his time is short? What are we looking at here? I'll delve into this in a later chapter.

CONCLUSION

I have held to the biblical account that these intruders are, in fact, interdimensional entities with a nefarious, dark, demonic agenda. Everything connects back to the breeding program that we first discover in Genesis 3:15. As I have stated throughout this book, this scripture is the gateway to the rest of the biblical prophetic narrative. Once we plug this in, everything becomes extremely clear. There is a breeding program. The seed of the Dragon continues, but they are not given in marriage the way they were in the days of Noah; however, it's similar. Jesus warned us of this. It's time to wake up and understand that we are living in perilous times when the final endgame of the Dragon is about to manifest—and millions of people will be deceived.

Chapter 16

THE FIFTEENTH RUNG: THE WHISTLEBLOWER— DAVID GRUSCH

David Grusch, former U.S. Air Force intelligence officer, giving testimony on July 26, 2023, before the U.S. House Subcommittee on National Security, the Border, and Foreign Affairs.

THERE WAS A hearing before the House Subcommittee on National Security, the Border, and Foreign Affairs, of the Committee on Oversight and Accountability, on July 26, 2023. The subject was "unidentified anomalous phenomena: implications on national security, public safety, and government transparency."[1] David Grusch appeared as a witness. What he stated on the record blew me away; it was profound.

Before I talk further about Grusch's testimony, I want to give you his background. Here is the transcript of his opening statement and his written closing statement (which was not delivered) to Congress:

Opening Statement

Mr. Chairman, Ranking Members, and Congressmen, thank you. I am happy to be here. This is an important issue, and I am grateful for your time.

My name is David Charles Grusch. I was an intelligence officer for 14 years both in the U.S. Air Force, both active-duty Air National Guard and Reserve at the rank of Major and most recently from 2021 to 2025—excuse me, 2023—at the National Geospatial Intelligence Agency, NGA, at the GS–15 civilian level, which is the military equivalent of a full bird colonel.

I was my agency's co-lead in unidentified anomalous phenomena and trans medium object analysis as well as reporting to the UAP Task Force—UAPTF—and eventually, once it was established, the All-Domain Anomaly Resolution Office—AARO.

I became a whistleblower through a PPD–19 urgent concern filing in May 2022 with the intelligence community inspector general following concerning reports from multiple esteemed and credentialed current and former military and intelligence community individuals that the U.S. Government is operating with secrecy above congressional oversight with regards to UAPs.

My testimony is based on information I have been given

by individuals with a long-standing track record of legitimacy and service to this country, many of whom also have shared compelling evidence in the form of photography, official documentation, and classified oral testimony to myself and many of my various colleagues.

I have taken every step I can to corroborate this evidence over a period of 4 years while I was with the UAP Task Force and do my due diligence on the individuals sharing it. It is because of these steps, I believe strongly in the importance of bringing this information before you.

I am driven by a commitment of both to truth and transparency, rooted in our inherent duty to uphold the United States Constitution and protect the American people. I am asking Congress to hold our government to this standard and thoroughly investigate these claims.

But as I stand here under oath now, I am speaking to the facts as I have been told them. In the U.S. Air Force in my National Reconnaissance Office—NRO—reservist capacity, I was a member of the UAP Task Force from 2019 to 2021.

I served at the NRO operations center on the Director's briefing staff, which included the coordination of the Presidential daily brief and supporting a variety of contingency operations, which I was the reserve intelligence division chief backup.

In 2019, the UAP Task Force Director asked me to identify all special access programs and controlled access programs, also known as SAPs and CAPs, we needed to satisfy our congressionally mandated mission and we would direct report at the time to the DEP/SecDef.

At the time, due to my extensive executive level intelligence support duties I was cleared to literally all relevant compartments and in a position of extreme trust both in my military and civilian capacities.

I was informed in the course of my official duties of a multi-decade UAP crash retrieval and reverse engineering program to which I was denied access to those additional read-ons when I requested it.

I made the decision based on the data I collected to report this information to my superiors and multiple inspectors general and, in effect, becoming a whistleblower. As you know, I have suffered retaliation for my decision, but I am hopeful that my actions will ultimately lead to a positive outcome of increased transparency.

Thank you, and I am happy to answer your questions.[2]

Closing Statement

It is with a heavy heart and a determined spirit that I stand, under oath, before you today, having made the decision based on the data I collected, and reported, to provide this information to the committee. I am driven in this duty by a conviction to expose what I viewed as a grave congressional oversight issue and a potential abuse of executive branch authorities.

This endeavor was not born out of malice or dissatisfaction, but from an unwavering commitment to truth and transparency, an endeavor rooted in our inherent duty to uphold the United States Constitution, protect the American People, and seek insights into this matter that have the potential to redefine our understanding of the world.

In an era, fraught with division and discord, our exploration into the UAP subject seems to resonate with an urgency and fascination that transcends political, social, and geographical boundaries. A democratic process must be adhered to when evaluating the data and it is our collective responsibility to ensure that public involvement is encouraged and respected. Indeed, the future of our civilization and our comprehension of humanity's place on earth and in the cosmos depends on the success of this very process.

It is my hope that the revelations we unearth through investigations of the Non-Human Reverse Engineering Programs I have reported will act as an ontological (earth-shattering) shock, a catalyst for a global reassessment of our priorities. As we move forward on this path, we might be poised to enable extraordinary technological progress in a future where our civilization surpasses the current state-of-the-art in propulsion, material science, energy production and storage.

The knowledge we stand to gain should spur us toward a more enlightened and sustainable future, one where collective curiosity is ignited, and global cooperation becomes the norm, rather than the exception.

Thank You.[3]

Before I get into the transcript of the testimony involving Representative Nancy Mace of South Carolina and the witnesses, I think it's necessary to look at Grusch's statements. First off, in my opinion, he is telling the truth—*as he knows it*. He might not have all the answers, but he has seen and heard enough to come forward and assume his whistleblower position. He has been met with hostility, and the media has done several hit pieces on him, attacking his credibility. As a side note, the powers that be—and make no mistake about it, our media is in their back pockets—always, and I mean *always*, engage in ad hominem attacks. This has become a common tactic of the Left, but it is also used by those in power who wish to obfuscate truth. I'm sure you've heard the all too familiar outcries: *you're a racist; you're a homophobe; you're a bigot; you're a conspiracy theorist; you're a right-wing loon; you're a communist; you're a Nazi!* The name calling goes on and on. Without the ability to engage in meaningful discussion and respectful debate in the public eye, the thirty-second sound bites are what remain.

Then we have this statement from Grusch:

> This endeavor was not born out of malice or dissatisfaction, but from an unwavering commitment to truth and transparency, an endeavor rooted in our inherent duty to uphold the

United States Constitution, protect the American People, and seek insights into this matter that have the potential to redefine our understanding of the world.[4]

This statement reflects *"of the people, by the people, for the people."*[5] I would state here that Grusch is a true patriot. He realizes the importance of what he has become privy to, and he knows that *the people of the world have a right to know.* Unfortunately, the powers that be really don't care about you or me; they care only about gaining power, and once they have achieved it, maintaining it. They certainly don't care about the truth.

I am reminded of a biblical prophecy, and I think it's very timely:

> Justice is turned back, and righteousness stands far away.
> Truth has fallen in the street, and honesty can't come in.
> —Isaiah 59:14, GW

I would say that we are living in a time when truth has fallen in the street. It is becoming increasingly difficult to tell truth from fiction—and with the advent of AI, it becomes almost impossible.

Bully for David Grusch! Here's the transcript of the exchange between Representative Nancy Mace and David Grusch and Commander Fravor in the halls of Congress.

———

Ms. Mace. Thank you, Mr. Chairman, and good morning to our witnesses who are testifying today. I want to thank each of you for being here to discuss a topic of grave importance to our national security.

Earlier this year a Chinese spy balloon was shot down off the coast of my home state of South Carolina. Since the Roswell incident in 1947, many Americans have wondered about the dangers of unknown objects crisscrossing our skies. Whether these are UAPs or weather phenomena, advanced technology from American allied or enemy forces, or something more out of this world.

So, my first question—I have several questions and I will—if we can just be quick on these first two. I am going to ask each of you the same question and then I will get to each of you individually. The first one, when you reported your experiences with a UAP did any of you face any repercussions with your superiors? Yes or no.

Mr. GRAVES. No.

Commander FRAVOR. No.

Mr. GRUSCH. I have actually never seen anything personally, believe it or not.

Ms. MACE. All right. And then do you believe there is an active disinformation campaign within our government to deny the existence of UAPs? Yes or no.

Mr. GRAVES. I do not have an answer to that.

Mr. GRUSCH. As previously stated publicly, yes.

Commander FRAVOR. Previously with, like, Project Bluebook, yes, but currently I do not speak for the U.S. Government.

Ms. MACE. OK. Thank you.

I have a few questions for Mr. Graves. What percentage of UAP sightings, in your belief, go unreported by our pilots?

Mr. GRAVES. This is an approximation based off of my personal experience speaking with a number of pilots, but I would estimate we are somewhere near 5 percent reporting, perhaps.

Ms. MACE. So, like, 95 percent basically do not report seeing UAPs?

Mr. GRAVES. That is just my personal estimate.

Ms. MACE. In the incident off Virginia Beach, do you believe the Navy took the danger to your aircraft seriously after it was reported?

Mr. GRAVES. Absolutely.

Ms. MACE. A few questions for Mr. Fravor.
As an expert naval aviator have you ever seen an object that looked and moved like the Tic Tac UAP?

Commander FRAVOR. No.

Ms. MACE. Did the Tic Tac UAP move in such a way that defied the laws of physics?

Commander FRAVOR. The way we understand them, yes.

Ms. MACE. Many dismiss UAP reports as classified weapons testing by our own government. But in your experience as a pilot does our government typically test advanced weapons systems right next to multimillion-dollar jets without informing our pilots?

Commander FRAVOR. No. We have test ranges for that.

Ms. MACE. It took over 15 years for your encounter with the Tic Tac to be declassified. Do you feel there was a good reason to prevent lawmakers from having access to this footage?

Commander FRAVOR. No. I just think it was ignored when it happened, and it just sat somewhere in a file. Never got reported.

Ms. MACE. In a drawer. It happens a lot up here. Shocker.

Mr. Grusch, a couple of questions for you too, sir, this morning. What percentage of UAPs do you feel are adequately investigated by the U.S. Government, of the 5 percent that are reported?

Mr. GRUSCH. I can only speak for my personal leadership over at NGA. I tried to look at every report that came through that I could triage.

Ms. MACE. Do you believe that officials at the highest levels of our national security apparatus have unlawfully withheld information from Congress and subverted our oversight authority?

Mr. GRUSCH. There are certain elected leaders that had more information that—I am not sure what they have shared with certain Gang of 8 members or et cetera. But, certainly, I would not be surprised.

Ms. MACE. OK. You say that the government is in possession of potentially nonhuman spacecraft. Based on your experience and extensive conversations with experts do you believe our government has made contact with intelligent extraterrestrials?

Mr. GRUSCH. It is something I cannot discuss in a public setting.

Ms. MACE. OK. And I cannot ask when you think this occurred. If you believe we have crashed craft, as stated earlier, do we have the bodies of the pilots who piloted this craft?

Mr. GRUSCH. As I have stated publicly already in my News Nation interview, biologics came with some of these recoveries. Yes.

Ms. MACE. Were they, I guess, human or nonhuman biologics?

Mr. GRUSCH. Nonhuman, and that was the assessment of people with direct knowledge on the program I talked to that are currently still on the program.

Ms. MACE. And was this documentary evidence, this video, photos, eyewitness? Like, how would that be determined?

Mr. GRUSCH. The specific documentation I would have to talk to you in a SCIF about.

Ms. MACE. Got you. OK.

So—and you may or may not be able to answer my last question, and maybe we get into a SCIF at the next hearing that we have. But who in the government, either what agency, sub agency, what contractors, who should be called into the next hearing about UAPs either in a public setting or even in a private setting?

And you probably cannot name names, but what agencies or organizations, contractors, et cetera, do we need to call in to get these questions answered whether it is about funding, what programs are happening, and what is out there?

Mr. GRUSCH. I can give you a specific cooperative and hostile witness list of specific individuals that were in those.

Ms. MACE. And how soon can we get that list?

Mr. GRUSCH. I am happy to provide that to you after the hearing.

Ms. MACE. Super. Thank you. And I yield back.[6]

COMMENTS AND CONCLUSION

As I mentioned earlier, when I heard this exchange between Representative Nancy Mace and the whistleblower David Grusch,

I was completely blown away. Here, in the halls of Congress, Representative Mace asked the $64,000 question: Were the bodies retrieved from the crash human or nonhuman? David Grusch looked right up at her and stated, on the record, in Congress, that the biologics that were recovered were nonhuman.

What are we to do with a statement like that? Please remember that this isn't some unprofessional conjecture on George Noory's *Coast to Coast AM* program. This is a professional career military person, part of the intelligence community, stating on the record that what he knows is the truth—nonhuman biologics were indeed recovered, so-called extraterrestrials.

You would've thought that my phone and my email box would've blown up like crazy, but here again, that was not the case.

The church, sadly, remains asleep. And as I have asked numerous times, Do we as Christians really believe what we read in our Bibles? The virgin birth, floating ax-heads, men that walked on water, water that changed into wine, men that were raised from the dead, and talking donkeys?

The statement that Grusch proclaimed in Congress should've made everyone on this planet sit up and take notice. Unfortunately, that did not happen. A statement like this has far-reaching implications. It means one of two things. One, that we are being visited by extraterrestrials, beings from other planets, who have come here perhaps for millennia. This view would state that they seeded us here, that they genetically manipulated early man, that they started the world religions and first civilizations, and that they have been monitoring us. This view is widely held as truth in the UFO community and with ufologists. But there is another paradigm, the biblical one. The Bible cautions us about a coming deception, a strong delusion, which will possibly deceive even the elect.

Another thing that amazes me is that essentially the American people didn't seem to care. And I would posit that the reason for this is that we have had decades of sci-fi movies and television shows presenting aliens visiting earth, such as *E.T.*, *Star Wars*, and

Star Trek. I would call this predictive programming. People have been so inundated with it that they have become numb to the idea. Then, when someone like David Grusch comes to the forefront with history-making testimony, most people don't even react.

What happened in the halls of Congress is the tip of the iceberg. It also lets us know that there is a shadow government, a deep state, a cabal of men and women who have information that they do not share with the American public. This is why the United States House Committee on Oversight and Accountability was formed in the first place.

In the months that followed this important moment before Congress, little to no information was released. If they wanted to come clean, they would show us the film from the 1947 Roswell crash incident. In our two films on Roswell, *Revisiting Roswell: Exoneration* and *Revisiting Roswell: Evidence From the Debris Field*, we show a black-and-white film clip.[7] My business partner, co-director, and producer of our UFO films, Gil Zimmerman, and I watched this clip numerous times, looking at it from all possible angles. With the information we have at this point, we both agreed that this clip is likely real, that it is genuine, and that the corpse being brought in on a stretcher is most likely from the 1947 Roswell crash. This is why these films are so important. There is a history that has been deliberately obfuscated from the peoples of the world.

Chapter 17

THE SIXTEENTH RUNG: "SCIENTISTS SAY EARTH NEEDS TO PREPARE FOR AN ALIEN ENCOUNTER NOW BEFORE IT'S TOO LATE"

WHEN I READ the headline in the chapter title,[1] I was immediately taken aback and began to wonder who these scientists were and why they were warning us that we need to prepare *before it's too late.* How many scientists are there in this think tank? What are they basing this warning on? Why aren't their names listed along with their credentials? More importantly, *how* do we prepare for an alien encounter before it's too late? And what does *too late* actually mean? I think it sounds ominous!

WHAT IS AN ALIEN ENCOUNTER?

This book is all about alien encounters. Our UFO series—which includes ten films—shows in-depth alien encounters of all sorts, everything from abductions and the breeding program to crop circles and cattle mutilations.[2]

I think that our government has been working side by side

with so-called ETs for decades—whistleblowers have come on the record and told me about this. In our film *UFO Disclosure Episode 1: Disclosure*, there was a man who would not show his face on camera, but he told us an interesting story.[3] A good friend of his had a son who was in the military, and one day he blurted out that he was working side by side with the "gray" aliens. I would posit that our government has been in contact with so-called ETs for decades. I also believe that we have craft in our possession, and we have reverse engineered these craft.

So what are we supposed to do, dust off our tinfoil hats? Journey to a high place and hold up signs saying TAKE ME? Watch hours of *Ancient Aliens* on the History Channel and take copious notes? Storm Area 51 or Wright-Patterson Field and demand they show us the recovered alien bodies from Roswell?

I'm being sarcastic here, but you get the point. How do the people of Earth prepare for what would be the most paradigm-changing event in all of history, apart from Jesus' resurrection? There is no way to prepare for this. When, not if, it happens, people will be forced to reorder their worldview. They will have to come to grips with the fact that we are not alone. But as most of you know by now, I truly think this is the *coming great deception* that we are warned about in the Bible. This is the *strong delusion* that God sends humanity because they did not believe the truth. And what is the truth? The truth is this:

> In the beginning was the Word, and the Word was with God, and the Word was God. He was in the beginning with God. All things were made through Him, and without Him nothing was made that was made.
>
> —JOHN 1:1–3

This scripture from the Gospel of John states very clearly that the Word—in other words, Jesus—spoke everything into existence.

We either believe what the biblical prophetic narrative says, or we are left with the Darwinian paradigm of evolution.

When "they," the so-called extraterrestrials, show up, they will tell us that they created all life on earth, that they genetically manipulated the DNA of early man, that they started the world's civilizations and the world's first religions, and now, at this critical juncture in human history, our space brothers are back to usher mankind into a golden age of enlightenment.

I heard this very thing fifty years ago when I was twenty-four and immersed in the New Age. I was also told that there would be people on the earth who would not be ready for this cosmic event, this evolution of human consciousness, and that they would be taken off the earth, removed to another place, so they could evolve spiritually.

We know that the Vatican has openly talked about their belief that intelligent life exists elsewhere in the solar system or universe. We covered some of this in our *Watchers* film, when we interviewed Chris Putnam. Putnam went on the record in the film and quoted a Vatican source who said that if aliens landed, they would baptize them.[4]

In our film *UFO Disclosure Episode 9: What is the Truth?*, Derrick Gilbert told us that *they* have been with us for thousands of years.[4] He's right, and the TV show *Ancient Aliens* promulgates this week after week. But the question is, Who are *they*? I know Derrick, and we have spoken at numerous conferences together over the years. He's talking about the fallen angels, not the so-called space brothers. However, the *Ancient Aliens* crowd is firmly entrenched in the *ancient astronaut* paradigm, which states that we have been visited by these entities for thousands of years. Like Derrick, I also believe we have been visited by nonhuman entities for thousands of years. But unlike the History Channel and the *Ancient Aliens* crowd, I do not believe for a moment that these entities are benevolent and have our best interest in mind, which is why we created our ten-part film series on UFOs.

What Do We Prepare For?

Just how do we prepare for a so-called alien encounter? Honestly I have no idea, and I'm sure you don't either. Why was this statement even released to the public? Who authored it?

Here's a *fictional account* of what could happen. A craft has appeared over Paris, and a representative from earth has been chosen to communicate with the ET. Our representative is from Israel, and his name is Uri. The ET's name is Kloto.

Uri: Where do you come from?

Kloto: We come from a star system known as Epsilon Eridani.

Uri: Why have you chosen this time to reveal yourselves?

Kloto: We have been visiting you for centuries, according to your concept of time. Because of your advancements in technology, we have revealed ourselves to make sure you do not harm your planet and each other.

Uri: I assume you are referring to the nuclear bomb that was detonated in the Middle East.

Kloto: Exactly. We and the Galactic Federation of Planets will not allow you to destroy yourselves. We have invested a great deal in you and your species and want humans to be part of the Galactic Federation. We were responsible for creating life on this planet, and in fact, we genetically manipulated the human species.

Uri: Are you saying you were responsible for humans on earth?

Kloto: Yes. As I stated, we were the ones who seeded all life on this planet millions of years ago. We have watched you all of these millennia. We have seen your advancements but also your devastating wars. This is why we have returned and chosen this time to reveal ourselves.

Uri: Many peoples of the earth believe in different gods, and we have different creation stories. Where did you come from? Is there a god on your planet that you worship?

Kloto: There is no god, only the force that is within everything. Essentially you and I are gods, and we are in the process of realizing this.

Uri: There is no supreme being?

Kloto: No. Only the *force* that is within every living thing.

Uri: So where did you come from?

Kloto: Millions of years ago the force directed us from one dimension to this one, to this universe.

I could go on, but I think you get the point. Even though the above dialogue is a fictional account, I've heard this from so-called New Agers for the last fifty years! You will also notice that Kloto is espousing the same old lie that the serpent told Eve millennia ago, which started the slippery slope that we find ourselves on today. Truly there is nothing new under the sun.

Of course the above dialogue is 100 percent in contradiction to what Bible-believing Christians hold to. I know that I have a Creator who loves me, fashioned me, put His gifts into me, and then sent His Redeemer, Jesus, to ransom me from death!

WHAT IS EXOPOLITICS?

I met Francisco Mourão Corrêa around 2017 when we arrived in Portugal to shoot some footage and interviews for our two films on Fátima. Francisco arranged the interviews in Portugal, and we had many wonderful and tasty late-night dinners, something I was not accustomed to. Here in the United States we have dinner in the evening around 6 p.m. Francisco insisted that we dine no earlier than 9 p.m. I must admit this was quite an adjustment for Peggy and me, but in the end, we came to enjoy these nighttime culinary adventures. The seafood in Portugal is second to none, and if I ever become an expat, I would move to Southern Portugal in a heartbeat. Two years later, in 2019, Francisco was once again our guide as we filmed in Spain, France, Portugal, and finally England. It is an honor to have Francisco comment on exopolitics here. As you will see, he is an authority on the subject.

The article on Exopaedia about him reads:

Born in 1973, Francisco Mourão Corrêa developed since a young age a growing interest in the possibility of intelligent life in other planets. With dedication and persuasion, he studied the long history of both Portuguese and international [UFO] cases, and with time, he was able to meet most of the pioneer researchers in Portugal, developing a respectful relationship, which quickly became a good friendship.

Feeling the sense of stagnation in the field of ufology, and motivated by the activism of people like Steven Greer, Stephen Bassett or Paola Harris, in 2009 Francisco founded the Portuguese Exopolitics Initiative, which was later registered as a non-for-profit organization.

Exopolitics Portugal works in coordination with CTEC, the Centre of Transdisciplinary Studies of Consciousness, a research and think tank department of the University Fernando Pessoa in Porto, Portugal. The members of this research centre are academics from different universities in Portugal.

Over the years, with the support of CTEC, Francisco has organized several conferences at the University Fernando Pessoa, with speakers like David Griffin, Frederik Uldall, Gary Heseltine, Olli Pajula, Paola Harris, Pepón Jover, Richard Dolan, Robert Fleischer, Stephen Bassett.

Besides Portugal, he has made presentations at UFO conferences in the Czech Republic, Denmark, Germany, Spain and the UK.

Francisco has been part of the production, and participated in the filming in Portugal, of documentaries like "UFO Europe" and "Planet UFO" both for National Geographic Channel, and "Extraterrestres" seasons 1, 2 and 3 for the History Channel. He has also participated in news segments of Portuguese TV channels, as well and radio shows, talk shows, and he also collaborates with the UFO Truth Magazine.

Along with other heads of international Exopolitics groups, he co-founded the Global Exopolitics Organization (GLEXO), and is part of the Advisory Board of the Exopolitics Institute.[5]

I had the pleasure of interviewing Francisco, and I asked him the following questions.

What is exopolitics?

Exopolitics is a field of study that projects the possible political, social, and diplomatic relationships between different forms of intelligent life in the universe, including possible extraterrestrial civilizations. It addresses issues such as the existence of life outside Earth, possible contacts with these life forms, and how humanity should deal with these situations.

Exopolitics explores topics such as the search for evidence of extraterrestrial life, sightings of UFOs (unidentified flying objects), theories about governments covering up information about extraterrestrial contacts, and even ethical and legal issues related to possible contact with alien civilizations. It is an area that falls within the social sciences, which involves some scientific speculation, and ethical and political considerations.

You are the head of Exopolitics Initiative. What do you espouse to those in your organization?

The Exopolitics Initiative in Portugal encourages rigorous and evidence-based study, so the organization's members must be serious people, who avoid unfounded speculation, and know how to argue the principles and objectives of exopolitics sensibly. They are also required to know how to work as a team and establish cooperative ties with other entities, promoting the good name of all colleagues and the movement in particular. What members can expect is no less than learning work, in order to be able to distinguish the different levels of evidence, the quality of information, and to be able to participate in a movement that aims to be an activist for transparency and availability of information, as well as in preparing society for a new paradigm, namely that we are not alone in the universe.

Do you think disclosure of the so-called extraterrestrial presence is in the near future?

At this moment it is more or less recognized by all those who seriously study the phenomenon, that the extraterrestrial hypothesis is reductive, with other hypotheses on the table, namely interdimensionality and extratemporality, so what the community calls disclosure will be near in the sense of admitting the existence of non-human intelligences interacting with our reality. The information and the evidence have long been available. The recognition that the phenomenon is real has already occurred. What is missing is official recognition that the nature of part of the phenomenon is intelligent and non-human. It is difficult to put the timing in perspective, given the history of cover-ups and the continuous play of forces between those who defend transparency and those who want to perpetuate the secret. But it is also true that there has never been as much motivation as there is now. We'll have to wait and see, and hope things keep going in the right direction of transparency.

How will this disclosure impact the people of the world?

Announcing the discovery of alien life out there in the universe, some light years away is one thing. Announcing the existence of an advanced non-human intelligence interacting with our reality is a different thing entirely. Who are they, what do they want, what's their agenda, is there a threat—all of these questions matter and have the potential to create turbulence in society.

It may have a different impact in different parts of the world. In the West, people are more aware of the possibility that we are not alone. In the rest of the world, like Africa and Asia, there are cultural traditions that speak about other beings and other worlds. But on those continents, there are so many other struggles and priorities that it's difficult to predict the reaction to a disclosure scenario.

Depending on what type of admission the governments put out, there are potential risks in the economic/financial sector, with different religions, and possible social unrest.

People tend to forget that the hypothesis of the existence of exotic alien advanced technology may have a disruptive impact on the stock market; given that the key high-tech companies promote themselves as the ultimate R/D (research and development), when facing that new reality of far more advanced technology, it will diminish their stock value. Also, the Energy sector will most probably face the same challenges. So the most important sectors of the global market will potentially lose a lot in a contact scenario. The consequences to the stability of society are tremendous, just on the economics/financial side.

There are many religions on earth. How will disclosure affect them?

Religions will have to adapt to that new reality. How they use the information is also critical for the stability of society. In my view, according to the evolution into a possible scenario of disclosure, there should be a preparation plan, and meetings among the main religions should take place in order to establish some guidelines. If religious leaders take very different interpretations, then it has the potential to be one more major issue of conflict. Some Catholic key players have already positioned themselves on the matter: Monsignor Conrado Balducci, Gabril Funes, and Guy Consolmagno have all tried to calm the waters, saying that the ETH (extraterrestrial hypothesis) does not go against the Bible, that Christians should be prepared to accept aliens as their brothers in Creation, or even open the doors to the hypothesis of extraterrestrials receiving baptism.

There is high potential for great confusion among the followers of the different religions in the world. How the institutions prepare will definitely make a difference.

Do you hold the position that perhaps we were created by ET, that they seeded us here?

There are several authors that defend that hypothesis, but it's pure speculation. It's a mind exercise in terms of projecting a speculative hypothesis, most of the time based on interpretations of ancient paintings and traditions, but with no direct, real evidence to support the claims. There is the tendency to extrapolate conclusions based on beliefs and not on evidence. But that is human nature in action, propelled by the lack of government transparency for the last almost eighty years.

With the current disclosure happening in the U.S. Congress where David Grusch stated that we have recovered non-human biologics, how does this affect your worldview?

It does not affect my worldview as the claim is not exactly something new. There have been many other witnesses and whistleblowers who have claimed the same in the past. So, for any researcher that knows the history of the field and has been paying attention, he/she will know that that allegation has been on the table for some time.

For society in general, if the allegations are confirmed to be true, then it certainly has the potential to further deepen the mistrust of the governments and militaries, and create some havoc in the stock markets like I said above.

How can the peoples of Earth prepare for contact?

People should be paying attention to the news and the findings that result from the many hearings that have been taking place in the U.S. and other countries.

People should also pay attention to the initiatives that different organizations have been developing, such as awareness courses, that may in some way help to prepare.

It will be up to the governments to embrace such initiatives and help society to be prepared. But we do need to understand that even when you think you are prepared, it is only when going through the real situation that you will feel the impact.[6]

Final Thoughts

We're going through some interesting times. Some unconscious political decisions allowed for the creation of the conditions that led to the insertion of UAPs into the current political arena.

There have always been opposite forces battling over transparency versus secrecy on the UAP subject. The old guard who are the keepers of the secret have been successful in maintaining the status quo, but the new generation got an opportunity and used it with intelligence to level the scenario.

The fight is on, and it seems there are still some rounds to go.

It will definitely help if the many different research groups could come together and join forces, but I recognize that there are some expressed views that are too far apart to be used in the same discussion. Reconciling those ideas would need steps that not everyone is willing to take. Although there's an opportunity with the political conditions that seem to be falling in the right place, there is still a big weakness, namely the incompatibility between groups, which in itself may also be a threat if rightly used by the old guard.

The issue of total disclosure is truly complex, and it will have severe ramifications in all sectors of society; with that in view, the prolonged secrecy is understandable. No one wants to take that responsibility and deal with it.

Chapter 18

THE SEVENTEENTH RUNG: THE ENDGAME

I REMEMBER WHEN I saw my first UFO at Camp Horseshoe in Rising Sun, Maryland. I could take you to that place today; it's still there. I was twelve years old, and I was taking a shortcut back to camp for lunch. I was with three other boys. We were hopping over boulders and making our way back. I was the last boy in line; the three other boys were all in front of me. Suddenly the lead boy shouted, "What's that?"

The other two boys shouted, "Wow, what is that?"

I said, "Where?"

The boys pointed and shouted, "There!"

I looked out and above me, and there, in the clear canopy of blue sky, was a metallic silver disc. It was hovering without a sound as the sun glistened off it. We all watched it for perhaps twenty-five seconds, then, in a flash, it shot straight up into the atmosphere and was gone. We were so excited that all four of us ran back to the camp.

"We saw a flying saucer! A UFO!"

The other scouts came running out of the cabins and were joined by the scoutmasters. Everyone wanted to know what the object that we saw looked like.

That was lunchtime. By the evening meal on the same day, the other boys denied that they had ever seen anything due to the teasing and ridicule they experienced. This event became an important life lesson for me. I learned that people will deny what they have seen in order to remain part of the herd.

I have never forgotten that lesson, and I've wondered about the other three boys that saw the UFO with me that day. I have called out to them on numerous podcasts and radio shows, hoping that one of them would contact me, but so far no one has.

When *Close Encounters of the Third Kind* came out, I was all in. I believed in our space brothers and wanted them to take me. Fortunately that never happened. When I became a Christian years later, the Lord changed my paradigm. I began to look at the UFO phenomenon through a whole different lens, and that lens was the biblical one. I realized that these so-called space brothers were anything but!

I have elaborated on this throughout the pages of this book, and so I won't reiterate it here. But I will say that the Lord has led me on a very interesting road, perhaps one that I would not have chosen.

We Have Been Visited for Thousands of Years by Ancient Astronauts...or Fallen Angels?

I've mentioned before that every Friday night on the History Channel's *Ancient Aliens*, they promulgate the *ancient astronaut theory*. This theory essentially states that we have been visited by extraterrestrials for thousands of years.

I appeared on the first two seasons of *Ancient Aliens*, and one of the reasons my late business partner, Richard Shaw, and I started the *Watchers* series was to counteract what the ancient astronaut theory and *Ancient Aliens* were promulgating. They have a large budget, and they can travel anywhere on the planet. However, we've been to many places that the History Channel later visited for their series. In fact, our *Watchers* series broke the story of the ancient megalithic structures that were in Peru before the History Channel did their segment on it, and it was the same story regarding the enigmatic Paracas skulls.[1]

The sixth film in our *On the Trail of Nephilim* series covers the groundbreaking DNA evidence that we published regarding elongated skulls. The shape of the skulls is *not* the result of cranial deformation or cradle head boarding but is, in fact, genetic. In the film we have doctors, surgeons, optometrists, an archaeologist, an anthropologist, and a chiropractor go on the record, telling us that what we are looking at is genetic.[2] We broke the story. The History Channel followed us; however, the channel's media footprint is far bigger than ours and obviously we can't really compete with them.

Let's just take one example of the vast differences in our paradigms, in our belief systems. We have been to the ancient megalithic site of Sacsayhuamán, in Peru; I have been there three times. I remember the first time I laid eyes on it. It took my breath away, seeing how these megalithic stones, some of them weighing over one hundred tons, are fit together with absolute perfection and no mortar.

The reason I chose the site was because it is very controversial. There are essentially three paradigms regarding the site. The first is what the docents, who are hired by the Peruvian government, tell the tourists who visit the site. They will say that the Inca were master stone builders, and they created the site. I have witnessed this with my own eyes and ears, and it makes me mad. The reason it's maddening is that the Inca only had copper chisels—you cannot cut and shape andesite stone with a copper chisel. Moreover, the stones are polygonal in shape, and no two stones are the same. And in addition to all that, the stones with impossible shapes and angles are fit together, one stone to another, with absolute surgical precision. So the view that the Inca built Sacsayhuamán is patently absurd!

The second position is what the History Channel's *Ancient Aliens* is promulgating. They claim that what we see at Sacsayhuamán is the handiwork of extraterrestrials who visited the planet thousands of years ago. This is the paradigm they put forth every Friday night—for fifteen seasons now.

The third position, and the one I hold to, is that Sacsayhuamán is a pre-flood structure the likes of which I have come to call *fallen angel technology*, or *Nephilim architecture*. None of the tools or machines that were used to create this site have ever been found by archaeologists. It is truly a very enigmatic and mysterious site.

In the Book of Enoch we are told that fallen angels came down and gave mankind certain technology:

> And Azazel taught men to make swords, and knives, and shields, and breastplates, and made known to them the metals of the earth and the art of working them, and bracelets, and ornaments, and the use of antimony, and the beautifying of the eyelids, and all kinds of costly stones, and all colouring tinctures. And there arose much godlessness, and they committed fornication, and they were led astray, and became corrupt in all their ways. Semjaza taught enchantments, and root-cuttings, 'Armaros the resolving of enchantments, Baraqijal [taught] astrology, Kokabel the constellations, Ezeqeel the knowledge of the clouds, Araqiel the signs of the earth, Shamsiel the signs of the sun, and Sariel the course of the moon. And as men perished, they cried, and their cry went up to heaven.'[3]

While the Book of Enoch is not part of the biblical canon, Jude does quote from it. It may be easy for some to dismiss the Book of Enoch and Jude's reference to it. However, in my opinion, if a person were going to keep one book away from people, it would be Enoch 1. Why, you ask? Because the Book of Enoch tells us exactly what happened in Genesis 6. It tells the story of the fallen angels coming to earth, taking human women as wives, and procreating with them, creating what has become known as the Nephilim. This is the amplification of Genesis 3:15 and the ongoing seed war.

There are three paradigms. And looking at the History Channel's position, in some ways they are right—extraterrestrials did build Sacsayhuamán. However, we need to define what an extraterrestrial is. In my opinion an extraterrestrial is any entity that does not originate on planet Earth, and the entities that built these structures did not originate on planet Earth. However, and I need to stress this, these entities are not interplanetary but interdimensional and are, in fact, fallen angels. This is why the Book of Enoch is so important. In my opinion it clears up any doubt as to what happened so long ago. These fallen ones were here and influenced mankind, and they continue to do so up to the present day.

THE SKY GODS

Chief Joseph RiverWind is a Taino chief. We interviewed Chief Joseph in our *Watchers* series and *On the Trail of the Nephilim* series. Chief Joseph brings to the table the oral tradition of Native American culture. In the interview I asked Chief Joseph about the sky gods. Without hesitation Chief Joseph told me that the sky gods came down, took human women, and had sex with them.[4] This, of course, hails back to Genesis 3:15 and also Genesis 6. In other words, we have here in the Americas an extrabiblical source that is telling us about the reality of fallen angels taking human women and creating a hybrid entity—the Nephilim.

We also know, once again from the oral tradition, that giants roamed the Americas. Of course, modern-day archaeologists scoff at this and make every excuse possible to discredit Native American or First Nation oral tradition. Sarah Winnemucca talked about the Si-Te-Cah—the red-haired giants that were cannibalistic. The Paiute went to war with the Si-Te-Cah and essentially herded them into a cave. The cave still exists today, the Lovelock Cave, in Nevada. I have visited the cave and explored it. I found that the roof of the cave was completely singed black, which corroborates Sarah Winnemucca's story that the Paiute piled brush and wood at the mouth of the cave and set it on fire, and then when the giants came out, they killed them.[5] We also filmed in the Humboldt Museum, which is the home of the Lovelock Cave artifacts. One pair of sandals at the museum was well over fifteen inches in length. There are also reports of a ten-foot skeleton and a nine-foot giant skeleton being found in the area. Of course, there's no way to vet the reports of ten-foot skeletons, but the Lord willing, someday we will find one.

Added to this is the account by Robert Mirabal, a Pueblo musician from Taos Pueblo, New Mexico, who created a performance of his song "Stiltwalker."[6] I contacted Robert and asked, "Where did you hear the story of the giants?" He told me he heard it from his grandfather; it was part of the tribe's oral tradition. At the very beginning of the video Robert quoted—almost verbatim—the Genesis 6 narrative, talking about the sky gods coming down. Then in the video you see the giant appear. It really is an incredible piece. The music is superb. The staging and lighting are excellent. Hats off to Robert Mirabal. The interview I did with him is in my book *On the Trail of the Nephilim*.[7]

To sum things up here, it's important for us to understand that fallen angels did the unthinkable—they came to earth, had sexual relations with human women, and created a hybrid being known as the Nephilim.

Jesus warned us that it will be like the days of Noah when He returns. It's important for us to realize that it's *like* the days of Noah, meaning similar, not *exactly* like the days of Noah. Immediately we must ask ourselves, What differentiates the days of Noah from all the rest of human history? Once again I call your attention to the Genesis 3:15 narrative, which results in the full-blown manifestation of the seed war in Genesis 6. Daniel 2:43 (KJV) states:

> They shall mingle themselves with the seed of men: but they
> shall not cleave one to another, even as iron is not mixed with
> clay.

The word *cleave* is from the same root word that we see way back in Genesis when a man leaves his father and mother and *cleaves* to his wife. This is a marriage contract. I got this from Jim Wilhelmsen, who stated that there are no marriage contracts in the modern-day abduction phenomena.[8] We delved into this in our fourth film in the *UFO Disclosure* series, on abductions. What we are seeing is the creation of modern-day hybrids, who are in a fixed state, who have no soul. The sky gods have returned. These are the intruders, the fallen ones, interdimensional beings, with a very dark agenda.

SITCHIN IS WRONG

The *Ancient Aliens* crowd and lots of New Agers point back to Zecharia Sitchin and his work, and they quote it endlessly. Dr. Michael Heiser created a website called Sitchin is Wrong. I have spent some time on the site. It is incredible that Dr. Heiser clearly shows that the translations Sitchin used to base his entire theory on are, in fact, *mistranslations*. As Dr. Heiser shows, Sitchin has essentially created a fantasy with the Anunnaki. In other words, it is a construct, and Sitchin's body of work rests on his translations of the ancient Sumerian clay tablets.[9]

There are also critics of the biblical narrative that point to the fact that the Sumerian clay tablets were created centuries before the Bible, and sometimes these critics argue that the Bible is borrowing the flood story from the Sumerians. In my opinion, this is a straw man argument. The God of the Bible is patient, and just because He waited centuries before bringing Moses and Aaron into the fray does not mean that the Sumerian clay tablets are the truth. In fact, I would say this is just another example of fallen angels—interdimensional entities—which have come to earth and set up shop. In my series *On the Trail of the Nephilim* we show that all over the world there are ancient sites, and many of them are built on an eighteen-and-a-half-year lunar cycle. Many of them point to the constellation Draco, or the dragon. Many of these sites engaged in human sacrifice.[10] Where did this knowledge come from?

I have speculated that these entities arrived at a certain location on the planet, and then they set up shop. They were worshipped as gods. They gave technology to the human population. The Book of Enoch makes this clear. I remember the first time I visited Caral in Peru. It is the oldest city in the Americas, reaching back over five thousand years. It reminded me of Teotihuacan in Mexico, and when I mentioned this to our guide, he agreed, "Yes, they are similar, but Caral is much older."

Rising from the plateau were three large step pyramids. This immediately begs the question, Where do the engineering skills, the mathematics, and the knowledge of lunar and solar procession, equinoxes, and solstices come from? Did they just fall out of the sky? Yes, they might have, in the form of a fallen angel who set up shop there. What has become an inside joke is that we are told that climate change had forced these people to abandon the site. Of course, this is complete speculation and, in my opinion, is another straw man argument that is repeated at other megalithic sites all over the world. There was a diaspora 3,500 years ago as Joshua and Caleb conquered the Promised Land, and the Nephilim tribes fled westward. We see their handiwork all throughout the Mediterranean and into Spain, Portugal, France, England, Ireland, and finally the New World.

Dr. Michael Heiser, who was able to read the ancient Sumerian tablets, has cleared up the canard of the Anunnaki that has been promulgated by the ancient astronaut theorists for now two decades. Once again there is another explanation for all this technology, and it is this fallen angel technology, Nephilim architecture. It makes perfect sense.

As I often say, "There is a hidden history that has been deliberately obfuscated from the peoples of the world. And this is why I am on the trail of the Nephilim."

WHAT IS THE TRUTH?

In the last two films of our ten-part *UFO Disclosure* series, we interviewed lots of researchers and showed the two main paradigms. The first is the extraterrestrial hypothesis, which states that we are being visited by so-called extraterrestrials from some other planet. The second is the interdimensional hypothesis, which states that these entities are from another dimension, which I'm sure you know by now is the paradigm that I tenaciously hold to. These interdimensional beings have a nefarious agenda, and I think we've covered that in this book. Certainly, when a person watches our films on the UFO phenomenon, specifically episode 4 on abductions and episode 6 on cattle mutilations, the conclusion, in my opinion, is overwhelming. There is a dark agenda to all of this, and it connects directly back to the biblical prophetic narrative that we see in the Bible. Once again I call your attention to Genesis 3:15. It is the gateway to the biblical narrative. We are, in fact, in a seed war.

For episodes nine and ten of our *UFO Disclosure* series, I interviewed over a dozen people, including Nick Pope, Nick Redfern, George Noory, Dan Heiser, George Haas, Gonz Shimura, Derek Gilbert, Josh Peck, Gary Stearman, Mondo Gonzalez, Pastor Matt Freeman, and Dick Oswalt.[11] At the very end of the film I weighed in one last time, and in some ways I have waited until now, this last chapter, to bring this to your attention. It is based on decades of research and work. I stand on the shoulders of those who came before me such as Dr. I. D. E. Thomas, George Pember, Chuck Missler, and Gary Stearman. I owe a debt of gratitude to these men who have come before me, and in many cases mentored me. I will tell you what I think is about to happen. It is conjecture on my part; however, it is biblically sound and ties into the prophetic narrative.

Fátima: Harbinger of Deception

I already covered in detail the events that happened in 1917 in Fátima. I've created two films on the Fátima apparitions. We went there during the one-hundred-year anniversary of the so-called apparitions. The films do a deep dive into what really happened at Fátima in 1917. The crowds in Fátima swelling to as many as seventy thousand people ties into what I believe is the *coming great deception*. In my opinion, Fátima was, literally, a *harbinger of deception*. It was *not* Mary of the Bible. It was, in fact, a UFO event. I encourage you to do your homework and watch the films we made on the subject. You can download each film for just a few dollars.[12]

Nuclear Saber Rattling and What That Might Bring

I remember vividly doing safety drills when I was in elementary school and hiding under my desk in case of a nuclear event. I was born in 1950, so I was right in the window of time when the Cold War and the threat of a nuclear event was a very real thing. I remember the Cuban Missile Crisis, which alarmed my parents very much. Cuba was under the control of communist dictator Fidel Castro. The Soviet Union was bringing missiles into Cuba. This was unacceptable, and President Kennedy created a naval quarantine to stop the Russian ships from reaching Cuba. It was as close as we have ever been to World War III and a nuclear exchange. The Russians turned around, and a nuclear event was avoided. Years later the Cold War ended, and the former Soviet Union collapsed under its own weight. For the record, though they have been tried many times, communism and socialism have never worked anywhere and, quite frankly, never will. It is a dead-end system that eliminates the entrepreneurial spirit.

Now in 2024 we are seeing saber rattling coming from Russia, specifically Vladimir Putin, who is threatening the use of his nuclear arsenal.

You may recall from the chapter about Robert Salas that a UFO appeared over the Malmstrom base in Montana and switched off all ten intercontinental ballistic missiles. These intruders seem to be obsessed with our nuclear armament. Is it any wonder they appeared in Roswell in 1947, when the 509th Bombardment Group was the only nuclear-capable bombing group in the world and, in fact, had dropped the atom bombs on Hiroshima and Nagasaki? Is it possible that a nuclear event triggers their arrival?

WE GO UP; THEY COME DOWN! WE GO UP; THEY SHOW UP!

I am going to present you with a scenario I think is extremely plausible and based on the biblical prophetic narrative. When Jesus cast out the demons from the man of the tombs, they said to Him, "'What have we to do with You, Jesus, You Son of God? Have You come here to torment us before the time?'" (Matt. 8:29). Think about it. How did these entities, these demons, know that it was not their time? How can they make a statement like that? I truly believe that the fallen ones see through time in greater ways than we humans do. I wrote about this in my book *The Cosmic Chess Match*. I will quickly repeat it here; I call it the *cornfield analogy*.

A person is standing in a cornfield. They see the corn in front of them and the corn to the left and the right and the corn behind them, but they can only see a very short distance in any direction. That's our perspective of time—we move through time one second at a time. We can't jump ahead; we can't go back. We are, in fact, stuck in the space-time continuum. We are grounded in linear time.

The Dragon pulls up to the same cornfield in a shiny red fire-truck with a ladder. He climbs up that ladder, and now he's two stories above the cornfield. The Dragon can see that cornfield plus several other cornfields around it. In other words, he is able to see through time in ways that we humans cannot. The fallen ones can see farther in time than we can, but they cannot see all of it as God can. The Dragon is *not* all-knowing and thus cannot pinpoint the future with the specificity of the Most High God![13]

> I am God, and there is none like Me, declaring the end from the beginning, and from ancient times things that are not yet done.
>
> —Isaiah 46:9–10

The God of the Bible is sitting in the space shuttle high above the earth with a telescopic camera. He looks down at the cornfield, and He can see the dime that just dropped out of my pocket because it had a hole in it. And that dime is next to my right shoe! But the telescopic camera can pan back and see not only you but the cornfields that the Dragon saw. Plus He can see the entire state of Kansas. And if He pulls back farther, He can see all of planet Earth![14] In other words, the God of the Bible is all-knowing, and He sees through time in ways that are incomprehensible to us. This is why He can call out with great specificity the end before the beginning and the beginning before the end. This is why prophecy is so important—it is His words of warning about what will happen!

Here's a question: Is it possible that the fallen ones know that there will be a nuclear event somewhere on this planet and that event will trigger their arrival? Is it possible that a nuclear event is their go button, as it were? Think about this: In 1945, when the atom bomb was dropped on Japan, there was no internet; people were not connected the way they are today. Fast-forward to 2024. There is a grid that connects all living beings on the planet. News travels at the speed of light. Satellites circle the earth, relaying information. I truly believe that this is the time of the end.

Think about it. If a nuclear device goes off anywhere on this planet, it will create the greatest fear that humanity has experienced collectively since the beginning of time. All eyes would be on this event, and people would panic. People would wonder if the whole world were going to come to an end. Fear is the calling card of darkness. Faith is the calling card of the kingdom of light, of Jesus' kingdom. If you have the greatest collective fear in the history of the world sparked by a nuclear device, is that when they show up since *fear* is their calling card, their gateway to the people of earth?

A few years ago I was at Prophecy Watchers, and Gary Stearman was interviewing me. I came up with this comment on the spot, during that interview: *We go up; they come down! We go up; they show up!*

Gary looked at me, and I could see he was startled and taken aback by what I had just said. He replied, "You should copyright that, LA!" From that saying, which acted like a springboard, Mondo Gonzales and Jeff Van Hatten inspired the following.

We know that when Elijah the prophet was taken up, Elisha watched him go up. We know from the biblical narrative that when Jesus was taken up, the apostles (and who knows how many other people; certainly Mary, His mother, and I would venture Mary Magdalene were there as well) watched Him ascend *into the clouds*. We have the two witnesses in the Book of Revelation; they are killed, and their bodies lie on the streets of Jerusalem. Then three days later, they are resurrected, and the entire world watches them ascend *into the clouds*. Finally, we are told in 1 Thessalonians:

> For the Lord himself shall descend from heaven with a shout, with the voice of the archangel, and with the trump of God: and the dead in Christ shall rise first: then we which are alive and remain shall be caught up together with them in the clouds, to meet the Lord in the air: and so shall we ever be with the Lord.
>
> —1 THESSALONIANS 4:16–17, KJV

The point I'm trying to make is that in all of these scriptures, human beings go up *into the clouds*. The passage from 1 Thessalonians makes it clear that we rise to greet the Lord in the air together with Him *in the clouds*. Is it possible that when we go up into the clouds, after we are gone, and millions of people have vanished in similar ways all over the earth, then one-mile-wide UFOs will appear out of that same cloud? I realize for some of you this might be a stretch. But I heard *this exact scenario* literally fifty years ago when I was in the New Age. I mentioned briefly in a prior chapter that I was told there would be some people who would be taken to another place by the space brothers because they were not ready for the paradigm shift in consciousness. *We go up; they come down! We go up; they show up!*

While the scenario above is conjecture, there are biblical precedents for it, and I truly believe we are on the cusp of seeing these events unfold. I will close with the statement that I have said perhaps thousands of times: *UFOs are real, burgeoning, and not going away.* It is time for the church to wake up and understand that we were warned by Jesus Himself that even the elect would be deceived if that were possible, that men would faint from fear of what was coming upon the earth. This is what I have come to call the *coming great deception*, and it is at hand. The time is now.

Appendix

WHAT IS THE TRUTH?
MY JOURNEY FROM THE
ASHRAM TO THE GREAT I AM

IN 1950, IN the northeastern United States, I was born to second generation Italian parents and a very Catholic family. As a child I was in awe of what happened at Mass every Sunday because the priest, who was dressed in robes and surrounded by lit candles and incense, seemed to my boyhood mind like some special magician between the people—sitting in typical sheep-like fashion—and God.

I didn't understand anything that was being said because it was all in Latin. I knelt, I stood, and I tried not to fidget, which was almost impossible in the wool pants my mother made me wear. When I was older, I served briefly, very briefly, as an altar boy.

One of the most traumatic events in my life was the death of my grandfather. Even though I was only five years old at the time and I didn't quite grasp the finality of it at that tender age, it was a blow to my spirit; it changed me.

Right before his untimely death, I remember grabbing his oversized Bible, constructing a make-shift pulpit in front of the long dining room table where my relatives were all eating and—though I couldn't read a word—giving my first sermon.

"What is the truth?" I shouted as I slapped my hand on the "pulpit."

I recently spoke to my parents about this memory, and they informed me that it was quite hysterical to everyone who witnessed the spectacle. The more they laughed, my parents recounted, the more insistent, passionate, and serious I became. This from a five-year-old! Looking back, I can see it was a foreshadowing of what I do today. But I'm getting ahead of myself!

When I was ten years of age, we moved from Waltham, Massachusetts to Berwyn, Pennsylvania, which is near Philadelphia. It took some time for me to adjust; my new school was Catholic, and for me it was torture. Like many young boys, I found it almost impossible to sit still and focus on what was being taught. All I wanted to do was go outdoors and play and run in the woods. This is the reason I am still trying to learn the art of punctuation, because I was totally checked out when it was being taught in the third grade. "Where do I place those pesky commas," I still ask myself.

At thirteen I decided to leave the church. I made this decision after going through confirmation, an unbearable process wherein we had to memorize a gazillion catechism questions and be prepared to answer correctly when quizzed by the bishop. We all spent weeks memorizing the questions and answers. When the bishop arrived, we were stupefied when he didn't ask us even one question—not one! Something in me gave up on the Catholic Church at that point. In fact, I announced that I didn't want to go to church anymore. My mother was aghast, but my father took it in stride. This began the years in which God—whoever I may have thought He was—took a back seat to everything else I deemed important. He was, for all practical purposes, at the bottom of my list. Well, more truthfully, He didn't make the list at all.

I went through my junior and senior years of high school and hated most of it. I didn't fit in. Music was my big out, and I was the coleader of the most popular band in the school. We rocked the house and looked as freaky as possible. This was the sixties, and I was desperately trying to be a hippie with my long, frizzy hair. And, like many others, I endured acne, which really is the bane of young people struggling through those teenage years.

I was a nature counselor at the local YMCA for one summer, and it was there, at the age of sixteen, that I met my first crush. Her name was Michelle, and she was only fourteen. Before I could take her to the YMCA dance, her father interrogated me—think the *real* Archie Bunker here! We were in love; at least as much as immature teenagers can be. We dated throughout the rest of high school, and then we broke up for some stupid reason that I can't remember.

It was during this high school period that the lead guitarist in the band introduced me to marijuana. The first time I took it I laughed and laughed and thought it was the greatest thing that had ever happened to me. Before long we moved from smoking pot to LSD, and right after graduation in the summer of 1969, I found myself sitting in a large field with thousands of other stoned-out hippies at what would be known as the legendary Woodstock concert. Unlike our former president,[1] I inhaled as often as I could.

Looking back on those days, I realize that my generation was hoodwinked and lied to. The Beatles and other bands at the time promulgated the use of drugs. As many of you who are reading this know, drugs have been the cancer of our society. When I speak at conferences, I sometimes ask the audience to give a show of hands if they themselves either have been to or know people in rehab. The hands go flying up, and to our dishonor, it is most of the audience. Drugs have changed the moral fabric of this country forever. But I digress.

That same summer I was sitting in my room—high on LSD— reading letters from Michelle and another girl while trying to decide between them. At the same time, I was trying to read the book of Revelation from the Bible, which was way too taxing for my drug-saturated brain. I was asking—actually more like challenging—that if there was a God, for Him to show me which girl I should be with.

About an hour later, around midnight, my father came into my room and told me that Michelle had been killed in a hit-and-run automobile accident. Remember that at the time I was high on LSD, so my emotions were like gelatin in a blender. I was stunned and I just sat there not being able to move for what seemed like a very long time. Eventually I went to bed, and when I woke up the next morning, I asked my father if Michelle was dead or if it had been a horrible dream. He said that it was true—it had not been a dream. She was sixteen; I was eighteen.

This single event changed my life. It sent me on a quest that didn't end until twelve long, weary years later. Her death was so final; there were no second chances or do-overs. It was a wake-up call, and I was cut to the quick by it. Michelle's death started me on a journey searching for the meaning of life; I was compelled to discover who God was, if He even existed at all.

I began to read everything I could get my hands on. I read books on the occult, tomes by Carlos Castaneda, Blavatsky, Euspensky and others who introduced me to the New Age paradigm. I continued to experiment with drugs as part of my search for enlightenment. I went on vision quests, and very often due to taking psychedelics I had horrible experiences. I realize now that all of these drugs were gateways into the occult, stepping-stones to the world of the Fallen One and his dark purposes.

What is the purpose of this life? Why are we here? What is the meaning of love? I pondered these and other questions, looking for answers but not finding any.

At the age of twenty-one and after three years of searching, I still had not found what I was looking for. It was 1972, and I had heard about a course called Silva Mind Control, which was developed by José Silva. I took a friend along with me, and we signed up for the course. I had no idea what I was getting into, but the promotional flyer that I had read promised me that I would have the ability to diagnose and heal those who were sick. We were told to lie down on the floor and visualize a workroom. Then we were told to create imaginary counselors to help us in this workroom. My counselors were Jesus, Curly of the Three Stooges, and the Lone Ranger. I laugh as I think about it now, but at the time I figured that each of them could be trusted. Much to my amazement they would appear with me in my imaginary workroom. Without realizing it, I was being indoctrinated into the occult, using meditation and what is known as guided imagery to catapult me into the unseen world of the spirit.

When we had completed the three-day seminar, for graduation we had to perform a test to see whether or not we could function as *seers*.[2] I was handed a 3x5 index card with a name on it, nothing more. I was then told to diagnose the illness this person had. I went into my workroom with Jesus, Curly, and the Lone Ranger, and together we diagnosed what was wrong with the person. I would use my hands, like a human X-ray machine, to scan the person while my eyes were closed. I "saw" what was wrong and announced it, "He has a growth on his brain." The instructor smiled at me while nodding and said, "Correct."

I had passed the test! What I wasn't told was that through the techniques of Silva Mind Control I had opened myself to real spirit guides. (For a more in-depth view of this, see Sharon Beekmann's book *Enticed by the Light*.[3] She vividly portrays what happens when people open themselves up to these entities.) Please remember that we are told in *The Guidebook to the Supernatural*, how I often refer to the Bible, to avoid all cooperative contact with these malevolent impostors!

I continued my esoteric studies, and now I was reading about the "holy men," the *mahatmas*[4] of India, and how they would sit and attain enlightenment. And how the *fakirs*,[5] denunciates of the world, could perform miracles and feats of superhuman strength and endurance. I was intrigued by what I was reading and began to think about going to India. It was around this time that someone gave me a poster that stated *the God of the universe had come to earth in the form of a fourteen-year-old boy named Guru Maharaj Ji.* The teenaged *guru*[6] was going to appear at a theater in Philadelphia.

I found myself sitting with hundreds of other hippies in a crowded, non-air-conditioned theater. There were no seats left, and my friend and I sat on the floor in the aisle. If I remember correctly, a band played, and we listened to their music as we waited for what seemed like forever. Finally, the guru showed up. There was a chair set in the middle of the stage on a *dais.*[7] It was more like a throne than a chair. It was draped with wreaths of flowers.

When the guru came out on the stage, most of the audience fell to their faces voluntarily. This is called *pranam.* It is meant as a sign of respect and submission. Much to my surprise, I found myself stretched out on the floor in this *pranam* position. Someone on the stage called out, *Bo-ley shri- Satguru Dev* and most of the audience replied, *Maharaj ki ji.* Looking back, it now reminds me of the mindless Nazi salute and cries of *Heil Hitler* by the masses in WWII Germany. I'm certainly not comparing the guru to Hitler, but I'm referring instead to the way people can respond in an entranced or controlled state.

At that point everyone settled back in their chairs as the guru began what was to be about a two-hour lecture. It went on and on and on! The central core of his message was that he was dispensing *knowledge.* This knowledge could only be given by him and was unknown to everyone else. Only through the guru's appointed mahatma, a holy man, could someone attain the bliss that he promised. He then went as far as to say that all the other gurus and masters before him were dead and that a person needed a living, "perfect" master to show them the way to peace and enlightenment. I believed every word of it. This seemed like what I was looking for, so I picked up a scrap of paper and feverishly scrawled the address of the place where this knowledge was going to be given out the next day.

SECRET KNOWLEDGE OR
DECEPTION A GO-GO?

Early on a Saturday morning I arrived at the house where the mahatma was going to give those in attendance the secret knowledge. The place was packed with hippies. We all sat on the floor. It was a hot summer day, and we were cramped in one large room spilling out into the hallway. The mahatma arrived and the session began. He talked all morning and most of the afternoon about how this knowledge was special and how the guru was the perfect master. He told us how important it was to practice the secret knowledge, and then he began to dispense it, going down the line to each of us one at a time. By then it was the end of the day and everyone was exhausted.

Before I get into what happened next, I want to relay to you an incident that made such an impression on me that even after nearly forty years I still remember it vividly.

There was a man named Dennis who was trying to get this knowledge along with the rest of us. He was crippled and deformed and had steel braces on his legs. The mahatma literally shunned him. He looked at Dennis with such disdain that it was obvious to everyone in the room. There was not an ounce of compassion from this so-called enlightened man—who was going to give us the secret knowledge so we could be just like him—and that hit me like a rogue wave breaking at Zuma beach! It shocked me, and although I wasn't able to articulate what offended me about the mahatma's actions then, I can do so now.

In Indian culture they believe in reincarnation. This is when a person is born over and over again and, depending on his or her actions, comes back in a higher or lower caste. It also has to do with the so-called laws of Karma. This is where actions that are deemed good or bad are carried over to the next incarnation and these actions decide where you are in the Indian caste system. Brahma caste is the highest, while the *untouchables*[8] are deemed the outcasts of Indian society. Some of this has changed in the last one hundred years, but the mindset is still very much alive in India today.

What the mahatma was reacting to with Dennis is this: In his worldview, that of believing in reincarnation, Dennis must have committed some grievous offense in his previous life for him to be crippled as he was in this lifetime. It was a glaring example of where this so-called enlightenment leads, and it is one of segregation and working one's way to a state of perfection by countless reincarnations. This is a false system, and the fruits of it are apparent as demonstrated by the mahatma's attitude toward Dennis and his unfortunate condition. There wasn't any compassion or empathy from the "enlightened one" toward Dennis; there was, in fact, open contempt of him to the point that others in the room began to shun Dennis too.

The mahatma was dressed in a saffron-colored robe, and his head was shaved. He had this blissed-out look on his face, meaning that he smiled and appeared holy and enlightened. Of course, he had a retinue of attendants who cared for his every need and whim.

He moved around the room and dispensed the secret knowledge. I was in a state of heightened awareness at this point and waited expectantly for my turn to come. The first thing he was going to do was to open our *third eye*.[9] This is the spot that is located between the eyes in the center of the forehead. It is where our pineal gland is located, and in many occult initiations opening the third eye is the springboard or gateway to the lower astral, or what I have come to call the second heaven.

I sat there waiting my turn, and then the mahatma was in front of me. My eyes were closed, and I felt him put his finger on my forehead. Nothing happened at first, and then suddenly I saw a circle that opened up and became a stream of colors and light images. I just sat there taking it all in and feeling special that I had now obtained the first part of this secret knowledge. I opened my eyes and looked around, and everyone had the same goofy, blissed-out smile on their faces. We had been initiated, and we had seen the light—literally!

The mahatma again went down the line, this time placing his fingers in our ears. When he did, I immediately began to hear flutes and the sound of rushing water. This really startled me because it was playing in my head. I opened my eyes, and the mahatma laughed at me and told me to close my eyes again. Then he took my hands and placed my own fingers in my ears. The music continued for some time, and then it slowly faded away.

At this time Dennis called out because the mahatma had passed him by with both the opening of the third eye as well as the music. He whined and looked and acted like a little boy who was being picked on. The mahatma grilled him for maybe ten minutes to the point where Dennis was literally groveling and begging him for the knowledge. Finally, the mahatma reluctantly gave in and dispensed the guru's knowledge to who I would now call the American untouchable, Dennis.

Next was the *nectar*.[10] He showed us how to put our tongues behind the uvula of our mouths and to keep it there until this divine nectar began to flow. Sure enough, I tasted something sweet trickle down into my throat from where my tongue was jammed against my uvula.

The last part of the initiation ceremony was receiving the "holy word" or *mantra*.[11] We were told that we were to meditate on this word day and night, that it was the *primordial vibration*,[12] and that we were to empty our minds and focus on this word.

The mahatma gave us the word and our initiation was complete. We had received the secret knowledge of inner light, music, nectar, and the primordial word. We were on the path to enlightenment— or so we thought.

In the Ashram

I got home and went to my room feeling elated then went to sleep. When I awoke the next morning, I remember feeling whole and good for the first time in my life, because I believed I had finally connected with God. I immediately sat up and stuck my fingers in my ears to hear more of the divine music. Sure enough, after a few moments it began, faintly at first, then louder.

This experience had a profound impact on my life. I felt that finally, after years of searching, I had found the truth. I changed my diet and became a vegetarian. I went to the local *ashram*[13] and listened to what is called *satsang*,[14] which is supposed to be divine discourse on the knowledge that Maharaj Ji was giving to all who asked. It wasn't long before I decided to give up worldly things and devote my life to the guru. So in 1971 I moved into the Philadelphia ashram and became a full-time devotee.

This was our schedule: We were up at 5 a.m. when we gathered in front of an altar and sang a devotional that is called *Arti*. It was the same song over and over again every day and one of the lines was *"rights and rituals won't reach the goal!"* But if that were true then why were we all engaging in the same rituals day after day? After we sang *Arti*, we would then have an hour of meditation. I remember sleeping through most of it because I was exhausted from only getting five hours of sleep a night! In spite of this, there were a few times when the light would explode in my third eye. Please don't be confused by this, it is nothing more than an occult practice that has deceived millions of people for thousands of years. It is nothing short of a demonic light show. After a vegetarian breakfast we would go to work. This was my routine day after day.

At one point I joined the orchestra of the guru's brother and found myself flying to England to play. For me this was a dream come true. The orchestra was about fifty-six pieces with another ten or so people to manage, provide food, and schedule events. We played at many of the guru's appearances. We were gearing up for an event called Soul Rush, a ten-city tour of the East Coast and the midwestern U.S. to attract people to the upcoming 1974 Houston Astrodome event known as the Millennium.

We finished the Soul Rush tour, settled into the long, hot summer days in an old hotel somewhere in Houston, and prepared for the big event. I thought at the time that this was it, the end of the world as we knew it. I remember calling my parents and friends and telling them to try to come to Houston. We were all that brainwashed and believed everything we were told.

The event came and the fifty-thousand–seat Astrodome was hardly filled by the estimated ten thousand people who showed up for the event. It was a far cry from what Maharaj Ji and the leaders at the top were expecting.

There was a large dais that was set up on the stage that was probably forty feet above the floor of the Astrodome. There were chairs on this dais for the members of the guru's family who were referred to as the "holy family." The orchestra was seated on the stage directly below the thrones.

The big night came and the holy family paraded out, followed lastly by the guru himself, who then perched on the highest throne. Now, I have told you all of this to get to this point—*the crowd began to worship the guru and the other members of the family.* At this point one of my bandmates nudged me and told me to look at the family on their thrones. When I did, I couldn't believe what I was seeing. The family was there but they had changed; they looked different—*there were other entities that manifested on that stage.* Looking back now, it is my opinion that what I saw was the demonic manifestation of what in-dwelt each of these people.

I stayed with the guru for another year and then I left. Here's why. When we were rehearsing for the big event in Houston that turned out to be anything but, I became disillusioned. At this point I had practiced meditation and done all that had been required of me, yet I had no peace. One night I went into the large hall that was used for *satsang* and meditation and lay down prostrate in front of the ever-present chair bedecked with flowers for the guru. I cried bitterly, my sobs coming in deep uncontrollable heaves. It awakened other people, as I would later discover, but no one came to see what was going on. Something broke in me that night. I realized that while I had practiced the knowledge that the guru had given to me, and had done so religiously, in my deep inner core, at the soul level of my being, in my spirit, *nothing had changed.* I had no terms to articulate it at the time, but it marked the beginning of my leaving the phony, blissed-out, mindless state of practicing meditation with the guru.

After the dismal turnout in Houston, the so-called holy family had a rift between them. This rift continues to the present day, and I included a link in the endnotes where you can check it out for yourself.[15]

Maharaj Ji is still telling people that they can have peace through his meditation, but take it from me, it's nothing more than New Age, phony baloney. There is only one Prince of Peace, and it certainly isn't this or any other guru.

The orchestra moved to Hollywood, California, to a seedy and unsavory hotel on Hollywood Boulevard. We were about four guys to a room that was supposed to hold one person. A drag queen lived across the hall, drugs were openly sold and used on the premises, homosexuality was practiced by so-called celibate followers in the orchestra, and, on top of all this, we were supposed to meditate and attain enlightenment. What a crock! And every night we would walk about eight blocks to the rehearsal hall to practice.

One amazing moment came when I borrowed a motorcycle and got on the Interstate 10 Freeway knowing that it would lead me to the Pacific Ocean. As I drove through the McClure tunnel I could smell the sea air, and as I came out of the tunnel into the light, the blue expanse of the ocean unfolded before me, sparkling in the midday sun. I have never forgotten that moment because it felt like I had found my home at last—California.

The orchestra moved to a place called Camp Joan Myer, a camp for the blind, located in the northern part of the city of Malibu. It is set on a hill overlooking the ocean. It was there that I really began to question the guru and the meditation. I was with another member of the orchestra, and we were both having difficulty believing the so-called party line. One day he said, "If you were told you were a god from the time you were a baby, what would you believe?" I nodded, and a few months later I left. Before my departure, however, a mahatma of great importance came to visit and I saw this man perform occult, demonic "miracles." Here's what I mean.

We were walking on the beach with this mahatma, who spoke little to no English. It appeared that he wanted to go into the ocean. He began to undress, and then I heard in my head, "*Hold these.*" I was taken aback; I didn't believe what was happening. The mahatma looked at me and shoved his clothes into my arms. I was stunned. We watched the "holy man" go into the water and submerge himself under a wave. When he came out, he put on his clothes and began to walk with us.

This next part is even stranger than the first, but I know what I saw and I'm not making this up. As we were walking, the mahatma suddenly vanished—he reappeared fifty yards farther down the beach. The other people with me were as shocked as I was. This man clearly demonstrated occult power by using mental telepathy and space-time travel. He had real power, but I believe that power was demonic in nature, given to him by a diabolical source.

The orchestra relocated to another residence in Malibu and downsized its numbers, and when it appeared that nothing more was going to come of it, the leaders decided to move into the city. This is when I jumped ship and left the guru. The northern part of Malibu in 1974 was quiet and serene with large amounts of vacant land. To my twenty-four-year-old brain, I had found paradise.

Now this is pertinent to this testimony. I began using drugs in high school. After Michelle's death in 1969 I immersed myself in esoteric and occult studies. In 1972 at the age of twenty-one, I graduated from the mind control seminar, then explored Eastern religions, served the guru 1972–1975, and until 1980 I meditated, sought after the occult, and read about the New Age. An important moment came in 1976 when I found a book, *UFO...Contact from the Pleiades* about Swiss farmer Edward "Billy" Meir's UFO encounters.[16] This book was pivotal for me as it *reintroduced* me to the UFO phenomena. I began to believe that aliens had seeded us here, that they were the gods of antiquity, and that they were going to come back for us. When I say it *reintroduced* me to the UFO phenomena, here's what I mean. I had seen a UFO when I was at Boy Scout camp around 1962. I didn't tell this part of the story earlier because I think it fits better here. Here's what happened.

My UFO Sighting

I was twelve years old and in love with Boy Scouts. I was at Camp Horseshoe, which is located in Rising Sun, Maryland. I was with three other boys taking a shortcut back to our camp so we wouldn't miss lunch. The lead boy who knew the shortcut led us up a boulder-covered ravine. As we were making our way up this ravine the boy who was in front said, "Wow, what's that?"

The other two boys chimed in, "Yeah, what is that?"

"What are you guys looking at," I asked.

"There, in the sky," they said, as all three boys pointed upward.

I looked up, and to my astonishment, there standing out against the cloudless, blue mantle was a silver disc. It was metallic and made no noise. It hovered motionless for maybe twenty seconds and then suddenly shot straight up into the sky. In the blink of an eye it was gone. We started shouting and ran as fast as we could back to the camp. When we got there we yelled, "We saw a UFO! We saw a UFO!"

The ridicule from the scoutmaster and other boys began almost immediately. By sundown that same night the three other boys denied that they had seen anything. But I held tenaciously onto my story. My campmates made fun of me the rest of the weekend, but I refused to change my story or deny what I had seen. It was my first experience with what I call "herd mentality."

VISION QUESTS

As I mentioned earlier, I read everything I could get my hands on by Carlos Castaneda, an anthropologist who wrote about his involvement with the spirit world using mescaline and marijuana as a springboard into the dimension where these beings reside. I was hitchhiking one day and was picked up by a guy who, like me, was a hippie. He had a joint going and offered me some. I eagerly took it and inhaled as deeply as I could, holding the smoke in my lungs while feeling the drug explode in my head. Even writing this I have to pray against the feeling, yet you couldn't pay me enough money to get stoned again, because I believe it is a gateway to the second heaven! He dropped me off at the bottom of Encinal Canyon, which is right off Pacific Coast Highway, and I started walking up the canyon.

The sun was beginning to set, and I was really wasted. I found a pathway that led off the road and followed it. It took me to a small clearing that overlooked the expanse of the Pacific Ocean. I sat down on the ground, cross-legged, in the *lotus position*.[17] I began to meditate and felt at one with the universe. The thought exploded in my mind that everything was connected, everything was one, there was no separation, and that if everything in the universe was connected and one, then there was nothing to fear. I pondered this for a while, and at the time it made sense to me. I felt like I had just been given one of the secrets of the universe.

Then, I suddenly heard a rattle sound coming from directly in front of me about twenty feet away. Startled, I opened my eyes and wondered what could be making that noise. I knew that rattlesnakes were common in these hills, but this was no rattlesnake. Then I heard the noise again, this time coming from my right, still about twenty feet away. The thought came to me that maybe someone was playing a trick on me, but I realized that there was no one in the area—I was alone. Besides, how could a person move noiselessly through the chaparral without me hearing them? I was getting scared and wondered what was going on. Again the rattle sounded, except this time it was directly behind me. Then I heard it in front of me, but this time it was closer.

The noise grew louder and louder as it continued to circle me. I suddenly became very afraid, and my mind raced back to the Carlos Castaneda books that talked of encounters with spirit beings similar to the one I was encountering now. Whatever it was circled again, growing closer with each pass that it made. Now it was right in front of me.

Remember that at this point I was still sitting cross-legged on the ground. Then something touched me, gently pushed me backward several degrees, and just held me there. If you are in the lotus position this is impossible to do because the weight of your upper body would cause you to fall all the way backward to the ground. But that's not what happened—I was held there. This demonic spirit, I call it that because that is what it was, held me there for a while and then slowly let me up. Once it did, I jumped to my feet and started slamming my open palms against my thighs. This was a technique that I had read about from Castaneda, who used it when a spirit that he did not want to deal with would come to him. This action would apparently repel the spirit. Once I had done this, another thought came into my mind from the outside. It said that if I had opened myself up to the spirit it would have been able to take me out of my body and show me the secrets of the universe.

I know some of you are reading this and thinking, *Where can I get some of this stuff?* Don't be swayed by the lie I was told, because that is what it is—a lie. Let's walk through this for a moment and examine the two messages I received.

The first message told me that I was connected to everything else in the universe, that we were all one, and that there was nothing to fear. This is called *pantheism*.[18] Briefly stated, it is the belief that we are all one. It is not true because you and your pet dog or cat are not connected! You may love your pet, but you are not your pet and your pet is not you. This philosophy is the basis of Hinduism, and I believe it is a lie. We are not all one—period!

The second message I received was that if I had trusted the spirit, I would have been taken out of my body and shown the secrets of the universe. These spirits can actually do this; however, there is a high price. When we give them our permission to take us on the journey, this familiar spirit, who is a demon, now has the right to possess us!

Now, back to the story. After the demonic spirit left me, I slowly made my way back home, unnerved and changed by the experience. Drugs are a springboard into the lower astral or the second heaven and should be avoided at all costs because we can pick up unwanted entities who will not readily leave us when we later realize who they are. This kind of experience can lead to possession. I was lucky that did not happen to me.

Chasing the Rock-and-Roll Carrot

During this time, I was performing with a band all over Los Angeles. We were chasing the ever elusive rock-and-roll carrot. We came close several times but never managed to snag the record deal. I was nearing thirty years of age, and it seemed my dream was never going to materialize. I had spent the previous five years of my life doing carpentry by day to survive and rehearsing, recording, and playing gigs around town at night. In short, it was a life that was going nowhere.

In 1978 I partnered with a friend and we built what is called a "spec house"[19] in Malibu Lake. I had sunk every dollar and all my energy into the project. We were hoping to turn it over quickly and build another. It seemed like a good way to make a living, and we were both good at it. The build was complete, and we were trying to sell the house when the real estate market collapsed and interest rates soared to 20 percent. The house sat on the market for two years, and I lost everything I had invested in it by the time my partner agreed to buy it for much less than our asking price.

I had also become somewhat of an agnostic. I'd had it up to my eyeballs with trying to find God and enlightenment. My new philosophy was eat, drink, and be merry because we're just going to reincarnate anyway, so who cares! Someone gave me some books by Taylor Caldwell,[20] and I read them. A couple of Caldwell's novels depict the lives of the apostles, and I found them fascinating. Then my girlfriend, Gail, gave me a book by David Hunt[21] titled *The Cult Explosion*. As I read it, I realized that I had participated in many of the cults that Hunt was warning about. At the end of his book was a short prayer that you could say if you wanted to ask Jesus into your life.

At this point my spec house was still on the market, but I was living with Gail and we weren't married, I was in debt up to my eyeballs, and I was spiritually bankrupt as well. As I read the prayer in the back of Hunt's book, I thought to myself, *I wonder if it's real?* So, I repeated the simple prayer asking Jesus into my heart. I asked Him to come into my life and change it. I looked around and waited but nothing seemed to happen. I shrugged it off and went about my life.

About a month later I awakened from a very vivid dream that left me weeping in Gail's arms. Something was going on deep inside the core of my being, and though I didn't know it at the time, Yeshua Jesus was beginning to work on me.

Later, I was at a dinner party when a friend asked me if I believed in Jesus. It was an out-of-the-blue question. Much to Gail's amazement, I replied, "I do believe in Jesus, and I consider myself a Christian."

About that time, I experienced something that I will never forget. It was when the Most High God took me out of the kingdom of darkness. One evening Gail set dinner in front of me, and suddenly an inner dam burst. I thought I was losing my mind. Out of nowhere, I was being bombarded by thoughts that weren't mine, unwanted thoughts. It was terrifying. I didn't know what was happening to me, but the thoughts kept coming, and they were horrible!

We went to bed, and I had a very difficult time trying to get to sleep. Gail called a friend of hers from work, and she was given the name of a pastor I was to call for help, Pastor Fred. The next morning, I called the number. I told him I thought I was having a nervous breakdown. We set up an appointment for later that day.

I also received a call from a man who would become my mentor for the next two years. His name was Wayne Kendall, to whom I dedicated my book, *The Cosmic Chess Match*. He told me that I wasn't going nuts, and though it was comforting to hear, it didn't stop the horrible, unwanted thoughts.

Later that day I met Pastor Fred, the man who would counsel me on a weekly basis for the next three years. In the beginning we met two times a week, and then it went to one time a week, and finally to once a month.

I then met Wayne, and we became good friends. Wayne was twenty years my senior, and we worked together in construction daily.

I want you to know that this part of my journey was like being in spiritual boot camp. I ate, breathed, and immersed myself in the Bible. I worked all day and went to all the Bible studies, home groups, and church services that I could find.

I returned home one day to find that Gail had moved out and taken everything with her, including her bed. That night I slept on the floor.

From that point, the nighttime was very difficult for me, and I slept with a Bible clutched to my chest; it was my spiritual teddy bear. When I woke up each morning, I would read Psalms and Proverbs and get on my knees in ardent prayer for peace. This went on week after week. Unfortunately, Pastor Fred and Wayne knew little about deliverance or putting on the armor of God as we are told to do every day in Ephesians 6. I was also never told about the authority I have in Christ.

One night as I put my head on my pillow, I heard a roar as something tried to enter my body. I cried out, "Jesus, help me!" The attack stopped, and I lay there for a few minutes paralyzed by what had happened. I called Pastor Fred, and we prayed on the phone and afterward I went to sleep.

I was under relentless attack for years, but the entire time the Lord was busy "rewiring" me, as Wayne liked to call it. There were days that I honestly could not have made it through without Wayne's and Pastor Fred's help. Thanks, guys. Remember, I had been willingly involved in the occult since the age of sixteen and had been meditating and doing other occult practices for fourteen years. I had been firmly entrenched in the camp of the fallen one without knowing it. How's that for deception? You see how subtle it is? The entire time I was in the New Age I thought I was on the right path toward spirituality and enlightenment. Instead, I was beginning to discover I had opened myself up to what the *Guidebook to the Supernatural* calls *the doctrine of demons.* (See 1 Timothy 4:1.)

One afternoon Wayne and I were going into a market to get something for lunch. I was exhausted, fed up with the more than two years of relentless attacks. I asked him, "How long do you think this is going to go on?"

I had asked that question of Pastor Fred too. He replied that he had never seen anyone struggle as much as I had, but he assured me that God knew what He was doing and that at some point, the struggle would end. Recall the book of Job here. It illustrates the point Fred was making, that the fallen one was allowed to attack Job only for a period of time before the Most High God stopped the attack and sent restoration.

So, I was in the market with Wayne getting my lunch, feeling overwhelmed with the thousands of brightly packaged products, the lights, and the bustling shoppers—in short, with everything. I put my things on the conveyor belt and waited anxiously in line.

The conveyor belt moved, and suddenly from underneath the cash register where the belt reappears, I spotted a piece of paper. It was an evangelism tract. I picked it up and opened it. How it got there, I have no idea. Typically, the cashier would have spotted something like that and disposed of it. Not this time. I was next in line and—holding onto the tract—I paid and left the store. I got back to Wayne's car and began to read it out loud. It was my first spiritual warfare lesson. *This was the day that I began to get free once and for all from the harassment of the enemy!*

The tract said that when we are hit with a thought—just like the ones I was having—we are to say, *I am dead to you and you are dead to me! I am a new creature in Christ, old things have passed away! I am dead to you and you are dead to me!*

Yet, the biggest weapon that I received that day was this life-changing phrase written in the tract: *the Blood of Jesus!*

The tract told of the blood of Jesus and why the demons flee upon hearing it. It spoke of the cross and of Jesus' battered body that bled for all humanity, and that His blood, once, for all mankind, paid the price for the sins of the world. *The Lamb of God who takes away the sins of the world!*

I put what I'd read to use immediately. I began to say out loud, *the blood of Jesus,* when the attacks would come, and I finally began to get the victory!

That was many years ago and I still say *the blood of Jesus* on a regular basis. It is our BIG cannon to fight the enemy! Remember Satan goes about as a roaring lion—I heard that roar—and seeks to rob, kill, and destroy.

I want you to know that not a day goes by that I don't put on the armor and get ready for battle! I got the victory because of the blood of Jesus. I am a new creature in Christ because of what He did on Calvary. His blood covers us, and it is what makes the fallen one and his minions tremble in fear! They know that on that day, when Yeshua's blood was shed as the Passover Lamb, it spelled their defeat and certain doom.

CLOSING

It was not my idea to write this, and it is the first time that I have endeavored to do so. I believe I was instructed by the Lord to document my testimony so people could understand where I am coming from, my history, my search for God before I was a Christian, and what I endured after I became born again. My first three years as a Christian were the most difficult of my life. I wouldn't wish them on my worst enemy. Yet He was with me even in the valley of death!

In 1984 it was Pastor Fred who performed the ceremony when I married my beautiful wife, Peggy. At the time of this publication, we've been married forty years. She has been and continues to be such a blessing in my life!

Everything that I am today is because of Jesus. If there is anything good in me, anything worthy of praise, anything that I might be remembered for, may it point to Him who is the Savior and keeper of my soul and spirit!

BIBLIOGRAPHY

- Beekmann, Sharon. *Enticed by the Light: The Terrifying Story of One Woman's Encounter With the New Age.* Wipf & Stock Publishers, 2011.

- Corso, Col. Philip J. with William J. Birnes. *The Day After Roswell.* Gallery Books, 2017.

- Stevens, Lt. Col. Wendelle C. *UFO...Contact From the Pleiades: A Preliminary Investigation Report.* Genesis III Publishing, 1980.

- Caldwell, Taylor. *Dear and Glorious Physician: A Novel About Saint Luke.* Doubleday, 1965.

- Caldwell, Taylor. *Great Lion of God: A Novel About Saint Paul.* Doubleday, 1970.

- Caldwell, Taylor and Jess Stern. *I, Judas: A Novel.* Atheneum, 1977.

- Caldwell, Taylor. *Dialogues With the Devil: A Novel.* Open Road Media, 2018. (This novel is a correspondence between Lucifer and Michael the Archangel.)

- Hunt, David. *The Cult Explosion.* Harvest House Publishers, 1980.

NOTES

FOREWORD BY KARIN WILKINSON

1. Wikipedia, s.v. "George Adamski," last edited April 23, 2024, https://en.wikipedia.org/wiki/George_Adamski.

PREFACE

1. J. Allen Hynek, *The UFO Experience* (H. Regnery Company, 1972), 56.

INTRODUCTION

1. Michael Kaplan and Steven Greenstreet, "UFOs Are Real, Feds' Cover-Up Fueled by Fear: Ex-Pentagon Whistleblower," *New York Post*, updated April 30, 2021, https://nypost.com/2021/04/30/feds-cover-up-of-ufos-puts-us-at-risk/.
2. "The Darwinian Paradigm and Modern Evolution: What Is Evolution?," Lab Xchange, updated April 5, 2023, https://www.labxchange.org/library/items/lb:HarvardX:a382330e:html:1, emphasis added.
3. Joseph Stromberg, "Some Physicists Believe We're Living in a Giant Hologram—and It's Not That Far-Fetched," Vox, June 29, 2015, https://www.vox.com/2015/6/29/8847863/holographic-principle-universe-theory-physics.
4. L. A. Marzulli, *The Cosmic Chess Match* (Spiral of Life, 2014).

CHAPTER 1

1. Most people have no idea that there were this many facilities in Hitler's Third Reich that were used to process people. Over six million Jews were exterminated and countless others in what I would posit was one of the greatest cases of genocide in human history.

2. Mark Johnson, "How Oppenheimer Weighed the Odds of an Atomic Bomb Test Ending Earth," *Washington Post*, updated July 24, 2023, https://www.washingtonpost.com/science/2023/07/22/oppenheimer-manhattan-project-history-atomic-bomb-test/.

3. Reanna Smith, "Oppenheimer's Nuclear Bomb 'Got Attention of Aliens Worried We Will Destroy the Earth,'" *Mirror*, updated August 7, 2023, https://www.mirror.co.uk/news/weird-news/oppenheimers-nuclear-bomb-got-attention-30621861.

4. Russell Lee, "1947: Year of the Flying Saucer," National Air and Space Museum, June 24, 2022, https://airandspace.si.edu/stories/editorial/1947-year-flying-saucer.

5. L. A. Marzulli, *UFO Disclosure: The 70-Year Cover-Up Exposed* (Spiral of Life, 2018).

6. Wikipedia, s.v. "1952 Washington, D.C., UFO Incident," last edited May 23, 2024, https://en.wikipedia.org/wiki/1952_Washington,_D.C.,_UFO_incident.

7. Don Berliner and Stanton T. Friedman, *Crash at Corona: The U.S. Military Retrieval and Cover-up of a UFO* (Paraview, 2004).

8. Jesse Marcel Jr. and Linda Marcel, *The Roswell Legacy: The Untold Story of the First Military Officer at the 1947 Crash Site* (Career Press, 2009).

9. Marzulli, *UFO Disclosure*, ch. 2.

10. Wilbur Wright Field, named after one of the Wright brothers, grew during WWII and absorbed Patterson Field. It was later renamed Wright-Patterson.

11. Wikipedia, s.v. "Barney and Betty Hill Incident," last edited June 1, 2024, https://en.wikipedia.org/wiki/Barney_and_Betty_Hill_incident.

12. L. A. Marzulli, *The Nephilim Trilogy* (Spiral of Life Publishing, 1999).

13. *Men in Black*, directed by Barry Sonnenfeld (Columbia Pictures, 1997), emphasis added.

14. The Free Dictionary, s.v. "UFO Researchers' Mysterious Deaths," accessed June 26, 2024, https://encyclopedia2. thefreedictionary.com/UFO+Researchers%27+Mysterious+D eaths.

15. L. A. Marzulli, *Nephilim: The Truth Is Here* (Zondervan, 1999).

16. Quest TV, "Nurse Who Saw Alien Autopsies in Roswell | Roswell: The Final Verdict," YouTube, March 4, 2022, https://www.youtube.com/watch?v=fe_NwCqfz6c; U.S. National Archives, "W. Glenn Dennis Interview, 11/19/1990," YouTube, July 7, 2014, https://www.youtube.com/watch?v=_ DA-g94RoII.

17. L. A. Marzulli, *Watchers 10: DNA*, https://lamarzulli.net/ product/watchers-10/.

CHAPTER 2

1. Jaded Truth, "David Fravor (Naval Pilot) Full Interview With Tucker Carlson About UFO Incident," YouTube, December 22, 2017, https://www.youtube.com/ watch?v=5gJF7x4H2dg.

2. Jaded Truth, "David Fravor."

3. To the Stars Academy of Arts & Science, "Gimbal: The First Official UAP Footage From the USG for Public Release," YouTube, December 16, 2017, https://www. youtube.com/watch?v=tf1uLwUTDA0.

4. "Retired Navy Pilot Who Spotted 'Tic Tac' UFO: There's Something Out There," Fox News, July 24, 2020, https:// www.foxnews.com/video/6174934355001.

CHAPTER 3

1. "Luis Elizondo – Biography," Luis Elizondo, accessed June 26, 2024, https://luiselizondo-official.com/lus-bio/;

Wikipedia, s.v. "Advanced Aerospace Threat Identification Program," last edited April 16, 2024, https://en.wikipedia.org/wiki/Advanced_Aerospace_Threat_Identification_Program.

2. Marshall Cohen, "Hillary Clinton Personally Approved Plan to Share Trump-Russia Allegation With the Press in 2016, Campaign Manager Says," CNN, updated May 20, 2022, https://www.cnn.com/2022/05/20/politics/hillary-clinton-robby-mook-fbi/index.html.

3. "Tucker Carlson: Source Says Yes, the CIA Was Involved in JFK's Assassination," Fox News, December 15, 2022, https://www.foxnews.com/video/6317311778112.

4. ABC15.com Staff, "Obama Birth Certificate Investigation: Sheriff Arpaio's Office Says '9 Points of Forgery' Found," ABC15, December 14, 2016, https://www.abc15.com/news/region-phoenix-metro/central-phoenix/sheriff-joe-arpaio-to-talk-obama-birth-certificate-investigation.

5. New Highlight Channels, "Tucker Carlson Tonight 5/31/19: UFOs—the Truth Is Out There," YouTube, May 31, 2019, https://www.youtube.com/watch?v=vwVj2jSKMG4.

6. Engaging The Phenomenon (@EngagingThe), "I reached out to Dr. Eric Davis for comment on Luis Elizondo's (@TTSAcademy) comment on the U.S. Gov being in possession of UFO Debris @TuckerCarlson show. This is what Dr. Eric Davis had to say," X, June 2, 2019, 6:24 a.m., https://x.com/EngagingThe/status/1135129992457838592.

7. U.S. National Archives, "Eisenhower's 'Military-Industrial Complex' Speech Origins and Significance," YouTube, January 19, 2011, https://www.youtube.com/watch?v=Gg-jvHynP9Y.

8. NBC News, "Trump Discusses Declassifying Roswell, Says He Knows 'Very Interesting' Information | NBC News

NOW," YouTube, June 19, 2020, https://www.youtube.com/watch?v=EWZWVEkqVS8.

9. "#1645 – Christopher Mellon," *The Joe Rogan Experience*, podcast, May 5, 2021, 1:38:10, https://open.spotify.com/episode/2V0uWX1C4m8xEL0HHYqbnE.

10. Ralph Blumenthal and Leslie Kean, "No Longer in Shadows, Pentagon's U.F.O. Unit Will Make Some Findings Public," *New York Times*, June 3, 2021, https://www.nytimes.com/2020/07/23/us/politics/pentagon-ufo-harry-reid-navy.html.

11. Vanessa Romo and Bill Chappell, "U.S. Recovered Non-Human 'Biologics' From UFO Crash Sites, Former Intel Official Says," NPR, July 27, 2023, https://www.npr.org/2023/07/27/1190390376/ufo-hearing-non-human-biologics-uaps.

12. "USG May Have Materials," UAP Guide, accessed June 27, 2024, https://www.uap.guide/quotes/USG-may-have-materials.

13. "#1645 – Christopher Mellon," 1:34:10.

14. Blumenthal and Kean, "No Longer in Shadows."

15. Google Dictionary, s.v. "ambivalence," accessed June 27, 2024, https://www.google.com/search?q=define+ambivalence.

16. George Knapp, "Pentagon UFO Study/Alien Civilizations," *Coast to Coast AM*, June 24, 2018, https://coasttocoastam.com/show/2018-06-24-show/.

17. Ross Coulthart, *In Plain Sight: An Investigation Into UFOs and Impossible Science* (HarperCollins, 2021), 204.

18. Christopher Mellon, "Unprecedented UAP Legislation," blog, December 24, 2022, https://www.christophermellon.net/post/unprecedented-uap-legislation.

19. Wikipedia, "Bob Lazar," last edited June 27, 2024, https://en.wikipedia.org/wiki/Bob_Lazar.

20. Philip J. Corso With William J. Birnes, *The Day After Roswell* (Pocket Books, 1997).

21. *UFO Disclosure Episode 7 - Revisiting Roswell: Exoneration*, created by L. A. Marzulli, https://streaming.lamarzulli.net/programs/ufo-disclosure-7-part-1-roswell-exoneration; *UFO Disclosure Episode 8 - Revisiting Roswell: Evidence From the Debris Field*, created by L. A. Marzulli, https://streaming.lamarzulli.net/programs/ufo-disclosure-7-part-2-roswell-debris-field.

22. Coulthart, *In Plain Sight*, 208.

23. Gideon Lewis-Kraus, "How the Pentagon Started Taking U.F.O.s Seriously," *New Yorker*, April 30, 2021, https://www.newyorker.com/magazine/2021/05/10/how-the-pentagon-started-taking-ufos-seriously.

CHAPTER 4

1. Anil Ananthaswamy, "Is Our Universe a Hologram? Physicists Debate Famous Idea on Its 25th Anniversary," *Scientific American*, March 1, 2023, https://www.scientificamerican.com/article/is-our-universe-a-hologram-physicists-debate-famous-idea-on-its-25th-anniversary1/.

2. "The Phenomenon on Tucker Carlson Tonight," YouTube, October 12, 2020, https://www.youtube.com/watch?v=eg6K4FRzqfc.

3. "Unidentified: Inside America's UFO Investigation—Cast," History, accessed June 28, 2024, https://www.history.com/shows/unidentified-inside-americas-ufo-investigation/cast/chris-mellon.

4. Phil Owen, "Tucker Carlson: It's 'Outrageous' the Government Is Still Hiding Evidence of UFOs (Video)," The Wrap, October 9, 2020, https://www.thewrap.com/tucker-carlson-its-outrageous-the-government-is-still-hiding-evidence-of-ufos-video/, emphasis added.

5. Owen, "Tucker Carlson."

CHAPTER 5

1. Blumenthal and Kean, "No Longer in Shadows."
2. "President Eisenhower Did Meet With Aliens in 1954, According to Former Politician," Journal Online, February 4, 2022, https://journal.com.ph/president-eisenhower-did-meet-with-aliens-in-1954-according-to-former-politician/.
3. Marzulli, *Nephilim.*
4. *UFO Disclosure Episode 2: The Expert Witnesses Weigh In,* created by L. A. Marzulli, Spiral of Life, https://lamarzulli.net/product/ufo-disclosure-part-2-the-experts-weight-in/.
5. Chuck Missler, "Mischievous Angels or Sethites?," Koinonia House, August 1, 1997, https://www.khouse.org/personal_update/articles/1997/mischievous-angels-or-sethites.
6. "This is the first promise given after...Adam and Eve ate the forbidden fruit in the Garden of Eden. Theologians call it the *protoevangelium*–or first gospel because these words spoken by God contain the first promise of redemption in the Bible. *Everything else in the Bible flows from these words in Genesis 3:15.* As the acorn contains the mighty oak, so these words contain the entire plan of salvation. The great English preacher Charles Simeon called this verse 'the sum and summary of the whole Bible.'" Ray Pritchard, "What is the Protoevangelium (Protoevangelion)?," Christianity.com, updated March 10, 2011, https://www.christianity.com/jesus/is-jesus-god/old-testament-prophecies/what-is-the-protoevangelium-protoevangelion.html.
7. "Roswell UFO Crash: USAF Confirmed 'Mystery Metal' Debris Tested," Phantoms & Monsters, February 11, 2022, https://www.phantomsandmonsters.com/2022/02/roswell-ufo-crash-usaf-confirmed.html.

8. FindingUFO, "Bob Lazar Explaining Element 115 from Area 51 (PART 1) – FindingUFO," YouTube, July 24, 2015, https://www.youtube.com/watch?v=oy-T_BsYLhE.

9. Norio, "1990 Photo of Object Above Area 51," Alien Hub, January 20, 2010, https://www.alienhub.com/threads/1990-photo-of-object-above-area-51.22525/; "Area 51. UFO Diaries," YouTube, March 15, 2014, https://www.youtube.com/watch?v=gmvGs0WPOv4.

10. Marzulli, *UFO Disclosure: The 70-Year Cover-Up Exposed*.

11. *UFO Disclosure Episode 7*; *UFO Disclosure Episode 8*.

12. *UFO Disclosure Episode 4: The Coming UFO Invasion*, created by L. A. Marzulli, Spiral of Life, 2023, https://lamarzulli.net/product/ufo-disclosure-part-4-the-coming-ufo-invasion/.

Chapter 6

1. "Preliminary Assessment: Unidentified Aerial Phenomena," Office of the Director of National Intelligence, June 25, 2021, https://www.dni.gov/files/ODNI/documents/assessments/Prelimary-Assessment-UAP-20210625.pdf.

2. Michael E. Salla, "Colonel Philip Corso and His Critics," Biblioteca Pleyades, January 2006, https://www;.bibliotecapleyades.net/exopolitica/esp_exopolitics_zzo.htm.

3. "Ep. #228: Stanton Friedman | Brennan Storr | D.B. Stearns," *Into the Parabnormal With Jeremy Scott*, podcast, November 4, 2017, https://music.amazon.com/podcasts/dd7406b6-a6e6-47a1-af16-cabe0d91d5e6/episodes/356d5ab5-b58a-4e5c-85c7-3b8a348f5df7/into-the-parabnormal-with-jeremy-scott-ep-228-stanton-friedman-brennan-storr-d-b-stearns.

4. Dwight D. Eisenhower, "President Dwight D. Eisenhower's Farewell Address (1961)," U.S. National Archives, January 17, 1961, https://www.archives.gov/milestone-documents/

president-dwight-d-eisenhowers-farewell-address, emphasis added.

5. "2.5 – Aliens & the Third Reich," Ancient Alienpedia, November 25, 2020, https://ancientalienpedia.wordpress. com/2-5-aliens-the-third-reich-alien-ingenuity/.

6. "2.5," Ancient Alienpedia.

7. "Preliminary Assessment," Office of the Director of National Intelligence, 8.

8. "Preliminary Assessment," Office of the Director of National Intelligence, 3.

9. knaps1, "Kumburgaz Turkey UFO - All Footage Stabilized," YouTube, November 26, 2018, https://www.youtube.com/ watch?v=Nhsz1Wkkp18.

10. *Watchers*, created by L. A. Marzulli and Richard Shaw, 2010– 2017, https://lamarzulli.net/product/watchers-11-dvd-set/.

11. "Preliminary Assessment," Office of the Director of National Intelligence, 5, emphasis added.

12. Norio Hayakawa, "Unknown Craft Over Area 51 in 1990, Filmed by TV Crew," YouTube, June 9, 2013, https://www. youtube.com/watch?v=TzbRiHjEdHg&t=0s.

13. "Preliminary Assessment," Office of the Director of National Intelligence, 5.

14. *UFO Disclosure Episode 7*; *UFO Disclosure Episode 8*.

15. knaps1, "Kumburgaz Turkey UFO."

16. "Preliminary Assessment," Office of the Director of National Intelligence, 5.

CHAPTER 7

1. WION Web Team, "NASA is hiring priests to prepare humans for contact with aliens," WIO News, updated December 27, 2021, https://www.wionews.com/science/ nasa-is-hiring-priests-to-prepare-humans-for-contact-with-aliens-440433.

2. Brooke Migdon, "NASA Used Religious Experts to Predict How Humans May React to Aliens," *The Hill*, December 28, 2021, https://thehill.com/changing-america/enrichment/arts-culture/587480-nasa-hired-religious-experts-to-predict-how-humans/.

3. Migdon, "NASA Used Religious Experts to Predict How Humans May React to Aliens."

4. "C. S. Lewis: Out of the Silent Planet," SuperSummary, accessed June 28, 2024, https://www.supersummary.com/out-of-the-silent-planet/summary/.

5. Abby Ohlheiser, "Pope Francis Says He Would Definitely Baptize Aliens If They Asked Him To," *The Atlantic*, May 12, 2014, https://www.theatlantic.com/international/archive/2014/05/pope-francis-says-he-would-definitely-baptize-aliens-if-they-wanted-it/362106/.

6. Ohlheiser, "Pope Francis Says He Would Definitely Baptize Aliens If They Asked Him To."

7. Wikipedia, s.v. "Catholic Church," last edited June 19, 2024, https://en.wikipedia.org/wiki/Catholic_Church.

8. Wikipedia, s.v. "Religion in the United States," last edited June 17, 2024, https://en.wikipedia.org/wiki/Religion_in_the_United_States.

9. L. A. Marzulli, *Countermove: How the Nephilim Returned After the Flood* (Spiral of Life, 2020).

10. Joaquim Fernandes and Fina D'Armada, *Celestial Secrets: The Hidden History of the Fátima Incident*, trans. Alexandra Bruce (Anomalist, 2006).

11. *Fatima 1: Miracle of the Sun or Harbinger of Deception*, created by L. A. Marzulli, https://lamarzulli.net/product/fatima/.

12. Joseph Ratzinger, "The Message of Fatima," The Vatican, accessed July 26, 2024, https://www.vatican.va/roman_curia/congregations/cfaith/documents/rc_con_cfaith_doc_20000626_message-fatima_en.html.

CHAPTER 8

1. *UFO Disclosure Episode 4.*
2. Michael Luciano, "Bret Baier Runs Bizarre Report Suggesting Link Between UFOs and 'Unexplained Pregnancies,'" Mediaite, April 6, 2022, https://www.mediaite.com/tv/bret-baier-runs-ufo-segment-suggesting-link-between-ufos-and-pregnancies/.
3. John E. Mack, *Abduction: Human Encounters With Aliens* (Charles Scribner's Sons, 1994).
4. Whitley Strieber, *Communion: A True Story* (William Morrow Paperbacks, 2008).
5. L. A. Marzulli, *Further Evidence of Close Encounters* (Spiral of Life, 2013), 17.
6. *UFO Disclosure Episode 4.*
7. *UFO Disclosure Episode 4.*
8. *UFO Disclosure Episode 4.*
9. Karin Wilkinson, *Stolen Seed, Evil Harvest* (Spiral of Life, 2023).
10. *Watchers.*

CHAPTER 9

1. *Watchers.*
2. *UFO Disclosure Episode 6: Cattle Mutilations*, Spiral of Life, 2023, https://lamarzulli.net/product/ufo-disclosure-part-6-cattle-mutilations-streaming/.
3. "Hemopure: An Alternative to Blood Transfusion," University of Florida, June 5, 2018, https://anest.ufl.edu/2018/06/05/hemopure-an-alternative-to-blood-transfusion/.
4. Fahad Khan, Kunwar Singh, and Mark T. Friedman, "Artificial Blood: The History and Current Perspectives of Blood Substitutes," *Discoveries (Craiova)* 8, no. 1 (January–March 2020): e104, https://doi.org/10.15190%2Fd.2020.1; Randolph Delehanty, "Historic California Posts, Camps,

Stations and Airfields: Letterman Army Medical Center," California State Military History and Museums Program, updated April 21, 2016, https://www.militarymuseum.org/LettermanAMC.html.

5. *UFO Disclosure Episode 4.*

CHAPTER 10

1. Jeffrey Kluger, "Congress Is Finally Taking UFOs Seriously, 50 Years After Its Last Hearing on the Mysterious Subject," *TIME*, May 17, 2022, https://time.com/6177650/congress-ufo-hearings/.

2. Josephus, the ancient historian, said the Nephilim, or giants, were "terrible to the hearing." Josephus, *The Antiquities of the Jews*, 5.125, trans. William Whiston, https://www.lexundria.com/j_aj/5.120-5.174/wst.

3. L. A. Marzulli, "The Giants of Kandahar!," YouTube, January 8, 2024, https://www.youtube.com/watch?v=5W8mb0I8N7k.

4. Osprey, text messages to author, emphasis added.

5. Chad Pergram, "Close Encounters of Congressional Kind: Lawmakers Struggle to Grasp Alleged 'Interdimensional' Nature of UFOs," Fox News, January 17, 2024, https://www.foxnews.com/politics/close-encounters-congressional-kind-lawmakers-struggle-grasp-alleged-interdimensional-nature-ufos.

6. Steph Whiteside, "'I Didn't Learn Anything:' Burchett on Classified UFO Briefing," NewsNation, updated October 27, 2023, https://www.newsnationnow.com/space/ufo/didnt-learn-anything-burchett-ufo-briefing/.

CHAPTER 11

1. Emma Bowman, "Pentagon Finds 'No Evidence' of Alien Technology in New UFO Report," NPR, March 8, 2024,

https://www.npr.org/2024/03/08/1237100622/pentagon-
ufo-report-no-evidence-alien-technology#.

2. Department of Defense All-Domain Anomaly
Resolution Office, "Report on the Historical Record
of U.S. Government Involvement With Unidentified
Anomalous Phenomena (UAP), Volume I," Department of
Defense, February 2024, https://media.defense.gov/2024/
Mar/08/2003409233/-1/-1/0/DOPSR-CLEARED-508-
COMPLIANT-HRRV1-08-MAR-2024-FINAL.PDF.

3. Jaded Truth, "David Fravor."

4. Shane Harris and Dan Lamothe, "Pentagon Report
Finds No Evidence of Alien Visits, Hidden Spacecraft,"
Washington Post, updated March 8, 2024, https://www.
washingtonpost.com/national-security/2024/03/08/no-ufo-
aliens-pentagon-report/.

5. Bowman, "Pentagon Finds 'No Evidence'"; see also
Bill Chappell, "The Pentagon Got Hundreds of New
Reports of UFOs in 2022, a Government Report
Says," NPR, January 13, 2023, https://www.npr.
org/2023/01/13/1149019140/ufo-report.

6. L. A. Marzulli, "BREAKING UFO NEWS!!,"
YouTube, March 12, 2024, https://www.youtube.com/
watch?v=p7EZyiv8dc0.

7. "*Roswell Daily Record* Articles," Geocities, accessed June
29, 2024, https://www.geocities.ws/rynnfrink/roswellnews.
html.

8. Bowman, "Pentagon Finds 'No Evidence.'"

9. "File: *Roswell Daily Record*. July 8, 1947. RAAF Captures
Flying Saucer on Ranch in Roswell Region. Full front
page.jpg," Wikimedia Commons, last edited February 20,
2024, https://en.wikisource.org/wiki/RAAF_Captures_
Flying_Saucer_on_Ranch_in_Roswell_Region, emphasis
added.

10. James McAndrew, *The Roswell Report: Case Closed* (Headquarters United States Air Force, 1997), https://archive.org/details/AFD-101027-030/page/n3/mode/2up.

11. Stanton T. Friedman, "Scientists Challenge Air Force Regarding UFOs," The Black Vault, November 13, 1997, https://www.theblackvault.com/casefiles/scientists-challenge-air-force-regarding-ufos/.

12. Friedman, "Scientists Challenge Air Force Regarding UFOs."

13. *UFO Disclosure Episode 7.*

14. Friedman, "Scientists Challenge Air Force Regarding UFOs," emphasis added.

15. McAndrew, *The Roswell Report: Case Closed.*

16. *UFO Disclosure Episode 2.* See L. A. Marzulli's interview with Francisco Corrêa, head of Exopolitics Portugal.

17. "Statement by Pentagon Press Secretary Maj. Gen. Pat Ryder on the Historical Record Report on Unidentified Anomalous Phenomena, Volume 1," U.S. Department of Defense, March 8, 2024, https://www.defense.gov/News/Releases/Release/Article/3700894/statement-by-pentagon-press-secretary-maj-gen-pat-ryder-on-the-historical-recor/.

18. Harris and Lamothe, "Pentagon Report Finds No Evidence of Alien Visits, Hidden Spacecraft."

19. *Men in Black*, directed by Barry Sonnenfeld.

20. Brett Tingley, "Pentagon UFO Office Finds 'No Empirical Evidence' for Alien Technology in New Report," Space.com, March 8, 2024, https://www.space.com/pentagon-ufo-office-aaro-historical-report-no-emprical-evidence-alien-technology.

21. "Statement by Pentagon Press Secretary Maj. Gen. Pat Ryder on the Historical Record Report on Unidentified Anomalous Phenomena, Volume 1," U.S. Department of Defense.

CHAPTER 12

1. "Garry Nolan," Stanford University, accessed June 29, 2024, https://profiles.stanford.edu/garry-nolan.

2. UAP Tracker, "Dr Garry P Nolan UAP UFO Tucker Carlson Full Interview 03/08/2022," YouTube, August 2, 2022, https://www.youtube.com/watch?v=T3sszdf_93w.

3. *Close Encounters of the Third Kind*, directed by Steven Spielberg (Columbia Pictures, 1977).

4. "Classification Systems: Hynek's Classification System," CUFOS, accessed June 29, 2024, https://cufos.org/types-of-ufos/classification-systems/.

5. "Classification Systems," CUFOS.

6. "Classification Systems," CUFOS.

7. "Classification Systems," CUFOS.

8. Wikipedia, s.v. "Close Encounter," last edited May 3, 2024, https://en.wikipedia.org/wiki/Close_encounter.

9. *Close Encounters of the Third Kind*.

10. *Taken*, Steven Spielberg and Leslie Bohem, 2002, on Sci-Fi Channel.

11. *UFO Disclosure Parts 9 & 10: What Is the Truth?*, created by L. A. Marzulli, https://lamarzulli.net/product/ufo-disclosure-episode-9-10/.

12. Wilkinson, *Stolen Seed, Evil Harvest*.

CHAPTER 13

1. *Alien Abductions*, Fox Nation, accessed June 30, 2024, https://nation.foxnews.com/alien-abductions-with-abby-hornacek-nation/.

2. Wikipedia, s.v. "Barney and Betty Hill Incident."

3. Wikipedia, s.v. "Barney and Betty Hill Incident."

4. Wikipedia, s.v. "Pascagoula Abduction," last edited June 26, 2024, https://en.wikipedia.org/wiki/Pascagoula_Abduction.

5. Matthew Phelan, "EXCLUSIVE: New Witness of 1973 Alien Abduction in Mississippi Featured in New Netflix Doc Claims She Saw the 5ft Creatures With 'Pincer-Like' Claws That Performed 'Examinations' on Two Fishermen,"

Daily Mail, updated April 11, 2024, https://www.dailymail.co.uk/sciencetech/article-13294539/mississippi-alien-abduction-1973-netflix-documentary-creatures-examinations-fishermen.html.

6. *UFO Disclosure Part 4: UFO Abductions*, created by L. A. Marzulli, https://www.lamarzulli.net/product/buy-stolen-seed-evil-harvest-bonus-dvd-ufo-disclosure-episode-4/.

7. Daniel Lavelle, "'What I Saw That Night Was Real': Is It Time to Take Aliens More Seriously?," *The Guardian*, September 12, 2021, https://www.theguardian.com/world/2021/sep/12/what-i-saw-that-night-was-real-is-it-time-to-take-aliens-more-seriously-.

8. Becca Martin-Brown, "One Man's UFO Story: Author Discusses Lifetime of Extraterrestrial Encounters," *Northwest Arkansas Democrat Gazette*, April 5, 2020, https://www.nwaonline.com/news/2020/apr/05/one-man-s-ufo-story-author-discusses-li/.

9. *Incident at Devil's Den: A True Story by Terry Lovelace, Esq.* (Lulu Press, 2019); "509th Bomb Wing," Whiteman Air Force Base, accessed July 24, 2024, https://whiteman.af.mil/About/Facts-Sheets/Display/Article/323963/509th-bomb-wing/; Martin-Brown, "One Man's UFO Story."

10. "Podcast: Terry Lovelace's Remarkable UFO Abduction at Devil's Den II Part 1," UFO World, February 2024, https://www.youtube.com/watch?v=SztzZK3VK1w.

11. Lavelle, "'What I Saw That Night Was Real.'"

12. Martin-Brown, "One Man's UFO Story."

13. *UFO Disclosure Part 4: UFO Abductions*.

CHAPTER 14

1. *The Best of Watchers*, Spiral of Life, https://lamarzulli.net/product/the-best-of-the-watchers-series/.

CHAPTER 15

1. Andrew Roberts, "UFOs Are 'Demonic' Aliens Visiting From Other Dimensions in Latest Theory," PopCulture, March 30, 2024, https://popculture.com/trending/news/ufos-are-demonic-aliens-visiting-from-other-dimensions-in-latest-theory/.
2. *Ancient Aliens*, created by Kevin Burns, 2009–2024, on History.
3. *Watchers.*
4. *UFO Disclosure Parts 9 & 10.*
5. Josephus, *The Antiquities of the Jews*, 5.125.
6. I. D. E. Thomas, *Omega Conspiracy* (Defender, 2008).
7. Graham Hancock, *Supernatural: Meetings With the Ancient Teachers of Mankind* (Disinformation Books, 2006).

CHAPTER 16

1. *Unidentified Anomalous Phenomena: Implications on National Security, Public Safety, and Government Transparency, Hearing Before the Subcommittee on National Security, the Border, and Foreign Affairs of the Committee on Oversight and Accountability*, 118th Congress, July 26, 2023, https://www.congress.gov/118/meeting/house/116282/documents/HHRG-118-GO06-Transcript-20230726.pdf.
2. *Unidentified Anomalous Phenomena*, 118th Congress, 15–16.
3. David Grusch, "Opening Statement," U.S. House of Representatives, accessed June 30, 2024, https://oversight.house.gov/wp-content/uploads/2023/07/Dave_G_HOC_Speech_FINAL_For_Trans.pdf.
4. Grusch, "Opening Statement."

5. Abraham Lincoln, "The Gettysburg Address," November 19, 1863, https://www.abrahamlincolnonline.org/lincoln/speeches/gettysburg.htm.

6. *Unidentified Anomalous Phenomena*, 118th Congress, 39–41.

7. *UFO Disclosure Episode 7*; *UFO Disclosure Episode 8*.

CHAPTER 17

1. Fiona Jackson, "Do You Speak Extra-Terrestrial? Scientists Say Earth Needs to Prepare for an Alien Encounter NOW Before It's Too Late," *Daily Mail*, November 4, 2022, https://www.dailymail.co.uk/sciencetech/article-11389643/Scientists-say-Earth-needs-prepare-alien-encounter-late.html.

2. *UFO Disclosure Episode 1: Disclosure*, created by L. A. Marzulli, Spiral of Life, https://streaming.lamarzulli.net/programs/disclosure.

3. *Watchers Episode 7: Physical Evidence*, created by L. A. Marzulli and Richard Shaw, Spiral of Life, https://streaming.lamarzulli.net/programs/watchers-7-physical-evidencemp4-f578e2?category_id=41163.

4. *UFO Disclosure Parts 9 & 10*.

5. Exopaedia, s.v. "Mourao Correa, Francisco," accessed June 30, 2024, https://www.exopaedia.org/Mourao+Correa%2C+Francisco.

6. Francisco Mourão Corrêa, in communication with the author.

CHAPTER 18

1. *Watchers*.

2. *On the Trail of the Nephilim Episode 6: DNA: The Final Result*, Spiral of Life, https://streaming.lamarzulli.net/programs/dna-the-final-results?category_id=39780.

3. "1 Enoch (Ethiopic Enoch)," Hanover University, accessed June 30, 2024, https://history.hanover.edu/courses/excerpts/260enoch.html.
4. *Watchers*; *On the Trail of the Nephilim*, created by L. A. Marzulli, https://www.lamarzulli.net/product/on-the-trail-of-the-nephilim-complete-series-1-8/.
5. Wikipedia, s.v. "Si-Te-Cah," last edited July 24, 2024, https://en.wikipedia.org/wiki/Si-Te-Cah.
6. Elios, "Robert Mirabal Stiltwalker," YouTube, June 19, 2015, https://www.youtube.com/watch?v=ROrieJx23Ak.
7. L. A. Marzulli, *On the Trail of the Nephilim: Definitive Proof of the Biblical Giants* (Spiral of Life).
8. Jim Wilhelmsen, *Beyond Science Fiction!* (iUniverse, 2009).
9. Sitchin Is Wrong, accessed July 26, 2024, https://sitchiniswrong.com/anunnaki/anunnaki.htm.
10. *On the Trail of the Nephilim.*
11. *UFO Disclosure Parts 9 & 10.*
12. *Fátima 1*; *Fátima 2: Strange Phenomena*, created by L. A. Marzulli, https://streaming.lamarzulli.net/programs/fatima-2-strange-phenomena.
13. Marzulli, *The Cosmic Chess Match.*
14. Marzulli, *The Cosmic Chess Match.*

APPENDIX

1. In 1992 President Bill Clinton announced on national television that he had used marijuana but claimed he did not inhale, which even today remains a pop culture comedy reference.
2. *seer* – "(noun) one that sees; one that predicts events or developments; a person credited with extraordinary moral and spiritual insight; one that practices divination especially by concentrating on a glass or crystal globe." https://www.merriam-webster.com/dictionary/seer.

3. Sharon Beekmann, *Enticed by the Light: The Terrifying Story of One Woman's Encounter with the New Age* (Wipf & Stock Publishers, 2011).

4. *mahatma* – from the Sanskrit word *mahātman*, "great souled." "A person to be revered for high-mindedness, wisdom, and selflessness...In India, it is used as a title of love and respect." https://www.merriam-webster.com/dictionary/mahatma.

5. *fakir* – "a Muslim or Hindu religious ascetic or mendicant monk commonly considered a wonder-worker." https://www.dictionary.com/browse/fakir.

6. *guru* – "a personal religious teacher and spiritual guide in Hinduism." https://www.merriam-webster.com/dictionary/guru.

7. *dais* – "a raised platform (as in a hall or large room)." https://www.merriam-webster.com/dictionary/dais.

8. *untouchable* – Hinduism. The name given to a member of a lower caste in India "whose touch was believed to defile a high-caste Hindu." https://www.dictionary.com/browse/untouchable.

9. "The *third eye* is a representation of mystical intuition and insight—an inner vision and enlightenment beyond what the physical eyes can see. It is traditionally depicted as being located in the middle of the forehead." https://www.dictionary.com/browse/third-eye.

10. *nectar* – the food of the gods; ambrosia or nectar. https://www.merriam-webster.com/dictionary/nectar.

11. *mantra* – "a mystical formula of invocation...or incantation as in Hinduism." https://www.merriam-webster.com/dictionary/mantra.

12. According to Eastern religions everything has come out of Primordial Vibration, which is represented by Om, a syllable and sound used in meditation. https://www.hinduamerican.org/blog/5-things-to-know-about-om.

13. *ashram* – "a secluded dwelling of a Hindu sage." https://www. merriam-webster.com/dictionary/ashram.

14. *satsang* – "from Sanskrit, meaning to associate with true people, or to be in the company of true people. It is also related to sitting with a sat guru." https://www.dynastyresort. com/satsang.php.

15. "Prem Rawat Was Disowned, Disinherited and Deposed," Prem Rawat Bio, accessed July 25, 2024, http://www. prem-rawat-bio.org/family/disinherit.html.

16. Lt. Col. Wendelle Stevens and Lee Elders, *UFO...Contact from the Pleiades* (Genesis III Publishing, 1980), out of print.

17. "*Lotus position* or *Padmasana* is a cross-legged sitting meditation pose from ancient India, in which each foot is placed on the opposite thigh. It is an ancient asana in yoga, predating hatha yoga, and is widely used for meditation in Hindu, Tantra, Jain, and Buddhist traditions." https:// en.wikipedia.org/wiki/Lotus_position.

18. *pantheism* – The New Age worldview "centers on *monism* (all is one), *pantheism* (all is God), and *mysticism* (the experience of oneness with the divine)." https:// answersingenesis.org/world-religions/new-age-movement-pantheism-monism/.

19. A house built on a speculative basis. The builder and/or investor makes the investment with the expectation of selling the home at or above market price once it is completed. https://www.bankrate.com/real-estate/what-is-a-spec-house.

20. Taylor Caldwell "wrote many historical novels, including several about famous religious figures." https://en.wikipedia. org/wiki/Taylor_Caldwell.

21. David Hunt "was an American Christian apologist, speaker, radio commentator and author." https://en.wikipedia.org/ wiki/Dave_Hunt_(Christian_apologist).

ABOUT THE AUTHOR

L. A. Marzulli is an author, lecturer, and filmmaker. He has penned fourteen books including *The Nephilim Trilogy*, which made the CBA bestsellers list. Based on his work on the trilogy, Marzulli received an honorary doctorate from his mentor, Dr. I. D. E. Thomas, who was the provost at Pacific International University. He was also presented with a Gold Medallion award by Chuck Missler at the K-House (Koinonia House) conference in 2014.

His book series *On the Trail of the Nephilim* volumes 1 and 2 are full-color, oversized volumes that reveal startling evidence of a massive cover-up of what he believes to be the remains of the Nephilim, the giants mentioned in the Bible.

Marzulli teamed up with film producer Richard Shaw to create the *Watchers* series, which grew to an eleven-episode catalog. One of those installments, *Watchers 7: Physical Evidence*, won both the UFO Best Film and People's Choice Award at the UFO Congress in 2014.

Marzulli created a "team" that legally extracted material for DNA testing from the enigmatic elongated skulls found in Peru. The results were released in episode 6 of the *On the Trail* series in late 2020. There are now eight installments in the series.

Marzulli toured Portugal for two weeks conducting extensive research and interviews, which resulted in the films *Fatima: Miracle of the Sun or a Harbinger of Deception* and *Fatima 2: Strange Phenomenon*. In part 2, the film releases a never-before-seen photograph that clearly shows a *disc-shaped object* directly above the so-called apparition site on October 13, 1917. This is groundbreaking information.

With the passing of Richard Shaw, Marzulli teamed up with Gil Zimmerman, and the two have completed ten films in their ongoing UFO series. This is the only film series that deals with the many facets of the UFO phenomenon from close encounters of UFOs to abductions, cattle mutilations, crop circles, and so much more! *UFOs are real, burgeoning, and not going away!*

L. A. Marzulli is a frank supernaturalist who lectures on the subjects of UFOs, the Nephilim, and ancient prophetic texts, presenting his exhaustive research at conferences and churches, through all media platforms, and through interviews on numerous national and international radio and television programs.